BURT FRANKLIN: RESEARCH & SOURCE WORKS SERIES
Philosophy & Religious History Monographs 143

THE

L I F E

OF

THE LEARNED

SIR JOHN CHEKE, K^T.

Engraved by James Fittler A.R.A. after a Drawing by W. Skelton, taken from an Original Picture in the Possession of the Dowager Marchioness of Downshire, at Ombersley Court, Worcestershire.

SIR JOHN CHEKE, K.ᵗ

Born June 16, 1514.   *Died Sept. 13, 1557.*

THE

L I F E

OF

THE LEARNED

SIR JOHN CHEKE, K^T.

FIRST INSTRUCTOR, AFTERWARDS SECRETARY OF STATE,

TO

KING EDWARD VI.

ONE OF THE GREAT RESTORERS OF GOOD LEARNING AND
TRUE RELIGION IN THIS KINGDOM.

A Work wherein many remarkable Points of History, relating to the State of
Learning and Religion in the Times of King Henry VIII. King
Edward VI. and Queen Mary I. are brought to light.

TO WHICH IS ADDED,

A TREATISE OF SUPERSTITION,

Writ by the said learned Knight.

———◆———

BY JOHN STRYPE, M. A.

———◆———

A NEW EDITION, CORRECTED BY THE AUTHOR.

———◆———

BURT FRANKLIN REPRINTS
New York, N. Y.

Published by LENOX HILL Pub. & Dist. Co. (Burt Franklin)
235 East 44th St., New York, N.Y. 10017
Reprinted: 1974
Printed in the U.S.A.

Burt Franklin: Research and Source Works Series
Philosophy and Religious History Monographs 143

Reprinted from the original edition in the University of Illinois
    Library at Urbana.

Library of Congress Cataloging in Publication Data

Strype, John, 1643-1737.
    The life of the learned Sir John Cheke, kt., first instructor,
afterwards secretary of State, to King Edward VI . . .

    "A treatise of superstition": p.
    Reprint of the "new edition," 1821, published at the Clarendon Press,
Oxford.
    1. Cheke, Sir John, 1514-1557. I. Title. II. Title: A treatise of superstition.
1974.
DA345.1.C5S9 1974   942.05'3'0924 (B)   78-183699
ISBN 0-8337-3446-6

THIS edition of Strype's Life of Sir John Cheke, as well as that lately published of Sir Thomas Smith, is printed verbatim from a copy corrected by the Author, which is the property of Mr. Watson Taylor, and with the use of which he was pleased to oblige the Delegates of the Clarendon Press.

Feb. 1821.

a 2

THE RIGHT WORSHIPFUL

EDWARD CHEEK OF PYRGO, ESQ.

SIR,

BE pleased to accept this book of the Life of the right worthy and ever memorable Sir John Cheke, your great great grandfather, who derives an honour upon you that are sprung in a direct line from him. To you therefore it most properly belongs. And further, it may be of this use to you, that by reading and knowing his extraordinary accomplishments, they may be your continual *mementos,* not to degenerate from, but to imitate, as much as may be, such a forefather.

The cause that moved me to write this Life, was the notable figure Cheke made in this island in his time; having been a rare instrument of doing good to his country, (the effects whereof remain to this day,) not only in the wise and happy modelling of an excellent Prince to govern the State, but also in furthering most successfully solid and useful learning in the University, and the pure religion of the Gospel in Court and kingdom: though it raised him up implacable enemies of the Popish faction, brought him into extreme troubles, and shortened his life. And therefore it is highly becoming, nay, I may say, a public debt, to preserve his name and memory.

It is true, Sir, I do not pretend to be either the first or only writer of his Life. For Gerard Langbain, D. D. in the time of the civil wars, and David Lloyd since, and Holland before them both, have done something that way. But their writings are so slight, superficial, and deficient, and so full of errors and impositions upon the reader's credulity, that something more full and correct was necessary, to give a better representation of this gentleman to the world: which I have endeavoured to do; and perhaps I have had greater advantages than others to do it.

My inclinations (I know not how) have carried me now for many years to search more curiously into the affairs of that age. And in my pursuits I have conversed with many records, manuscripts, original letters, as well as other old thrown-by printed books, and some of them rare ones too. And from the multifarious collections and transcripts taken thence, I have been furnished with materials for the composing this tract. Which (whatever it be) I have done with all care, faithfulness, and integrity. For as I love not to be imposed upon myself, so neither to impose upon others. The opportunities I have had (I will not say, the pains I have taken) in making myself acquainted with Cheke's life and actions, may appear by that catalogue of books and papers set down afterwards, which I have made use of.

There was, Sir, another reason excited me to this undertaking. It was not long ago I printed the Life of Sir Thomas Smith, his dear friend and contemporary in the same University; both joint-promoters of true religion and good literature; both King Henry's Scholars; both raised and brought to Court by the fame of their learning; and both at length Privy Counsellors and Secretaries of State, and both sufferers for religion; so that I reckoned my work but half done, while Cheke's Life remained unwritten. Which therefore I have now done; and do shew (somewhat to my own satisfaction) this incomparable pair to the English world.

And, Sir, methinks it is not to be passed over without a remark, how the parallel between these two great men still continues; that the heirs of both flourish to this day, in two noble seats in the same county, mounted upon two pleasant hills, in prospect one of another, *viz.* Hillhall and your Pyrgo; remaining lasting remembrances of the names of Smith and Cheke. But as God hath blessed each of you with an hopeful heir male, so may they prove the best monuments of their blessed ancestors: and may they become excellent patterns of wisdom, sobriety, and usefulness; the best way to entail God's blessing upon both your houses and families, and to perpetuate them in wealth and honour. Which is the prayer of,

Sir,

Your most humble Servant,

JOHN STRYPE.

ADVERTISEMENT.

At the end of this Life is added a Discourse made by Sir John Cheke concerning Superstition; which he set before his Latin translation of a tract of Plutarch upon the same subject, by way of dedication to King Henry VIII. It hath lien, for ought I know, this hundred and fifty years and more in obscurity; but lately discovered in the library of University college, Oxon, by the Reverend Mr. W. Elstob, then a Fellow of that house: who did not only courteously transcribe it for me, but hath now voluntarily taken the pains to translate it out of Cheke's elegant Latin into English, for the more common benefit. It is indeed imperfect, and defective of some pages, which is great pity; but the greatest part is remaining, and worthy to be preserved, to shew the learning of the writer, and likewise his good intention and desire of forwarding a reformation of the Church of England in those times, and of exciting King Henry, as far as he durst, to cast off the superstitions and corruptions mixed with the public worship of God then used.

And as we have retrieved this piece of this learned man, so it is heartily to be wished that other of his works and writings might come to light.

J. S.

CHAPTERS AND CONTENTS.

CHAP. I.

A VIEW of Sir John Cheke, from his birth to his leaving
the University, and advancement at Court.　　　P. 1

CHAP. II.

From Cheke's coming to Court, to his advancement to the
Provostship of King's college in Cambridge.　　　P. 22

CHAP. III.

From Cheke's retirement to Cambridge, to his receiving
the honour of knighthood.　　　P. 39

CHAP. IV.

CHAP. V.

REMARKABLE LETTERS OF SIR JOHN CHEKE AND OTHERS, COLLECTED IN THIS HISTORY.

BOOKS AND MANUSCRIPTS MADE USE OF OR MENTIONED IN THIS WORK.

VARIA penes me MSSta.

Visitation Books in the Office of Arms.

Weever's Funeral Monuments.

Bishop of London's Register.

Fuller's Worthies.

Fox's Acts and Monuments.

His Martyrology, the first edition.

A MS. of Dr. Sloan's.

Checi de Recta Græcæ Linguæ Pronuntiatione.

Epistola D. Winton Checo in libro præfat.

Cælii Secundi Curionis Epist. Dedicatoria eidem Libro.

Aschami Epistolæ.

Lelandi Epigrammata.

Dixoni Poemata, MSS.

Volumen Epistolarum in Biblioth. C. C. C. C.

Dr. Langbain's Life of Cheke.

Haddoni Epistolæ.

Register of the University of Oxon.

Johan. Foxii MSS.

Sir John Hayward's Life of King Edward VI.

The Hurt of Sedition, written by Cheke.

Holinshed's Chronicle.

Warrant Book of King Edward VI. Of his Gifts, Grants, Sales, &c.

Council Book of King Edward VI.

Athenæ Oxonienses.

Order of the Policy and Offices of the Realm.

Bracton.

Bale's Centuries, first edition, in quarto.

Dr. Laurence Humphry de Nobilitate.

Dr. Ponet's Treatise of Politick Power.

MSS. of William Petyt, Esq. Keeper of the Tower Records.

The Decretals.

Petri Martyris Epistolæ. Edit. Genev.

MSS. of Sir Henry St. George, Knight, Garter King at Arms.

H. Holland's Heroologia.

Sir Thomas Chaloner's Miscellanea.

Dugdale's Baronage.

Dr. Thomas Wylson's English Translation of Demosthenes' Orations.

Epistola Nic. Carri de Morte Buceri.

Life of Sir Thomas Smith, Knight.

Miscellanea D. in Biblioth. C. C. C. C.

State Worthies, by Lloyd.

Grotii Annotationes in Novum Testamentum.

Monasticon Anglicanum.

THE

L I F E

OF

THE LEARNED

SIR JOHN CHEKE.

CHAP. I.

*A view of Sir John Cheke, from his birth to his leaving
the University, and advancement at Court.*

SIR JOHN CHEKE was raised purely by his learned _{Anno 1514.} abilities, and his name requires a place among the most memorable men of those times, being one of the completest scholars for Latin and Greek learning in that age; and having the happiness to be the chief instructor of the blessed King Edward's youth, a Prince so singular for learning, knowledge, and religion, that he wanted nothing but a longer life to render him one of the most illustrious monarchs in the world: in the praise whereof, Cheke, his guide and teacher, must have a share.

Being minded to revive the memory of this gentleman, I shall endeavour to give a view of him; first, from his birth to his leaving of the University, and coming to Court; next, from his coming to Court, to his travels abroad and exile; and lastly, from his exile to his return and death.

SECT. I.

*Cheke's birth and family; vindicated. His nativity.
Parents.*

IT is one of the chief honours of the town of Cambridge, _{Cambridge,} that Cheke was born there; at which place his father set- _{Cheke's birth-place.}

tled, upon occasion of his matching with a gentlewoman of that county. For the family was anciently of the Isle of Wight, where it long flourished in wealth and reputation, and received accessions of honour by divers intermarriages. For Hayward, who wrote the life of King Edward VI. must be corrected, who, in that book, hath done this gentleman wrong, in disparaging his pedigree, as though it were obscure; where, speaking of the Prince's tutors, Dr. Cox and Sir John Cheke, he describes them to have been " of mean birth; and that they might be said to be " born of themselves, for the esteem of their virtue and " learning, by reason of the place of their employment."

The family of the Chekes.

He was the son and heir of Peter Cheke, a younger brother of the ancient house of the Chekes of Motston in the Isle of Wight. For to fetch his genealogy for some generations backward, as it lies in the visitation-books of the heralds; Richard Cheke of Motston, in the time of Richard II. married one of the daughters of Montacute, or Montague. His son was called Edward, who married a daughter of Trenenian. By whom he had John Cheke of Motstone, that matched with a daughter of Tremain. By whom he had issue John, whose wife was a daughter of Glamorgan, of the county of Southampton. His son was Robert, who married the daughter of Bremshot of Bremshot. Whose sons were David and Peter, the father of John Cheke, the subject of our story. David's line for divers generations after him enjoyed Motstone.

Peter Cheke's stock.

Peter, the second son, married Agnes, daughter of Dufford [i. e. De Ufford, a great name once] of the county of Cambridge, a grave, wise, and good woman. Ascham, in one of his epistles, styles her *venerandam illam fœminam,* i. e. that venerable woman. By whom Peter had Anne, married to George Allington; Alice, to Dr. Blithe, the first public King's Reader of the Physic Lecture in the University of Cambridge. He was of King's college, and sometime Proctor there; and a traveller beyond sea: Elizabeth, to Spering; Mary, matched with Sir William Cecil, afterwards Secretary of State to King Edward and Queen

Elizabeth; and Magdalen, first married to Eresby, then SECT.
to John Purefoy of Leicestershire. And besides these ___I.___
daughters, he had, by the same Agnes, John his son and Anno 1514.
heir.

If one were minded to seek further after this family, we Others of
might be told of one Margaret Cheke, who obtained a li- of the
cence from King Richard III. to found a chauntry for one Chekes.
Priest, in the parish church of Long Ashton, nigh Bristol; book of that
which bespake her a person of quality and wealth. We King.
might be told, that some of this name were dispersed in
Suffolk, where, in the parish church of Debnam, anno 1440, Weev. Mon.
was buried John Cheke, gentleman. There also lay buried p. 783.
Robert Cheke, and Rose his wife, as appears by a monumental inscription there. The name also flourished in the
city of London in Queen Elizabeth's time: where was also
one John Cheke, a wealthy citizen of the Company of
Mercers; who, upon a loan from the city, anno 1588, that
memorable year, (when the richest sort of all the companies lent their proportions to the Queen,) for his share lent
her 100*l.* To which I add another Cheke, named also
John, ordained Deacon anno 1560, by Grindal, Bishop of
London; which John is charactered in the Book of Ordina-
tions to be *liberæ conditionis, et laudabilis commendatio-* Regist. Bp.
nis, i. e. of genteel extract, as well as laudable life and Lond.
conversation.

These I the rather mention, to extinguish that ill report Cheke's
Sir John Hayward had suggested to the world of our dicated.
Cheke's mean birth; whom Dr. Fuller also hath taken
notice of with some just indignation, leaving him this character for his pains, that " he was a learned pen, but too Full. Wor-
" free in dealing disgraceful characters on the subjects thies.
" thereof:" adding this further account of Cheke's family,
that the paternal estate was 300*l.* per annum, never increased nor diminished till twenty years ago, [that is, so
many years before the time of Fuller's writing this,] when
it was sold outright; and that one of those Chekes in
Richard the II.'s days married a daughter of the Lord
Mountague's; though it may be inquired, whether that

CHAP.
I.
family were advanced to the honour of barons so anciently as that King's time.

Ann. 1514,
et seq.
In what
year born.
Acts and
Mon. first
edit. p. 807.
A MS. of
Dr. Sloan's.

The gentleman of whom we are to write was born in the year 1514, as I collect from his age, when he was called in for a witness to answer certain interrogatories concerning Bishop Gardiner, in December or January, anno 1550, being then set down to be thirty-six years of age: and more certainly from his nativity, calculated by his dear friend Sir Thomas Smith, that he was born the same year, on the 16th day of June, at two of the clock five minutes afternoon. And perhaps it may not be unacceptable to some to exhibit this scheme of his nativity, drawn up by so notable a man.

Cheke's
nativity.

1514 Die 16° Junii

Ho. 2. Mi. 5° post

Meridiem Cantabrigiæ.

JOANNES CHÆCUS.

His parents'
character.

His parents bore a repute in Cambridge for their honesty and integrity: and that character Gardiner Bishop of Winchester himself gave of them; who, while he lived

in Cambridge, and resided in Trinity hall there, maintained a good acquaintance and friendship with them, as
in one of his controversial letters to Cheke he hints; tell-
ing him, that he had his ᵃeducation under honest parents,
and such as were among the number of the best.

SECT. II.

*His education, proficiency; usefulness at St. John's
College.*

HE was bred up to learning, and from the grammar
school was admitted into St. John's college in Cambridge.
Which, as it communicated good literature and sound religion to him, so he afterwards proved a singular ornament
to it. For here he seemed not only to receive the grounds
of learning, but also the principles of true religion, and
the knowledge and love of the Gospel, which he so closely
adhered to, and so heartily professed, and endured so much
for afterwards. For this was one of the colleges in that
University, which in Cardinal Wolsey's days was noted
for reading privately the holy Scriptures and Luther's
books, and for their discovering thereby the abuses of religion. In this college, in the middle and latter times of
King Henry VIII. many excellently learned persons sprang
up, who unveiled and exposed the gross errors and corruptions wherewith the Popes of Rome and their party
had imposed upon the Church of Christ. Here were the
Levers and the Pilkintons, afterwards exceeding useful
preachers under King Edward, and exiles under Queen
Mary. Here was Taylor, afterward Bishop of Lincoln,
turned out of the House of Lords in Queen Mary's first
Parliament, for no reason, whatsoever was pretended, unless for his religion. Here were Roger Ascham, Hutchinson, Raven, Grindal, (tutor to the Lady Elizabeth,) and
divers others, who disputed at home, and offered to do so
more publicly in the Schools, against the Mass.

ᵃ Educatus ex parentibus probis atque adeo optimis. *Ep. D. Winton. Checo,
de Pronunt.*

Cheke so closely plied his studies, that he soon became a scholar of note, and, though but young, arrived to excellent skill in the learned languages. So that the commendation of him, and of his parts and abilities, came to the King, chiefly by the means of Dr. Butts, the King's Physician, who was Cheke's great friend, counsellor, and the encourager of his studies, and whom he called his *patron;* and to whom he once wrote a pious letter from Hartford, (where he was with Prince Edward,) upon a fit of sickness. For Cheke being once at Court with Butts, he took occasion to recommend him to the King for a singular scholar, and particularly for his study and proficiency in the Greek tongue. And being thus known to the King, he soon after advanced him to the honour to be his Scholar, together with one [b] Smith of Queen's college, afterwards sufficiently known, being Secretary of State, and employed in embassies abroad. To both whom the King exhibited for the encouragement of their studies, and for the bearing of their expenses of travel into foreign countries. A very good practice formerly used by our Princes, to fit and train up young scholars for the service of the King and Court, to be Ambassadors, Secretaries, Privy Counsellors, Bishops, Tutors to the nobility, and the like; having learned the languages of other countries, acquainted themselves with their customs, and visited the Courts of Princes. This qualified Cheke to be sent for to the Court, and to have the young Prince Edward committed to his care and charge, as we shall see by and by.

And as he and Smith were partners and consorts in the King's favour, so were they constant companions, being both of like age, conditions, studiousness, and pursuing the same methods of good learning. And though there was an emulation between them, who should outdo the other, yet so generous were the tempers of these young men, that it was so far from begetting envy between them, that, on the contrary, it knit them together in the most intimate friendship and endearments, like natural brethren.

[b] Sir Thomas.

But this distinguishing favour of the King, and that start SECT.
II.
they got in their studies beyond others, kindled a secret _____
hatred and malice against them in the minds of many of Ann. 1540,
et seq.
the rest of the University, and which they more manifestly
shewed in that opposition they made to them afterwards,
when they attempted the bringing in a more correct way
of reading the Greek tongue.

While Mr. Cheke was in the college, what with his St. John's
college
flourishes
by the means
of Cheke in
learning.
exemplary industry in his own studies, what with his dili-
gent instruction of the youth under him, St. John's flourished. He directed to a better method of study, and to
more substantial and useful learning: so that he was said
by one that knew him very well, " cto have laid the very
" foundations of learning in that college." Under whom,
or with whom, were bred Denny, Redman, Bil, Lever,
Pilkington, Tong, Ayre, Ascham, Cecil, and others, spread
abroad afterwards in Court, and in places of trust and honour both in Church and State. The two last mentioned
were his scholars of such a size and magnitude, that they
deserve to be mentioned again. Sir William Cecil was one, Cecil, his
pupil.
whom Leland in one of his epigrams to him takes notice
of for this:

Candidus erudiit noster te CHÆCUS amicus,
    CHÆCUS Cecropii gloria prima gregis.

And one Dixon, a good poet in those times, in certain
verses dedicated to him, when he came to speak of his
education at Cambridge, thus expressed it:

Atque frequentabas tunc numina docta sororum,
    Sub CHECO humano, doctiloquoque viro.

And what an honour must the education of such a man as
Cecil derive upon his tutor; that proved afterwards one of
the wisest, justest, and most fortunate Statesmen in Europe;
and to whose counsels and deliberations, the wonderful and
long successes of Queen Elizabeth must, under God, be

---

c Literarum fundamenta, te authore, in nostro collegio jacta sunt. *Ascham.*
Epist. ii. 45.

CHAP.
I.

Ann. 1540,
et seq.
Ascham, his
scholar.

And Dr.
Bill.

Vol. Epist.
in C. C. C.
C. Arch.
Ep. V. 50.

chiefly attributed? The other was Roger Ascham[d], one of the politest Latin writers of that generation, or any after. Whose learning and ingenuity appear in those two books[e] he left behind him, *The Schoolmaster*, and *The Art of Shooting out of a Bow.* He was tutor in the Latin and Greek tongue to the Lady Elizabeth, afterwards Secretary of an embassy from King Edward to the Emperor; and, upon the decease of that King, Latin Secretary to Queen Mary and Queen Elizabeth successively, as he was designed for that King[f], had he lived.

And all that good service that that well known person, Dr. Bill, afterwards did in the Church and University, was in a great measure owing to the instruction and friendship of Cheke, whose scholar he seemed to be: Dr. Bill, I say, that was Master of St. John's college, Dean of Westminster, Almoner to Queen Elizabeth, one of the Visitors of the University, and concerned in making the statutes for that collegiate Church, and (if I mistake not) Provost of Eton, and in his time a great promoter of virtue and true religion in these capacities. This man, when a student in that college of St. John's, was very poor; and being Bachelor of Arts, when he should have been chosen Fellow, had not wherewithal to discharge the arrears of college debts; a thing necessary in order to his election. By which means it was deferred, and perhaps he might have been forced at last to have quitted his course of studies, and left the University. At this pinch Cheke procured him a friend at Court with Queen Anne Bolen, a lady extraordinary munificent towards deserving scholars that needed supportation in their studies. So that nothing was wanting but the recommendation of such to her by Skip or Parker, or some other of her chief Chaplains, and the business was effected. Cheke about Michaelmas earnestly despatched

[d] This Ascham, shewing the rules for true imitation, which he calls the
Schoolmas- necessary tools and instruments wherewith it is wrought, saith, "I openly
ter, p. 48. " confess they be not of mine own forgeing, but partly left unto me by the
" conningest master, and one of the worthiest jentlemen, that ever England
" bred, Syr John Cheke."
[e] Epistles also. [f] Edw. VI.

a letter to Parker, laying open the condition of Bill to him, SECT. II.
giving him the character of *literatus et honestus, qui et*
rerum cognitione abundat et integritate morum; i. e. Ann. 1540, et seq.
learned and honest, plentifully endowed with knowledge
of things, and incorrupt in his manners: that he had come
into his fellowship before Easter, but that he could not get
his money ready. He prayed Parker to acquaint the Queen
with his condition, and to procure him favour from her;
which if he would do, it would be a thing pious and holy,
in promoting the studies and good learning of such as were
overburdened with the misfortune of poverty: and that if
he obtained this for him before All-Saints day, he would
hereby do a further good deed; that is, not only to put Bill
in possession of his fellowship, but give an opportunity to
others to come into his room, there being then to be an
election of Scholars to succeed into the empty scholar-
ships; and him, *viz.* Cheke, he should infinitely oblige.
And this no question was compassed by this seasonable
mediation, and a foundation laid for Dr. Bill's useful learning, preferments, and influence on the public. He preferred ingenious and studious scholars of his college, as it
lay in his way. William Grindal, bred up under Roger
Ascham, and the best Grecian one of them in the University, he took from the college; and after some time
keeping him with him, preferred him, in King Henry the
Eighth's time, to read Greek to the Lady Elizabeth. Ascham recommended him to Cheke, with a great character Ascham Ep. ii. 15.
(as fit for a Court) for his learning and studiousness, for
his taciturnity, fidelity, and abstinence; and ready to take
any business Cheke should put him upon. He died in the
Lady Elizabeth's family, a young man of great hopes.

And this then was the flourishing estate of the college,
while Cheke, and his friends, and scholars were there. But
to keep up the former good condition of that house, Ascham, after some discontinuance, desired of Secretary Cecil to have leave to return back there again, when all the
rest were gone, like seed to propagate true learning and
piety. Wherein he thus expressed himself: " Seeing the Mr. Cheke's crop at St. John's.
" goodly crop of Mr. Cheke was almost clean carried from

" thence, [*i. e.* the college,] and I in a manner alone of
" that time left a standing straggler, peradventure though
" my fruit be very small, yet, because the ground from
" whence it springs was so good, I may yet be thought
" somewhat fit for seed, when all you the rest are taken
" up for better store; wherewith the King and the realm is
" now so nobly served."

In short, Cheke promoted good religion as well as learning in his college by his labours, which had a very good
influence upon that society long after.   So that these two
things he made his great aim: the one was to set on foot
universal learning in the college; that it might not be
without some that were well studied in each liberal science,
and that each scholar, according as his genius prompted
him, might make either one or other the main subject of
his study: and so St. John's g become a storehouse of all
good learning.   The other thing he aimed at, was to bring
into the college the study especially of divinity: not such
a divinity as prevailed then in the world, corrupt and con-
founded with such principles and doctrines as were easily
discovered to be brought in by designing men, on purpose
to obtain secular ends, and to aggrandize the Bishop of
Rome, and make all the world dependent on him: but
such a divinity as was from God, stripped of all such gross
frauds and abuses.   And, for that purpose, he advised that
a man should come to the study of divinity, without being
at all prepossessed with the commonly received notions;
but that he should fetch the whole doctrine of Christ out
of the fountains of Scripture, where the avowed principles
of Christianity lie; and next unto them, from the primitive and apostolical writings, which were the nearest to
those fountains.   And withal he particularly recommended
this rule, that the greatest care and caution should be had,
that nothing be derived from the sink of Pelagianism h, to
infect these divine studies.

g Ut singuli sic in singulis, natura duce, elaborarent, ut universa illa literarum societas in hac societate nostra [S. Johannis] contineretur. *Int. Ascham.*
Epist. iii. 35.
    h Ascham, ii. 45.

What effect these directions of Cheke had in the college, for the study of divinity, may appear from a passage
that happened there some time after he was gone, *anno*
1548; a disputation was held in course. The *thesis* was, *de*
Missa, ipsane Cœna Dominica fuerit, necne : i. e. concerning the Mass, whether it were the Lord's Supper or no.
It was managed very learnedly by Tho. Lever and Roger
Hutchinson. Some in the University took this private disputation very ill. The matter was brought to that pass at
length, that Ascham undertook, by the encouragement of
many in that college, to dispute this question in the public schools, and to bring it forth out of their private college
walls before the public University; and that for this end
and intent, to learn freely from learned men what could
be produced from the fountain of holy Scripture to defend
the Mass; which had not only taken up the chief place in
religion, and in the consciences of men, but had, by the
common practice and custom of Christians, taken away all
the faithful ministry of God's word and sacraments. And
for this purpose, the men of St. John's had conference
among themselves. They resolved that the canonical Scripture should be the authority that they would desire to
have the whole matter decided by. They also heaped together the old canons of the primitive Church, the councils
of Fathers, the decrees of Popes, the judgment of Doctors,
the rout of Questionists, all later writers, both Germans[i]
and Romanists. All these, as far as they could, they got
together, for the furnishing themselves the better to state
this question. But the matter got wind, and the noise of it,
though they went about it with all the quietness, went abroad
in the University; insomuch as some took public notice of
it, and at last obtained so much of the Vice-Chancellor, Dr.
Madew, that he, by his letters, stopped this disputation.
Nay, it fled as far as to Lambeth, where their enemies, with
loud outcries, made complaints to Archbishop Cranmer
against them: and they called them rash and heady. But
though their disputation was by this means hindered, yet
their studies proceeded still upon the same subject of the

---

[i] Lutherans.

CHAP.
I.

Ann. 1540,
et seq. Mass: and in short time they digested their arguments
into a just book, which they intended to present to the
Lord Protector, unless Cheke and Cecil (unto whom they
discovered all this) thought it more convenient to forbear so
to do. Thus inclined and affected stood this college to true
religion: a great cause whereof was Cheke's influence. In
short, while Cheke was a member of the college, he in-
fluenced much, not only in a diligent promoting learning
and religion, but in wisely pacifying and quieting domestic
commotions. After he was gone, he was dearly missed in
both respects. Of this Ascham, remaining behind there,
Epist. p. 77.
li. 15. takes notice, and complained once to him of the ill times
that followed his departure from them, for the want of his
counsels.

SECT. III.

*Made the King's Greek Professor. Reforms the pronun-
ciation of Greek.*

A great
light to the
University. ALL this he was to the college; but his light diffused
itself over all the University, to the benefit of it, as well as
for his own glory. He was of chief esteem for all human
learning, and was a great judge of it. Leland, one of the
floridest scholars there, teaches as much, whilst he submits his epigrams to his censure, and bids his book strive
to make itself approved and acceptable to Cheke.

> *Si vis Thespiadum choro probari,*
> *Fac, ut consilio, libelle, nostro,*
> *Facundo studeas placere CHECO.*

For he was a great master of language, and a happy imi-
tator of the great orator: and *Facundus, i. e.* Eloquent,
was the epithet Leland thought proper for him. His presence and society inspired the University with a love of
learning: and the youth every where addicted themselves
to the reading and studying of the best authors for pure
Roman style, and Grecian eloquence; such as Cicero and
Demosthenes; laying aside their old barbarous writers and
schoolmen, with their nice and unprofitable questions.
The benefit whereof was, that as good learning increased

there, so also did true religion and the knowledge of the SECT. III.
Gospel; Popery being sheltered with nothing so much as
barbarism and ignorance. And as it was thus with the Ann. 1540, et seq.
University, while Cheke was there, so when he was
gone from it, learning and religion seemed with the absence of him to wither and languish. A thing which Cheke
himself could not but take notice of with trouble, in a letter to a friend of his in the University, that the Cantabri- Aschami
gians τὰ πολλὰ ὑστερίζειν, *i. e.* were wanting in many things, Epist. fol. 104. ii. 45.
or went much backward. Such a want had the University
of the daily incitements and good example of some such
an one as he.

But that that gave a great stroke to Cheke's endeavours Made the
for the restoration of learning here, was that the Univer- King's Greek Lec-
sity chose him their Greek Lecturer; and this he per- turer.
formed without any salary. But the King, about the year
1540, having founded a Greek lecture, with the salary of
40*l.* a year, for the encouraging that study, (not long after
he had made him his Scholar,) constituted him his first Greek
Professor, being now Master of Art, and about twenty-six
years of age. Together with Cheke, were now constituted
other very learned Professors in the University, which
made it flourish. For as Cheke was Reader of the Greek
lecture, Wiggin read Divinity, Smith Civil Law, Wakefield
Hebrew, and Blith (who married Cheke's sister) Physic;
being all the King's Professors, with the salary of 40*l.* a
year: as Ascham acquainted a friend of his, speaking of Epist. Bran-
the flourishing state of the University at that time. And disbæo.
that which was an addition to Cheke's honour, as well as
the repute he had for his excellent skill in the Greek, we
have been told by one that hath given some short notes of Dr. Lang-
his life, that when this lecture, with the salary before bains's Life of Cheke,
mentioned, was to be disposed of, Cheke was absent; and before his
though there were three competitors earnestly making edition of the True
their interest for it, yet Cheke's name obtained it from Subject,
them. This place it seems he was so well pleased with, &c.
that he held it long after he left the University, *viz.* until
October 1551.

CHAP.
I.

Ann. 1542,
et seq.
Reforms the
pronuncia-
tion of
Greek.
Hereby Cheke, together with his learned contemporary, Smith, (who ever went along with him in promoting good literature,) was highly instrumental in bringing into more request the study of Greek, in which language all learning anciently was contained; and from Greece it flowed into Italy, and other parts of the world. This language was little known or understood hitherto in this realm. And if any saw a piece of Greek, they used to say, *Græcum est; non potest legi,* i. e. "It is Greek, it cannot be read." And those few that did pretend to some insight into it, read it after a strange corrupt manner, pronouncing the vowels and diphthongs, and several of the consonants, very much amiss: confounding the sound of the vowels and diphthongs so, that there was little or no difference between them. As for example, αι was pronounced as ε, οι and ει as ιωτα; η, ι, υ, were expressed in one and the same sound; that is, as ιωτα. Also some of the consonants were pronounced differently, according as they were placed in the word; that is to say, when τ was placed after μ, it was pronounced as our *d.* And when π was put after ν, then it was sounded as our *b.* The letter κ was pronounced as we do *ch,* β as we do the *v* consonant. But since different letters must make different sounds, Cheke, with his friend Smith, concluded these to be very false ways of reading Greek, and sounds utterly different from what the ancient Greeks read and spake. But what the true way was, that they both earnestly set themselves to consider and find out; which at length they did, partly by considering the power of the letters themselves, and partly by consulting with Greek authors, Aristophanes and others; in some whereof they found footsteps to direct them how the ancient Greeks pronounced.

These errors then Cheke in his lectures plainly discovered, and at length exploded. And the more studious and ingenuous sort of scholars being convinced, most gladly forsook their old way of reading Greek, for this more right and true, though new found out, shewn them by their learned Reader. But there was a party in the

University, who, disliking any thing that was new, and
dreading alterations, and blindly admitting every thing
that was old, would by no means allow of this pronunciation, but opposed it with all their might, by disputing
against it, and at last, by complaining to Gardiner, Bishop
of Winchester, the Chancellor of the University, against
Cheke and his adherents for this great misdemeanor. Who
being of the same mind with the complainants, and fear-
ing innovation more than was need, made a solemn decree, dated the calends of June 1542, confirming the old
corrupt sounding of Greek, and enjoining the scholars to
make no variation, and that upon these pains, *viz.* If he
were a regent, to be expelled out of the senate; if he
stood for a degree, not to be admitted to it; if a scholar,
to lose his scholarship; and the younger sort to be chastised. And in short, the decree ran, " That none should
" philosophize at all in sounds, but all use the present.
" And that if any thing were to be corrected in them, let
" it all be left to authority ᵏ."

SECT. III.

Letters pass between Cheke and the Chancellor of the
University about it.

AND besides this, the Chancellor sent a Latin letter to
Cheke, the Greek Lecturer, to forbear any farther men-
tioning his new way of pronunciation in his lectures:
however treating him like a man of learning, and arguing
with him in an humane and scholar-like manner. Beginning his letter in this obliging style: " Stephen Bishop
" of Winton, Chancellor of the University of Cambridge,
" to John Cheke wisheth health. That which the Chan-
" cellor according to his right should do, namely, by his
" authority as a magistrate to abate and restrain unwary
" rashness, when it waxeth wanton in learning, I thought
" rather to be attempted by friendship. That I might ob-

ᵏ In sonis omnino ne philosophator, sed utitor præsentibus. In hiis siquid
emendandum sit, id omne autoritati permittite.

" tain that by fair means from a mild nature, and im-
" proved by human studies, which power would exact of
" the rude and barbarous. Therefore I purpose to deal
" with you in this epistle, not as a Chancellor with a
" scholar, but as a man somewhat versed in learning with a
" hard student; and to talk at the least with a young man
" of very great hopes, if the heat of age do not add a hurt-
" ful and too daring excess; a thing which (I must tell
" you) many dislike in you. For your attempt, as I hear,
" not so much with the derision of all, as with their anger
" also, to bring in a new sound of letters, as well in the
" Greek as in the Latin, and to settle it among the youth.
" And you, who have by the King's munificence obtained
" the office of teaching a tongue, do destroy the use of it
" by a new sound," &c.

Cheke an-
swers the
Chancel-
lor's letter.
But Cheke could not be persuaded to let go this enterprise of restoring the true and graceful pronouncing the
Latin, and especially the Greek; which he had upon so
good and sure grounds undertaken. Yet thought fit to
give a very submissive answer in Latin to the Chancellor;
expressing much deference towards him, and yet freely
discoursing the matter with him, and shewing in much
exquisite learning upon what reasons and authorities he
went. And thus he began his address to him:

" How much pleasure, most worthy Prelate, I took in
" the first letter privately to me sent, wherein I saw my-
" self treated so friendly and obligingly," &c. But the controversy afterwards grew more warm between the Chancellor and Cheke; who had seriously, and with an ingenuous freedom, expostulated with him about the decree he
had made, whereby so commendable a reformation of a
considerable piece of learning was checked, to the grief
and discouragement of the best scholars. This bad effect
he plainly set forth to the Bishop; and shewed how fully
he acquitted the place and office the King's Majesty had
set him in, in making him his Greek Reader; and how
much the Bishop's late orders had obstructed his Majesty's noble designs in this lecture: which was for put-

ting scholars upon the study of that learned language, and
for the further advancement of it. For, as he wrote to the
foresaid reverend person, " Is this," said he, " to err from
" my office, [as it seems the Bishop had laid to his charge,]
" and from the place wherein the King hath set me, to
" teach what is most ancient, what is most profitable,
" what most distinct? Which, since it was granted me
" by the King, it afflicts me not a little, that it is by you
" lessened and abridged. For had the University be-
" stowed this lecture on me, I could not without great
" trouble of mind have been drawn away from it, while I
" profitably and honestly performed my duty therein.
" With what mind then must I bear it, when the King
" himself hath bestowed it on me? And by reason of the
" rejection of that right pronunciation, neither have I the
" fruit of reading, nor they that come the desire of hear-
" ing; and almost all have cast off the study of the Greek
" tongue. For, when I entered upon this royal office of
" reading the Greek lecture, I found all my auditors well
" instructed in this way of pronouncing, and earnestly ap-
" plied themselves to the study of the Greek; and all (one
" or two only excepted) with all cheerfulness addicted to
" this way. Since therefore this pronunciation hath been
" received now a good many years, and is widely scat-
" tered among men by a customary use of it, should I
" alone, for no cause, reject that hath been received by all
" upon very great cause? Should I envy them so great a
" benefit, by removing it from them, or take it away by
" disparaging it? Or rather, should not I pursue this
" most glorious institution of the King, by the fruitfulest
" way of reading that I could."

Then he freely told the Bishop the success of his letter
to the University, " That since the order therein con-
" tained, many had departed from his lecture; and they
" that came, came with so sad and melancholic minds, as
" one would think they were mourning for the death of a
" friend. For, as he went on, with reluctancy of the best
" learned, and in effect of the whole University, you have

Marginal notes: SECT. IV. Anno 1542. De Pronunciat. p. 102. Cheke shews the Chancellor the ill effect of his letter to the University.

c

" again shut them up in this corrupt confusion; which is " so gross that we may almost feel it with our hand. " Wherefore, if any thing hereafter happen otherwise than " the King's Majesty expecteth, it is not to be ascribed to " me, who have taken the best way, and followed the me- " thod used among us; but it will lay on them who move " things well placed," &c. He subjoined, " Truly, I fear, " we must have no more declaiming in Greek, which we " daily practised before, since that which was distinct and " clear is taken away, and that which is confused and un- " sound is only left. For that pronunciation, which our " ears so liked and approved, is now gone into the utmost " parts of the earth: nor, however profitable it be, how- " ever true, however noble and magnificent, can longer " tarry at Cambridge by reason of the punishments and " mulcts threatened."

Thus did Cheke with an ingenuous boldness express his mind, and argue with the Bishop about this matter: wherein he shewed as well his eloquence, as his conscientious care of discharging the office committed to him by the King, and his zeal for the promoting of learning.

But whatever opposition of injunctions, decrees, and penalties were made against it; yet, as it was said of truth, it is great, and will prevail, so this true way of speaking and reading Greek got the day in the University.

Cheke's way of sounding Greek prevails.
And those that were the greatest ornaments of learning then in Cambridge, Redman, Smith, Ponet, Pickering, Ascham, Tong, Bill, and all others, who either read any thing publicly in the schools, or privately in the colleges, gave themselves wholly to this correct way.

Seven letters pass between Gardiner and Cheke.
In fine, there passed seven learned epistles between the Chancellor and our Greek Professor; wherein was comprised, I think, whatsoever could be said on this argument pro or con, containing considerable learning in them. The originals whereof were left in the hands of Cælius Secundus Curio, a learned man of Basil, by Cheke himself, as he passed through that place in his journey into Italy, in the beginning of Queen Mary's reign. From which ori-

ginals Cælius printed them anno 1555: dedicating them
to the learned Sir Anthony Cook, Cheke's dear friend,
and fellow instructor of good King Edward; giving him
this reason for publishing them, that after he had diligently perused them, he saw nothing in that kind ever
more perfectly written. And therefore judged so great a
good was by all means to be communicated to all that
were studious of good literature.

SECT. V.

What and how Cheke read.

BUT let us go and hear our Greek Lecturer read. In Cheke reads
his readings, among other authors he read Herodotus; and Herodotus.
in that ancient historian particularly, the books entitled
Euterpe and Polyhymnia, where Cheke had occasion to
speak of some places in Italy and Greece, and to describe
them. Which he did with that life and advantage of expression, [a] that one of the most ingenious of his auditors
ever after had a most ardent inclination to travel, and see
those parts of the world: so that he confessed it could
not be quenched by any fears of labour or danger, which
commonly are the attendants of travel. It was Ascham,
whom we have had occasion several times to mention already. Who afterwards being Secretary to Sir Richard
Morisin, King Edward's Ambassador, and now in Germany, had a fresh mind to pursue his long desire, of which
he remembers Cheke in a letter to him; adding, that
though for the bearing of travel, he had not a robust body,
yet that he could bear labour, and cold, and heat, and any
kind of food and drink, (the necessary qualification of a
hard student, and fit as well for a traveller,) wanting nothing but a purse; praying him, his friend, to assist him
by his interest with the rich, to supply him with travelling
expenses; promising him, as some recompense, that he
would bring him home a fair account of the customs, manners, and fashions of those places, whereof Cheke was

[a] Asch. Epist. iii. 16.

c 2

ever held with an admiration. He signified what a good
husband he would be; and that a little would serve a little ordinary man as he was. No annual pension it was
that he desired, but only a little money for the present
expedition to set him out. That he had made noble
friends in England, and particularly his lady, the Lady
Elizabeth, who, he made no doubt, would upon the motion
contribute largely to his petition. And the Duchess of
Suffolk would be another, who had already promised him
largely and nobly: whose son, the Lord Charles, he had
instructed for some months in Greek: and her liberality
he had reserved for this time and use. The Duke of Suffolk, the other son of the Duchess, favoured him also;
since by his means and teaching, he wrote so fair a hand
as he did. From both the Marquisses also, viz. Dorset
and Northampton, he had also great expectation. But
the imparting of these his requests, he left to be managed
by his friend Cheke, who, as we heard before, had blown
up these desires in him; and in his ancient goodwill to
him he confided.

The benefit
of Cheke's
lectures.
    Thus did the lectures of Cheke inflame his auditors to
noble desires and virtuous enterprises; and tended not
barely to instruct them in the understanding of a language, but to enlarge their faculties with good knowledge,
and to furnish their minds with principles of wisdom, by
his learned expositions and commentaries upon the authors he read to them. In short, we must dismiss our
Greek Reader with the character Leland gave him:

Chæcus Cecropii gloria prima gregis.

" Cheke the chief glory of th' Athenian tribe."

SECT. VI.

Cheke University Orator.

Cheke Uni-
versity Ora-
tor.
    CHEKE was an orator as well as a linguist; and the
University made him some time their Orator. And in that
office he adorned the Roman language, as well as in his

lectures he did the Grecian. Which place he held till he
removed to Court; and then was succeeded by Mr. Ascham
of the same college.

It was about the year 1543, that Cheke, being still at
Cambridge, gave the first specimen in print of his Greek
learning, as well as public testimony of his gratitude to
the King. For having gotten an authentic Greek MS. of
two of St. Chrysostom's Homilies, he translated them into
elegant Latin, and printed them at London, with a dedication thereof to his sovereign prince and patron the
King. Wherein he took occasion to acknowledge and
extol the King's free and voluntary munificence towards
him, in making him first his Scholar, and then his Greek
Lecturer. Dating it from Cambridge, at Christmas 1543,
subscribing himself, *Tuæ Majestatis Scholasticus, et assi-
duus Precator ;* i. e. " Your Majesty's Scholar, and daily
" Bedesman," as the phrase then was.

But Cheke was now to be transplanted into another
soil, and his learning and virtues were preparing greater
honours for him.

CHAP. II.

From Cheke's coming to Court, to his advancement to the
Provostship of King's College in Cambridge.

SECT. I.

Cheke removed to the Court.   Instructs the Prince.   The
loss of him at Cambridge.   Canon of Christ's Church.
His usefulness.

Anno 1544.
Becomes
schoolmas-
ter to Prince
Edward.

HIS first remove from the University was to the Court;
King Henry VIII. calling him from thence July the 10th,
1544, as judging him a fit person to be schoolmaster to his
only son Prince Edward, in the room, as it seems, of Dr.
Richard Cox, now preferred in the Church, who yet was
much about him, and his Almoner, as he was when he was
King.   To him, joined with Sir Anthony Cook, a man of
exquisite learning and true virtue, were the tender years
of that royal youth committed, to instruct him in learning,
manners, and religion.   Both which men, by their joint and
happy endeavours and counsels, framed a young King of
the greatest, nay, of divine hopes.   There are yet remaining some in print, and more in private libraries, written
with his own hand, (particularly in the library at St.
James's,) several of his pretty elegant Latin epistles to
the King, his father; to Queen Katharine Par, his mother-
in-law; to the Duke of Somerset, his uncle; to Cranmer
Archbishop of Canterbury, his godfather; and to his two
sisters, when he was as yet very young, as likewise other
of his exercises; which shew both his own forwardness in
his learning, and the diligence of his instructors.   Nor did
he intermit his studies, when he came to wear a crown;
but Cheke was always at his elbow, both in his closet and
in his chapel, and wherever else he went, to inform and
teach him.   And that with so much sweetness and easi-
ness, that he took a pleasure and delight in his book; and

observed his set hours constantly at his study. So that in SECT.
fine, one that knew Cheke and Cook well, writing to the ___I.___
latter, had these words : " ª That divine youth drew that Anno 1544.
" instruction from you both, *Qua neque Cyrus nec Achil-*
" *les, neque Alexander, neque ullus unquam Regum poli-*
" *tioremque sanctioremque accepit;* i. e. Than which
" never did Cyrus, nor Achilles, nor Alexander, nor any
" other Kings, receive more polite and holy. With which,
" could he have but grown up to man's estate, and arrived
" to the government of the kingdom, what kingdom in
" earth had been more happy? What nation ever extant
" more blessed?"

But if we look back to the University, what a want
Cheke left there is not easily to be spoken; being a man
that seemed to surpass the rest not only in learning, but
in the free communication of it, and that accompanied
with a marvellous affability and obligingness, and a most
holy and virtuous behaviour; whereby he became a public pattern and example to the youth there. This loss of
Cheke may be better understood by a part of a letter, one
of his University friends wrote to him not long after he
was gone to Court. " My condition," said he, " is harder The want of
" than the rest. They saw how you excelled in parts Cheke in
Cambridge.
" and learning; I not only well knew this too, but was Int. Had-
" throughly acquainted with your more interior orna- don. Epist.
" ments, which diffused themselves through all the parts
" of your life. Which when I then duly weighed, how
" great they were in you, I do so much the more want
" them now, and so much the less am able to bear the
" trifles, the levities, and the ignorances of many of our
" men. But because this was owing either to your hap-
" piness, that you should especially be there, where your
" diligence might flow abroad most extensively into the
" commonwealth; or to our unhappiness, that we should
" undergo the loss of your divine mouth, the loud trum-
" pet, as one may call it, of all good discipline, our trouble
" ought to be abated, lest if we appear over-much dis-

ª Cælius Secund. Curio. Epist. Dedic. ante libr. de Pronunciat.

" quieted, we may seem either not to love the common-
" wealth enough, or ourselves too much. It was a very
" good thought of your Plato, that some changes of com-
" monwealths are natural, that when there happens an
" alteration in the state of our affairs, we should not be
" much moved. And although your body be snatched
" from us, yet your obliging behaviour, your wit, your
" study, your eloquence, and learning, is present in all our
" schools, and in each of our private thoughts." And another of his learned acquaintance and collegians, Roger
Ascham, thus writes of the want of him in the University.

" As oft as I remember the departing of that man from
" the University, (which thing I do not seldome,) so oft do
" I wel perceive our most help and furtherance to learning
" to have gon away with him. For by the great commo-
" dity that we took in hearing him read privatly in his
" chamber, al Homer, Sophocles, and Euripides, Herodo-
" tus, Thucydides, Xenophon, Isocrates, and Plato, we feel
" the great discommodity in not hearing of him Aristotle
" and Demosthenes, which two authors, with al diligence
" last of al, he thought to have redd unto us. And when
" I consider how many men he succoured with his help
" and his ayd, to abide here for learning; and how al men
" were provoked and stirred up by his counsil and daily
" example, how they should come to learning, surely I
" perceive that sentence of Plato to be true, which saith,
" ' That there is nothing better in any commonwealth,
" then that there should be always one or other excellent
" passing man; whose life and virtue should pluck forward
" the wit, diligence, labour, and hope of al other; that
" following his footsteps, they might come to the same
" end, wherunto labour, learning, and virtue, had conveyed
" him before.' "

" The great hindrance of learning in lacking this man,
" greatly I should lament, if this discommodity of ours
" were not joined with the commodity and wealth of the
" whole realm, for which purpose our most noble King,
" ful of wisdom, called up this excellent man, ful of learn-

" ing, to teach noble Prince Edward : an office ful of hope,
" comfort, and solace, to al true hearts of England. For
" whom al England daily doth pray that he, passing his
" tutor in learning and knowledg, following his father in
" wisdom and felicity, according to that example which is
" set afore his eyes, may so set out and maintain Gods
" word, to the abolishment of al Papistry, the confusion
" of al heresy, that therby he, feared of his enemies, loved
" of al his subjects, may bring to his own glory, immortal
" fame and memory; to this realm, wealth, honour, and
" felicity; to true and unfaigned religion, perpetual peace,
" concord, and unity."

King Henry, having lately new founded the college of St. Frideswide in Oxford, (founded first by Cardinal Wolsey,) granted Cheke one of the Canonries of that church soon after he became tutor to the Prince, as some reward and token of his favour towards him. Which was about the year 1544, when, according to the registers of that University, he was incorporated into Oxford, and studied there some time. But the rents of the Canons decaying, the King, anno 1545, added special pensions to some of them; as to Peter Vannes, the learned Italian, and sometime Ambassador for the King into Italy; Richard Croke, S. Th. P. employed also abroad by the King; and our Cheke. Which said pensions were 26*l.* 13*s.* 4*d.* to each. By this preferment we may conclude him to be now in holy Orders.

Cheke, as he had now great opportunities by the place wherein he was put, so he had as great designs of making himself useful to the public. For he set before himself, how that he was now to instruct a Prince, that was one day to take on him the government of a mighty kingdom. And therefore he suited his readings and discourses with the Prince thereunto; that he might go out of his hands an excellent monarch, and become a true father of his country. But besides this, considering how his office required him to be always about the Prince's person, whereby he should have the opportunity of having his ear frequently, he resolved to improve it not so much to his private benefit, as to the benefit of the public, of the University, and of the deserving men there; to get them removed, and placed about the nation in Church and State; that by their influences, truth and virtue might every where be promoted. Thus he spent his time and cares at Court; and ever was a fast friend, and gave his helping hand to learning and religion: which appeared more manifestly afterwards, when his royal scholar, by the death of his most noble father, was advanced to the crown.

SECT. II.

His offices to his friends.

His letter consolatory to Dr. Butts, being sick. NOR did this learned man in the midst of the splendors of a Court neglect his private studies, nor his offices to his friends. Dr. William Butts, M.D. (and a Knight according to his monumental inscription,) domestic Physician to King Henry, had taken notice of Cheke from his youth, and been always a favourer of his hopeful parts, performing the part of a father to him, and Cheke styled himself *his son*. By this physician's interest he seems to have been first made known to the King, and to have received from him those marks of royal favour bestowed upon him, while he lived in the University; and afterwards by him preferred to the Court. For Butts was a friend to good religion and learning. While Cheke was at Hertford, (where the Prince's Court was mostly kept, in the latter times of his father,) this gentleman, in the year 1545, was seized with an afflicting dangerous fit of sickness; which gave a concern to his grateful friend; who composed a pious consolatory epistle to him, suitable to his condition: which being so expressive of his gratitude to the doctor, and withal of piety, and a sense of God, and of his dispensations, I cannot but here transcribe it, as from whence some character may be taken of the writer.

The original by time is somewhat defaced in some places, which I have been fain to supply by some words, which are put in Roman.

Johannes Checus, D. Guilielmo Butts, M. D.

Non dubito quin hanc perturbationem valetudinis tuæ, Vir ornatissime, imitatione *Christi æquissimo animo feras. Nam qui fide intelligunt* illum *omnia administrare, iis nihil potest malum videri, quod* ab illo proficiscitur. *Et qui Deum sapientissimum ac optimum judicant,* sciunt *consilio cuncta ab illo gubernari, et bonis ab illo ad salutem* mitti. Et quanquam *ægritudines aut alii cruciatus pios vexent, non ita* autem iis casu *aliquo objiciuntur, sed divinitus mittuntur hominibus a* Patre eorum cælesti. *Nam prudentissmè Propheta dixit, non est malum in* civitate, et ego non feci. *Et alio loco scribitur, Dominum mortificare et vivificare,* deducere ad inferos et reducere. *Ut negari non potest, Deum hiis ærumnis ac vitæ miseriis, ad gloriam suam, uti, et pro voluntate sua hominibus has quasi medicinas ad salutem et conservationem hominum adhibere. Cum enim judicamur a Domino, castigamur, ne cum mundo condemnemur. Quod si hæc, morborum, ærumnarum, variaque crucis genera depellunt supplicia æterna, viam ad salutem muniunt, condemnationem tollunt, exercitia pietatis* excitant, *et fide Domini nostri Jesu Christi nituntur, et totos se illius misericordiæ tradiderunt* afflicti, hilari *ac lubentissimo animo sustinenda nobis ac perferenda sunt. Neque tam* reputanda *quæ noster sensus ferat, quam lætandum, cum causam cur a Deo missa sint* perpendamus. *Certus, inquit Paulus, sermo est, siquidem compatimur, et* conregnabimus. *Relinquendus ergo hic doloris sensus, vel abjiciendus potius* a pio viro, *quia minimus dolor maximam habet adjunctam gloriæ ac* gaudii remunerationem. *Sed tu ista omnia per te melius ac planius intelligis, qui* fide Jesu Christi per gratiam *Dei inniteris, qui mortem Christi, remissionem peccatorum,* et reconciliationem *tuam esse putas, qui omnium redemptorem Christum, qui* fidelium præcipue credis; adeo *ut cum*

Thoma Didymo ingenue clames, Deus meus, et **Dominus**
meus. Quare *te in hac tristi ægritudine, quam tu, ut*
spero, tranquillissimo ac serenissimo animo fers, non deti-
nebo *longior. Hoc unum a Deo patre Domini nostri Jesu*
Christi assidue precor, ut quem ego in loco *patris in terris*
habui, sanum atque incolumem aliquando ab hac ægritu-
dine propter gloriam *nominis sui liberet. Atque utinam*
certe, quemadmodum præsens, tecum animo *ac voluntate*
sum, sic liceret mihi corpore tecum adesse, quo mihi, perci-
pere solatium conspectus tui, *sed aliter tum voluntate tua*
tum negotiis meis impedito, fas esset, si non morbum tuum
tollere ad te veniendo, saltem dolorem meum minuere,
quem ex invita *absentia mea capio. Dominus Jesus, cujus*
est omnis potestas, pro beneplacito suo *uxorem, liberos,*
familiamque tuam conservet, ac ab hac ægritudine eruat.
Harfordiæ xiii. *Octobris.*

Tuus animo filius,

Ornatissimo viro D. Guliel-   *JOANNES CHECUS.*
mo Butts, Regio Medico,
ac Patrono suo singulari.

To this tenor in English.

"Sir,

"I doubt not but in imitation of Christ you bear with a
"most equal mind this loss of your health. For to them,
"who by faith understand that he disposeth all things,
"nothing can seem evil which proceeds from him. And
"they who think God to be very wise and good, know
"that he governs all by counsel, and that he sends all
"things to good men for their salvation. And howsoever
"sicknesses, or other afflictions, do disturb those that are
"godly, they are not so thrust upon them by some chance,
"but sent to them from above by their heavenly Father.
"For the Prophet spake very wisely, [or rather God by
"the Prophet,] *There is no evil in the city, and I have*
"*not done it.* And in another place it is written, that *the*
"*Lord killeth and restoreth to life,* that *he bringeth down*
"*to the grave, and bringeth back again.* So that it can-

" not be denied, that God maketh use of these troubles
" and miseries of life to his glory, and according to his
" pleasure prescribes men these medicines, as one may
" call them, for their health and preservation. For when
" we are judged of the Lord, we are chastised, that we
" may not be condemned with the world. But if these
" divers sorts of diseases, troubles, and crosses, drive
" away eternal punishments, make a way to salvation,
" free from condemnation, stir up the exercises of piety,
" and if the afflicted depend upon the faith of our Lord
" Jesus Christ, and have submitted themselves wholly to
" his mercy, we should with a cheerful and most willing
" mind suffer and undergo them. For we are not so much
" to regard what things we feel by our senses, as to re-
" joice when we well weigh the cause why they are sent
" by God. *It is a faithful saying*, saith Paul, *if we suffer*
" *with him, we shall reign with him.* A godly man there-
" fore should lay aside, or rather cast off this apprehension
" of pain. Because a very little share of grief hath a very
" great recompense of glory and joy annexed to it.

" But you, Sir, of yourself understand better and more
" plainly all these things, who rest firmly on the faith of
" Jesus Christ by the grace of God; who reckon the
" death of Christ, the remission of sins, and reconciliation
" to be yours; who believe Christ to be the Redeemer of
" all men, but to be the Redeemer especially of those that
" believe; so that you may freely cry out with Thomas
" Didymus, *My God, and my Lord.* Wherefore I will not
" detain you longer in this doleful sickness, which you, I
" hope, bear with a very calm and composed spirit. This
" one thing I daily beg of God the Father of our Lord
" Jesus Christ, that him whom I had here on earth in the
" stead of a father, he would restore to health, and for
" the glory of his name at length deliver from this sick-
" ness. And I wish surely, that as I am present with you
" in mind and will, so I might be in body; whereby I
" might partake of the comfort of seeing you, being other-
" wise hindered as well by your will, as mine own busi-

" ness, if not to take away your disease by coming to you,
" at least to lessen my sorrow which I have from my
" forced absence. The Lord Jesus, who hath all power,
" according to his good pleasure, preserve your wife, chil-
" dren, and family, and restore you from this sickness.
" At Hartford the xiii of Octob.

" Your Son in heart,

" JOHN CHEKE."

This pious letter was the more seasonable, since this
gentleman must now have been very ill, this disease
proving .mortal, and within little less than a month after
ending his life; as appears by his monument in Fulham
church, against the wall in the chancel, which I will here
set down, and the rather, he having been Cheke's chief patron and dear friend, and that the memory of so worthy
a man might be preserved :

Cheke's pa-
tron's death
and epitaph.
*Epitaphium D. Guil. Buttii Eq. Aurati, et Medici Regis
Henrici VIII. qui obiit anno Dom.* 1545, 17 *Novembr.*

Quid medicina valet, quid honos, quid gratia regum,
  Quid popularis amor, mors ubi sæva venit?
Sola valet pietas, quæ structa est auspice Christo,
  Sola in morte valet; cætera cuncta fluunt.
Ergo mihi in vita fuerit quando omnia Christus,
  Mors mihi nunc lucrum, vitaque Christus erit.

And what if I should think that this was the issue of
Cheke's own pious fancy, as his last respects to this
man, for which he had so high and deserved a veneration?
This epitaph, when time had almost defaced, after four-
score years and upwards, Leonard Buttis, of Norfolk, Esq.
(*viz.* in the year 1627,) renewed.

SECT. III.

His private studies.

NOW also some of the spare hours Cheke could re-

deem to himself, he employed in reading of Chrysostom in
Greek. With whom he was so conversant, that one of
his friends, speaking to him of that author, called him, Anno 1547.
Tuus Chrysostomus, i. e. your own Chrysostom. And Sets forth
Chryso-
to make his studies useful to others as well as to himself, stom's ora-
he translated the six orations of that eloquent and pious tion's concerning
Father, *De Fato*, that is, Of Providence, out of Greek Fate.
into Latin, and published them about the year 1547, (as he
had translated some before,) where Cheke lively expressed
his own style, language, and affection. Insomuch that his
contemporary at the University, and his good friend told
him in a letter, " [b] That his book conveyed with it an ear-
" nest desire to enjoy his voice, his conversation, his wit :
" all which that writing as a certain picture of his mind
" did admirably represent. So that the voice in this dis-
" putation seemed not to be so much Chrysostom's, as
" Cheke's own. So plentiful was this whole volume of
" most noble sentences concerning God, so handsome the
" placing them, words so well suited to the matter, such
" elegant translations, so familiar and delightful narra-
" tions, so great a contexture of arguments, such agree-
" ment of the whole oration with the cause. Which were
" all properly Cheke's own virtues, partly natural, and
" partly obtained by study and knowledge." And as Haddon had a poetical vein, so on a sudden in some heat of
fancy, when he had read this translation of Cheke's, he
wrote this tetrastich upon it :

Divus Joannes Chrysostomus aurea Græca,
Fundere quod posset, nomen suscepit ab auro.
Noster Joannes sit nomine Checus eodem,
Aurea qui Græcis verbis dat verba Latina.

And besides the royal youth, Cheke seems to have the Takes care
care of his sister, the Lady Elizabeth's studies, at least of the Lady
Elizabeth's
studies.

[b] Maximum iste liber mihi desiderium attulit tuæ vocis, tuæ consuetudinis,
tui ingenii, quæ sane omnia hoc scriptum tanquam effigies quædam animi tui,
repræsentavit, &c. *G. Haddonus Joan. Checo.*

sometimes. When the Prince was once at his honour of Ampthil in Bedfordshire, (as at other times, for changing of air, he was at Hartford, and at Hatfield,) his said sister was with him. And she was then under Cheke's instruction, as may be gathered from a copy of verses made by Leland to that lady, to this import; that once going to Ampthil to see Prince Edward, and Cheke, his tutor; Cheke brought him also to the Lady Elizabeth, to have a sight of her, when Cheke also prays her to salute that learned man, and speak to him in Latin, which she did. Which honour done him, Leland expresses in these verses:

Tempore quo Chæcus, musarum cura, politus
Me commendavit, voce favente, tibi.
Utque salutares me tunc sermone Latino,
Egit, ut hinc scirem, quantus in ore lepos, &c.

SECT. IV.

Cheke's interest under King Edward. Applied to.
Marries.

Cheke's
condition
under King
Edward's
reign.

WHEN Cheke's royal charge and care came to reign, our learned man began to move in an ampler sphere: preferments and favours began to be accumulated upon him by his loving and grateful scholar, now his Sovereign; and applications began to be made to him by men of desert. And he ever readily used his interest with his Prince, (to whom he was very dear,) to promote and further all worthy and commendable both men and enterprises. And the University of Cambridge, knowing what a careful friend he was already, and would be to it on any occasion they might have of application to the Court, now near the beginning of King Edward's reign, addressed a letter to him of high respect, full of his deserved praises, and expressive of the assurance they had in his assistance at all times: which, because it will serve to give a light to our history, and shew in part our learned man, I cannot omit

setting it down in the English for the benefit of the SECT.
reader, though written originally in elegant Latin; which IV.
cannot be reached in a translation.   Anno 1547.

Ex universo illo numero, &c. " Of all that number of The Uni-
" very eminent men, most eminent Cheke, that ever went versity's
" forth from this University into the commonwealth, you tory letter
" alone are the man, whom she, above all others, loved be- to him. In-
" ing present, and being absent admired: which you also Epist. II.55.
" in recompense had adorned more than all the rest, when
" you were present, and now being absent afford your help
" unto. For being present, you delivered such rules of
" learning for all instruction, and propounded such ex-
" amples of ingenuity to all imitation, as when every one
" followed for their greatest benefit, none perfectly and
" completely attained. There is none indeed among us
" all, either so ignorant as knows not, or so envious as to
" deny it, that these most fortunate fountains of our stu-
" dies, which many with great industry, pains, and hope,
" have drunk at, have flown from your wit, tuition, ex-
" ample, and counsel. And the perpetual preservation of
" your memory, is consecrated to those monuments of
" your humanity, parts, and learning. But being gone,
" you have heaped upon us greater assistance, and surer
" defence, than either the rest of our friends could ever
" think, or we ourselves expect. For whilst a King, in-
" structed by your precepts, becomes such a patron of
" learning by your counsel, we are not ignorant what the
" rest either will, or at least ought to contribute to our
" University. We have drawn this our hope, and this dis-
" cipline out of your Plato, to Dionysius, a very bad king;
" yet we have had experience lately of the fruit and use of
" it, by your aid in our best Prince Edward. Therefore,
" since so many mutual offices, so many pious closenesses
" and ties are between you and the University, that in
" fetching back the remembrance of it from your very
" cradle, to the honour in which you now are, there is no
" benefit of nature, or fruit of industry, or praise of wit, or
" defence of fortune, or ornament of honour to be found in

D

" you, whereunto our University either hath not contri-
" buted for your use, or whereof it hath not partaken to
" her glory: we do not doubt, but the University may
" hope and receive from you this fruit of the ornaments
" she hath conferred on you; that whatever interest and
" power your honourable place and station may hereafter
" put into your hands, you will employ it all in preserving
" the dignity of the University. We do not commend any
" one, but all our causes to you, wherein we hope you will
" take such pains, as either you ought to bestow upon us,
" or we to expect from you."

Marries.　　In this year I place Mr. Cheke's marriage, being confirmed by a passage in his eldest son's letter to Cecil, that
he was nine years old when his father died, which was in
the year 1557. She whom he chose for his consort was
Mary, a young gentlewoman, daughter and heiress of Ri-
Mrs.
Cheke's fa-
ther.　　chard Hill, by Elizabeth, daughter of　　　　Ilsley, Esq.
This Hill lived, as it seems, in the Vintry, London, and
was a wine merchant, and died young; yet not before he
had ten or eleven children by his wife. He had also a
place of credit at Court, being master or sergeant of the
wine cellar to King Henry VIII. as appears by his monumental inscription in the church of St. Michael, Queen-
hithe, London, where he was buried: which was to this
Weev. Mon.
p. 405.　　tenor: RICHARDO HILL potentiss. Regis HENRICI Octavi
cellæ vinariæ prefecto, Elizabetha conjux mœstissima,
facta jam undecimorum liberorum mater, marito optimo,
immatura tandem morte sublato, (quod solum potuit) po-
steritati commendaturum cupiens hoc monumentum, po-
suit. Obiit, an. Dom. 1539, die mensis Maii 12.

As for this young lady, (daughter to this good widow
Mrs. Hill,) we shall meet with a passage concerning her
hereafter.

SECT. V.

*His preferments and benefits obtained from King
Edward.*

THE first benefit I find bestowed on Cheke by the

King, was an hundred mark rent for twenty-one years, by
a patent dated at Westminster, Aug. 26, an. 2. Edward
VI. which, it seems, was the way of gratifying the King's
instructors. So I find John Belmain, who was his master
for the French language, had, in the year 1550, a lease
granted for twenty-one years, (that is, of the same space
of time that Cheke's grant was,) of the parsonage of Mine-
head and Cotcomb, with the appurtenances in the county
of Somerset, and divers other lands, but with a certain
yearly payment out of it. But this grant to Mr. Cheke
was followed soon after with others.

George Day, a learned man, Bishop of Chichester, was
Provost of King's college in Cambridge; which provostship he had held *in commendam* from King Henry VIII.
to this time: but was deprived of his bishopric in the
year 1548, for his disobedience to the King's proceedings,
in refusing to take down the Popish altars in his diocese.
It was also thought convenient to displace him from his
provostship. Then all the talk was, that Cheke should be
made Provost of King's. And in St. John's college there
was great and glad expectation and desire that it might
be so. For thus I find [a] one of the chief of that house expressed his mind in this matter to the Lord Protector's
Master of Requests; " [b] It is the common wish among us
" here at Cambridge, that at length, yea, very shortly, we
" may see John Cheke Provost of King's college. That
" Bishop [*i. e.* the Bishop of Chichester, the present Pro-
" vost] does not promote studies; I wish he hindered them
" not. And this I do not speak for any one's favour, but
" for the benefit of the whole University. There are many
" things that make us of this judgment, and many more
" your own prudence sees. Thus we friends talk among
" ourselves, perhaps not so very wisely, yet warily, and at
" least very affectionately. Think, Sir, as you please of
" this affair, yet further it as much as you can." Nor was

---

[a] Ascham.

[b] Commune votum est apud nos, &c. *Asch. ad Cicell. int. Epist. MSS.*
iii. 35.

CHAP.
II.
Ann. 1548,
et seq.
By the
King'sman-
damus.
it long after that this preferment, according to these his friend's good wishes, fell upon him. For the King, his loving scholar, in that year granted him a *mandamus*, directed to the college, (upon Day's resignation,) to elect him their Provost. A place which suited best with his studious mind, that ever laboured for retirement, and affected contemplation. It is true, the statutes of that college were against him. And therefore the *mandamus* ran to dispense with three qualifications required in a Provost of this college, *viz.* to be a Doctor, a Priest, and of the foundation. Which they would scarcely have complied with, (as they have since refused such dispensations, being against their statutes,) had it not happened at that time, when the University wanted some notable reformers, and in respect of the extraordinary person recommended to them, so eminent for his virtue and his learning, and with some regard also to his greatness at Court. So at length he was chosen by the Vice-Provost and Fellows; who wrote letters both to the King and him. This place he held about five years, till the beginning of Queen Mary, when being found tardy [c], he was glad for his safety to resign, though the instrument ran *ex mero motu*, according to the common form.

The King grants him lands.
The King expressed also his gratitude to him, by bestowing considerable lands and lordships upon him; namely, out of such as fell to the Crown by the dissolution of religious houses, colleges, and chantries. For in the third year of his reign Cheke obtained of him, (as it is expressed in the patent,) *propter industriam in instituenda adolescentia Domini Regis; i. e.* " for his industry in in- " structing the King's youth," the house and site of the late priory of Spalding in the county of Lincoln, the manor of Hunden in the same county, and divers other lands and tenements in the counties of Lincoln and Suffolk, to the value of 118*l.* 11*d. q.* and no rent reserved. And the year before he obtained another estate of the King; wherein he and Walter Moyle were joint purchasers; and no

[c] In respect of Popery.

question a good pennyworth. The sum to be paid was 958*l.* 3*s.* 5*d. ob.* a sign that Cheke had by this time got money in his purse. It was the college of St. John Baptist de Stoke juxta Clare in Suffolk; and likewise, all the messuages, tenements, cottages, cellars, solars, chambers, stables, &c. with the appurtenances belonging to the college of Corpus Christi, in the parish of St. Laurence Poultney, London, lately dissolved; together with divers other lands and tenements in the counties of Suffolk, Devon, Kent, and in London. The Head of the foresaid college, who was styled the Dean of it, was Dr. Matthew Parker, afterwards Archbishop of Canterbury. He indeed by founding a free school in it for education of children, and by good statutes making it an useful foundation, deserved still to have enjoyed it. But by the act of Parliament in the first of the King, it fell under the same fate with the rest of the colleges superstitiously founded. So when Parker could not obtain the continuance of it, (which he endeavoured,) he gave Cheke (to whom it was granted) such friendly counsel and advice concerning the state of it, and for the better improvement of it, that he professed his great obligations to him in a letter, promising to take care that he should be the first to whom a pension should be appointed, as soon as the commission came out for stating the pensions; and so rewarded, that, as he trusted, no pensioner better: writing thus to him;

SECT. V.

Ann. 1548, et seq.

Dr. Parker Dean of Stoke.

" Mr. Doctor,
" After most hearty commendation, I am as diligent in
" your behalf as I would be in my own; and labour as
" sore, that you may think yourself to have found some
" kind of friendship at my hand, as indeed I think I have
" received at yours. When the commission is once come
" out, you and yours shall be the first to whom pensions
" shall be appointed: and for your part, I trust so or-
" dered, that no pensionary better. The time is not now
" long, within this sevennight or more, it is thought you
" shall be despatched; wherefore you need not much now

Cheke to Dr. Parker, MSS. C.C. C.C.

D 3

" to accumber yourself with any unquietness or delay;
" thinking that ratably you shall be despatched the best
" and soonest.   Fare you well.

7th of June, from   " Your assured,

Westminster.   " JOHN CHEKE."

He promised Dr. Parker also to take his opportunity
with the King effectually to recommend him for some
preferment, when it should fall.   But Parker remaining
two years after *in statu quo prius*, upon another occasion
of writing to him to Cambridge, Cheke voluntarily took
notice, that he had not yet done for him as he would; yet
assuring him, " that he did not forget his friendship
" shewed him aforetime, and was sorry no occasion
" served him to shew his good will.   But bid him assure
" himself, that as it lay long, and took deep root in him,
" so should the time come, he trusted, wherein he should
" understand the fruit thereof, the better to endure, and
" surelier to take place.   Which might as well shortly be,
" as be deferred.   But good occasion, he said, was all."
So that we may hence conclude Cheke had a great hand
in the places and dignities that afterwards were obtained
by the said Dr. Parker.

CHAP. III.

From Cheke's retirement to Cambridge, to his receiving the honour of knighthood.

SECT. I.

Goes to Cambridge. Visits the University by commission from the King. Resides there. Writes a book against the rebels.

IN May this year 1549, I find Cheke gotten to the be- Anno 1549. loved place of his nativity and education; and, as it seems, Cheke re-
tires to settling himself in his provostship lately granted him. Cambridge. Whither it appears he was now gladly withdrawn from the Court, and all its gay but ticklish splendours, and the frowns as well as the flatteries of it: the former whereof he had lately experienced. Here he is now busy, in order to his residence, fitting up his chamber and study; and sends to his friend Peter Osborn, at London, to convey down to him thirty yards of painted buckram, to lay between his books and the boards in his study, which he had trimmed up; a ream of paper, a perfume pan, and some other furniture. And to shew that he was now under some cloud at Court, and how glad of this his present recess he was, these words fell from him in a letter to his above mentioned friend; " That he now felt the calm of " quietness, having been tossed afore with storms, and " having felt ambition's bitter gall, poisoned with hope of " hap. That he could therefore be merry on the bank- " side, without endangering himself on the sea. Your " sight," added he, " is full of gay things abroad, which I " desire not, as things sufficiently known and valued. Oh! " what pleasure is it to lack pleasures, and how honour- " able to flee from honour's throes!" Our philosopher esteemed this the truest pleasure and the best honour, and much beyond that of a Court. And there being a visita-

CHAP.
III.

Anno 1549.

Cheke a Vi-
sitor of the
University.
tion of the University instituted by the King this summer,
Cheke, being now at Cambridge, had the honour to be nominated for a Commissioner; joined with Goodrick and
Ridley, Bishops of Ely and Rochester; Sir William Paget,
Comptroller of the Household; Sir Thomas Smith, Secretary of State; Dr. May, Dean of St. Paul's; and Dr. Wen-
dy, the King's Physician; all formerly choice learned men
of the said University. The disputations that were now performed before the Visitors, the correction of superstitious
practices, the furtherance of the King's good proceedings,
the reforming of the old statutes of houses, managed and
provided for by Cheke and his Fellows' care, I leave to other
historians to relate.

SECT. II.

Cheke's Book, viz. *The true Subject to the Rebel.*

THIS visitation being over, Cheke, who I conclude was
still in Cambridge, employed his thoughts (and that perhaps by order from above) in composing an expostulation
with the rebels; who this summer brake out, partly for
enclosures, and partly for religion, into an open and formi-
dable insurrection, in most counties in England, and especially in Devon in the west, and Norfolk in the north[a].
It was framed by way of a plain and earnest address
from himself to them: and being finished, was committed to the press to be dispersed, as well among them, as
elsewhere in the realm. The book was entitled, *The
Hurt of Sedition: how grievous it is to a Commonwealth.* The running title, *The true Subject to the Rebel.*
And as there were two sorts of these mutineers, who pretended two virtuous causes for their complaints, so Cheke
suited his discourse to each. Those in the west made their
disturbances for the restoring the old Popish religion.
Those in Norfolk and Suffolk would have amendment in
the commonwealth; that the gentlemen should not be put
into places of honour and trust, and the poor commons

---

[a] Rather east.

partake of none of these benefits and advancements; but that all ranks of people should be brought to an equal level.

The former of these thus did our learned man in his said book accost: " Ye rise for religion: what religion
" taught you that? If ye were offered persecution for reli-
" gion, ye ought to flee; so Christ teacheth you, and yet
" you intend to fight. If ye would stand in the truth, ye
" ought to suffer like martyrs; and ye would slay like ty-
" rants. Thus for religion ye keep no religion; and nei-
" ther will follow the counsel of Christ, nor the constancy
" of martyrs. Why rise ye for religion? Have ye any thing
" contrary to God's book? yea, have ye not all things
" agreeable to God's word? But the new [religion] is dif-
" ferent from the old, and therefore ye will have the old.
" If ye measure the old by truth, ye have the oldest. If ye
" measure the old by fancy, then it is hard, because men's
" fancies change to give that is old. Ye will have the old
" style. Will ye have any older than that as Christ left, and
" his Apostles taught, and the first Church did use? Ye will
" have that the Canons do establish. Why, that is a great
" deal younger than that ye have of later time, and new-
" lier invented; yet that is it that ye desire. And do you
" prefer the Bishops of Rome afore Christ? men's inven-
" tions afore God's law? the newer sort of worship before
" the older? Ye seek no religion; ye be deceived; ye
" seek traditions. They that teach you, blind you; that
" so instruct you, deceive you. If ye seek what the old
" Doctors say, yet look what Christ the oldest of all saith:
" for he saith, *Before Abraham was made, I am.* If ye
" seek the truest way, he is the very truth: if ye seek the
" readiest way, he is the very way: if ye seek everlasting
" life, he is the very life. What religion would ye have
" other now than his religion? You would have the Bibles
" in again. It is no marvel, your blind guides would lead
" you blind still.———But why should ye not like that
" [religion] which God's word establisheth, the primitive

" Church hath authorized, the greatest learned men of this
" realm have drawn, the whole consent of the Parliament
" hath confirmed, the King's Majesty hath set forth? Is it
" not truly set out? Can ye devise any truer than Christ's
" Apostles used? Ye think it is not learnedly done. Dare
" ye, commons, take upon you more learning than the
" chosen Bishops and Clerks of this realm have?———
" Learn, learn to know this one point of religion, that God
" will be worshipped as he hath prescribed, and not as we
" have devised; and that his will is wholly in his Scrip-
" tures, which be full of God's spirit, and profitable to
" teach the truth," &c.

And about
the com-
monwealth.
As for the other malecontents, the other rabble of Norfolk rebels, thus he proceeded to argue with them : " Ye
" pretend a commonwealth. How amend ye it by killing
" of gentlemen, by spoiling of gentlemen, by imprisoning
* Ket, their
ringleader,
was a tan-
ner.
" of gentlemen? A marvellous *tanned** commonwealth.
" Why should ye thus hate them for their riches or for
" their rule? Rule they never took so much in hand as
" ye do now. They never resisted the King, never with-
" stood his Council; be faithful at this day, when ye be
" faithless, not only to the King, whose subjects ye be, but
" also to your Lords, whose tenants ye be. In this your
" true duty, in some of homage, in most of fealty, in all of
" allegiance; to leave your duties, go back from your pro-
" mises, fall from your faith; and, contrary to law and
" truth, to make unlawful assemblies, ungodly compa-
" nies, wicked and detestable camps; to disobey your
" betters, and to obey your tanners; to change your
" obedience from a King to a Ket, to submit yourselves
" to traitors, and to break your faith to your true
" King and Lords?———If riches offend you, because
" ye would have the like, then think that to be no com-
" monwealth, but envy to the commonwealth. Envy it is
" to appair another man's estate, without the amendment
" of your own; and to have no gentlemen, because ye be
" none yourselves, is to bring down an estate, and to mend

" none. Would ye have all alike rich? that is the over-
" throw of labour, and utter decay of work in this realm.
" For who will labour more, if, when he hath gotten more,
" the idle shall by lust, without right, take what him list
" from him, under pretence of equality with him? This is
" the bringing in of idleness, which destroyeth the com-
" monwealth, and not the amendment of labour, which
" maintaineth the commonwealth. If there should be such
" equality, then ye take all hope away from yours, to come
" to any better estate than you now leave them. And as
" many mean men's children come honestly up, and are
" great succour to all their stock, so should none be here-
" after holpen by you. But because you seek equality,
" whereby all cannot be rich, ye would that belike, where-
" by every man should be poor: and think beside, that
" riches and inheritance be God's providence, and given
" to whom of his wisdom he thinketh good," &c. After
this manner did he excellently and popularly reason in
this book, for the reducing these men to more sobriety.

This book was reprinted anno 1576, as a seasonable
discourse upon apprehension of tumults, by malecontents
at home, or renegadoes abroad. Holinshed also thought
fit to add it in his Chronicle there, where he speaks of this
rebellion; as it was his practice to insert divers tracts and
discourses in suitable places of his history. And since that,
Dr. Gerard Langbain, of Oxford, about the year 1641, published the book once again, intending it for the use and
consideration of the rebels against King Charles the First,
in the time of the civil wars.

We are told also, that about these times Cheke penned, One of the
and perhaps published, several other learned and useful Commissioners for
tracts, both for Church and State. And whereas, in the the ecclesi-
month of October, thirty-two Commissioners (consisting astical laws.
of an equal number of Bishops, Divines, Civilians, and
common lawyers) were appointed for the examining the
old ecclesiastical law books, and drawing thence a body of
good and wholesome laws for the government of the
Church, and decision of other civil matters, Cheke was

CHAP.
III.

Anno 1549.

named one of the eight Divines selected for this great work; Taylor, Dean of Lincoln; Dr. Cox, the King's Almoner, and one of his teachers; Dr. Matthew Parker, Master of Bene't college, Cambridge; Latimer, (afterward a martyr;) Sir Anthony Cook, another of the King's instructors; Peter Martyr, the King's public Professor at Oxford; and Joannes à Lasco, a nobleman of Poland, and Superintendent of the German congregation in London; being the other seven. With such learned company was Cheke thought fit to be associated. And again, three years after, upon a new Commission for the same purpose, he was again nominated one to whom the Commission was directed, with the rest above named.

SECT. III.

Returns to the Court. His troubles there. His wife offends the Duchess.

Cheke at Court.

CHEKE'S stay was not long at Cambridge, his royal master no doubt wanting him to assist him in his studies, and to be about his person, whom he so much affected. For I find him at Westminster this winter, viz. anno 1549. And this is the first time I meet with any passage about his wife, who seemed to be a dependent on the family of Anne, Duchess of Somerset, and now with child. This first occasion I find mention made of her by Cheke, her husband, was an unhappy one, she having given some offence unwarily to the Duchess; or the Duchess, a very imperious woman, having taken some offence against her for some words spoken, or some matters concealed of, I know not what. This female fraction employed Cheke to obtain a reconciliation for his wife, and to qualify the lofty Peeress's mind towards her. Therefore he takes his pen[a], and

His wife.

The Duchess of Somerset offended with her.

Cheke's address to her in his wife's behalf.

[a] *Mr. Cheke to the Duchess of Somerset, Januar.* 1549, *upon some offence the Duchess had taken against his wife and himself.*

L. 20.

Your Graces singular favour towards me hath always been one of my chief comforts in my diligent service of the Kings Majesty, which was the easier to me, because it was wel taken; and altho in this desert of other mens trou-

with words of the lowliest submission makes his application to her; not in the least excusing his wife's fault, but
only using arguments proper to move and mollify the
Duchess's great spirit, after this manner: "That he could
" not choose but make half a suit for half himself, that is,
" for his wife, in regard of her misbehaviour towards her
" Grace: for which, whosoever was sorry, he was most
" sorry. And yet not ready to excuse that which was

ble, and mishap of mine own, I know not precisely of your Graces favourable goodness toward me, yet I judge that your good Graces mind towards
me, undeserved to be gotten, and undeserved to be lost again, is sich [such],
that I pass the quieter through the whole course of my danger, and feel the
less storm of causeless hap, because I do mich [much] stay myself in your
Graces wisdome of taking things truly, and in your goodness of helping the
honest favourably.

Wherefore, presuming to give your Grace thanks for myself, because I trust
well, and most humbly requiring your Grace of continuance of your favour,
worthily, as I trust, to be bestowed on me, I cannot chuse but make half a
suite for half myself, being dissevered as yet from the other half of myself,
in my wifes misbehaviour towards your Grace. Whosoever is sorry for it, I
am most sorry; not ready to excuse that which is faulty, but desiring of pardon where forgiveness is plentiful; and knowing that forgiveness of faults
past is amendment of time to come; and no vice in a mean woman to be so
great, but the vertue of nobility is as large to mercy. My most humble request
therefore is, that your Graces gentleness overcome my wifes faults; to favour
of clemency, where justice would have straitness; to be more noble in vertue
than others be in offence; that, wheras fault is greatest, your grace may most
appear. In other matters I have charged her to be plain; and I trust her
honest nature will content your Grace. Wherin if she be faulty (for I must
needs naturally pitty her) justly, I cannot speak for her; and yet, as I trust
she wil shew herself true and plain, so I would fain speak, if I thought there
were need, and put your Grace in mind that you of wisdome consider, that in
youth there may be pardon, where experience lacketh; and sich [such] we
pitty, as wisdome cannot be looked for of; and toward women with child, favour for the innocents sake.

But what mean I to enter into sich matters, as your Grace knoweth best;
and tel your Grace, that of yourself you consider. Onely I beseech your Grace,
and that most humbly, to extend your gracious favour so far above the required
desert toward my wife and me both, as my good mind toward your Grace,
which is equal with your greatest clients, is above mine habilitee, which is un-
derneath the common state of wel minded. God send your Grace most plen-
teous estate, and long quietness to his mighty will. From Westminster, the
XXVII. of January, 1549. 2 Edv.

Your Grace's most bounden Orator,
JOAN. CHEKE.

" faulty, but desiring pardon where forgiveness was plen-
" tiful, and knowing that forgiveness of faults past, was
" amendment for time to come. That no vice in a mean
" woman was so great, but the virtue of nobility was as
" large to mercy. That his humble suit was, that her
" Grace's gentleness might overcome his wife's faults;
" and to be more noble in virtue than others were in of-
" fence; and that where fault was greatest, there her
" grace might most appear. That of her wisdom she would
" consider, that in youth there may be pardon where ex-
" perience lacked; and towards such women pity, of whom
" wisdom cannot be looked for, and toward women with
" child, favour for the innocent's sake." Thus was he fain
to strain his rhetoric, to pacify the wrath of this lofty lady
toward Mrs. Cheke. And because she was to come under
examination, he told the Duchess, " he had charged her to
" be plain. And so he trusted her honest nature would
" content her Grace."

Cheke himself was scarce yet got out of his own troubles, occasioned, as it seems, by the troubles that lately
befel the Protector, the Duke of Somerset, Cheke seeming
first to be charged as one of the number of those that had
suggested ill counsels to the said Duke, and after of some

falseness to him. But the Duchess herself saw his innocency, and stood his friend, and that behind his back.
Which favour, therefore, he thought fit to make an ac-
knowledgment of by his pen; " Professing still to depend
" upon her protection and patronage, and protesting that
" he passed the quieter through the whole course of his
" danger, by means of her favourable goodness and good
" mind towards him; and felt the less storms of causeless
" hap, since he so much stayed himself in her Grace's
" wisdom of taking things truly, and in her goodness of
" helping the honest favourably. And that, in a word, it
" was her Grace's singular favour towards him, that had
" always been one of his chief comforts in his diligent
" service of the King's Majesty: which was the easier to
" him, because it was well taken."

SECT. IV.

Preferred at Court, and does good offices for men of religion and learning.

WHEN Cheke had undergone, and well got over this Anno 1550. shock at Court, he stood the firmer afterwards, and remained fast in his royal master's favour, and his interest and authority daily increased: so that he became the great Becomes patron of religious and learned men, both English and the patron of learning foreigners, and, together with Cecil and Gates, their chief and religion advocate with the King. So well did Ridley, Bishop of at Court. London, know this, that he called him *one of Christ's special advocates, and one of his principal proctors.* And Ascham Ascham, joining Cecil and Cook with him, as the great Epist. ab triumvirate at Court for favouring all good causes that miss. respected either religion or learning, bespake him once in these words: " If you, with Cecil and Cook, [the other " instructor of the King,] defend, as you have opportunity, " the causes of virtue and learning, ye shall answer the " opinion that all have of you."

And his great parts and abilities were now so well Made chief known, and his wisdom so tried, that by this time (*viz.* gentleman of the Privy 1550, the fourth of the King) he was made one of the chief Chamber. gentleman of the Privy Chamber, a high place in those times, and was preferred also, as it seems, to a participation of the public cares, and involved in the matters of State. Certainly very great and weighty business lay upon him: for Ascham, in one of his letters to him, excused III. 9. himself for the letter he wrote, not expecting long answers again, because he saw he was detained with weightier matters. And the King's Ambassador in Germany wrote weekly to him privately, as well as to the Privy Council, concerning the public affairs abroad. The foresaid Ascham, that elegant scholar, was Secretary to this Ambassador, concerning whom I shall here take occasion to set down a few things.

SECT. V.

*Procures Ascham to go Secretary to an Embassy to the
Emperor.*

AN embassy being to be despatched to the Emperor,
Charles the Vth, the charge of it was committed to Sir
Richard Morison, a learned Knight, and a brave gentleman;
and Ascham, by the means and recommendation of Cheke,
was appointed Secretary of the said embassy: two very
fit persons to be companions, and well sorted for their
tempers, learning, and judgment. This favour obtained
by Cheke, Ascham gratefully remembered, and professed
that he made it a spur to him, not to be wanting in any
respect to the Ambassador with whom he went, lest his
neglect might reflect any blame upon his friend that preferred him; for he bore, he said, that sentence of Cicero
in his mind, *graviorem esse sponsionem alienæ honestatis
quam alieni æris;* i. e. that it is a greater matter to pass
one's word for another's good behaviour, than for his debt.

Ep. III. 2. The day before the Ambassador went away, Ascham repaired unto Cheke's chamber in London, (in White Friars,
I suppose, for there his house was,) being retired thither
Cheke's ad- for his health's sake. Here coming to take his leave,
vice to As-
cham going Cheke, like a Christian philosopher, held a large conference
into Ger- with him, both concerning true religion, and the right
many. method of instituting studies. Which subjects were so
wisely and gravely handled, that the discourse made such
a mighty impression upon Ascham, that, as he sent him
word in one of his letters, he should never forget it. It
was no doubt intended by our learned man to fortify Ascham, now going abroad, and to confirm him in the good
principles he had imbibed and entertained at Cambridge;
and that in his travels he might be secured from gathering
any infection by the various conversation he must necessarily meet with; and so be in danger, without some fore-
arming, of forsaking religion, or that course of solid learning that he made so good progress in.

Of this communication, the next day after, *viz.* Sept. 21, SECT.
Ascham gave his fellow collegian and friend, Edward Ra- V.
ven, an account from Gravesend; which was to this pur- Anno 1550.
port, that from noon to nine at night, they two passed the Communi-
time in various philosophical discourses. They handled tween
many things relating to religion, to the Court, to the com- Cheke and
monwealth, and to the University: and particularly that Asch. Epist.
Cheke hugely approved of the state of St. John's college, III. 2.
and the discipline and course of learning there used.
Ascham, out of his love to the learned men there, and his
desire of their promotion, took this occasion to speak much
of the Pilkingtons, the Leavers, Wylsons, Elands, and
other good and deserving scholars of that college, and
particularly his friend Raven, (to whom he now wrote,)
whose sweetness of manners, wit, prudence, diligence, and
judgment, he commended and recommended to Cheke;
and chiefly a troublesome business of his, wherein he
might need the assistance of the Court: which the other
readily promised that he would get despatched.

Cheke's great mind towards the advancement of learn- Intelli-
ing and religion contained not itself within the limits of him of the
these nations united under the English government; but state of
the good-will he bare thereto made him heartily desirous and religion
of the propagation of these excellent things abroad in abroad.
the world. And some tidings of the present posture of
them, in the parts beyond seas, came to him now in the
month of November, from the pen of his before-men- Asch. Ep.
tioned learned friend, who was (with the Ambassador) by p. 433.
this time got as far as Ausburg. He shewed him first, in
general, how he had visited monasteries, churches, libraries; seen ancient both books and coins, a number whereof,
both very old and very fine, he promised him at his return:
also, how he had taken notice of the customs of cities,
their situation and discipline; diligently viewed their build-
ings, walls, strength, ports, and all opportunities of land and
water round about: and that he had made memoranda of
all these things: whereof Cheke was to be partaker when
Ascham came home. He proceeded to particulars: he

E

CHAP.
III.

Anno 1550.
An ill cha-
racter of
Lower Ger
many.

spake first of Lower Germany, which he called the *lowest*
indeed, and the deepest, as, he said, was easily perceivable,
and that in all respects; (except only in the mighty con-
course of merchants;) for into it flowed a sink of Roman
dregs and filth, and now seemed there to stagnate. This
was the ill character he gave of that country, which afterwards, by the vindication of its liberty from oppression
and superstition, is become in these our days one of the
richest and most considerable places in Europe. At Antwerp he saw a commentary upon Plato's Timæus, but of
some Latin writer. At Louvain, in the college, he heard,
for the space of an hour, Theodorus Candius, a man of
fame, read upon Sophocles's Tyrannus: where, by the
way, he acquainted Cheke, that in his reading he read and
pronounced according to the late way discovered by him,
when he read the Greek lecture at Cambridge. " But,"
said he, " if that reader were compared with Car, [who
" was the present reader of Greek there,] Louvain with
" Cambridge, both the former would fall much short of
" both the latter." That at Colen, Justus Velsius, once
of Argentine, now an Herodian, [*i. e.* I suppose a complier
with the *interim,*] read in Greek Aristotle's Ethics; whom
indeed he [Ascham] did approve, though he did not ad-
mire. That the same day he heard Alexander Blancart, a
Carmelite, reading upon the Acts of the Apostles. This
man he described to be a notable Papist; that he turned
the ninth epistle of the first book of Cyprian for oblations
in favour of the dead; and that he was esteemed to be
learneder, and worse [*i. e.* in respect of his rigour against
Lutheranism] than Edvardus Billicus, who there publicly
professed to read on Genesis. That for the fame that this
Billicus carried, he repaired to his monastery, and there
he saw the man; and having a mind to enter into discourse with him, he signified to him, that he was told he
had certain books of St. Bernard, as yet never printed.
This he said, that he might provoke the man to some discourse, and so make some trial of his parts and abilities.
But being full of business, as his servant told Ascham, he

was not then at leisure : so as being cast off to another SECT.
time, he cast off that proud Papist. He proceeded in his   V.
relation; that he had looked over many libraries in those Anno 1550.
parts, but saw not one eminent book. That at Spire,
the report was, there was an excellent library, well furnished with ancient Latin, Greek, and Hebrew books : but
the library-keeper being absent, he saw not the books,
which otherwise he had taken a view of. That at Gaves-
burgh, a town nine German miles distant from Ausburg,
many Jews dwelt : where he was, and saw many Hebrew
books well written; but they would not sell him so much
as one, though he offered them money. He also saw ancient coins there; and bought two, a Nero and an Au-
gustus. Also they shewed him an old Hebrew piece of
money, of gold, with very handsome Hebrew letters;
which he had bought, had not the price been too unrea-
sonable. That the city Ausburg, where he now was, had
a very copious library, furnished with very many ancient
Greek and Hebrew books. They that had the care of it
had laid aside threescore of their best books, lest the Emperor (now at Ausburg) or the Imperialists should take
them away, [either perhaps for their choiceness and excel-
lency, or containing some things contrary to the Imperial
or Popish interest.] There was a whole Chrysostom in
Greek, together with other very valuable books : and
though he had not yet seen them, he was promised that
he should.

This for the state of learning. Next he acquainted Cheke
in what condition religion was in those parts. That it flourished at Ausburg, though the Emperor himself were at
that time in person there : " Just, methinks," said he, " as
" your pronunciation of Greek flourished at Cambridge,
" even under the contrary commands and injunction of
" Winchester. At this success of religion, we all," added
he, " do rejoice, and I congratulate the same ; but fear, lest
" Cæsar, while present he shews himself, with fraud, easy
" in the cause of religion, when he is absent, more easily,
" without being suspected, break all their political power ;

" and that, by the ruin of their policy, religion also should
" be ruined with it." That the cities of Hamburg, Breme,
and Magdeburg defended religion with their minds, their
pens, and their swords. That he saw the Magdeburg
Confession. That the argument of the book was this, *Si
superior magistratus vim exercet in subditos contra jus
aut naturale aut divinum, licet tum inferiori magistratui
resistere ;* i. e. " That if the superior magistrate exerciseth
" force upon his subjects contrary to the law, either natural
" or divine, in that case it is lawful for the inferior magistrate
" to resist." That for the city of Magdeburg, and their
spirit, he could not but praise both, but this thesis he liked
not ; for that hence might great commotions and disturbances easily arise. This book, very scarce to be got, he sent
to Cheke for a present ; and would, as he wrote to him, have
sent him many other tracts concerning the *interim* and the
adiaphorists, but that Gipkin (who was a Dutch book-
seller in London) had taken care of procuring them for
him. That the city of Wittenburg with Melancthon, and
Leipsic with Camerarius, the chief Doctors in those cities, were blamed by many good men, that they admitted
the *interimistical* and *adiaphorical* doctrine. That Joa-
chim Camerarius, in an oration delivered at Leipsic the
last year, had disturbed the minds of a great many at that
time in matters of religion. Finally, that as soon as any
thing of certainty, either relating to religion or the civil
state, came to his hand, he would write all at large ; but
that now, upon their first coming, he had not much, nor of
much consequence, to impart.

Cheke put
upon trans-
lating De-
mosthenes
into Latin,
In this correspondence Ascham descended from public
to more private matters. He took occasion now to remember Cheke of that admirable discourse that he entertained him with at their parting at London, and how
much he spake concerning Demosthenes, declaring how it
rejoiced him to perceive that noble Greek orator was so
familiar with him, who was also the great subject of Ascham's delight and study. And here he took occasions
(knowing the excellent Latin style of Cheke) to put him

upon translating the oration of Demosthenes, and of his SECT.
antagonist Æschines, into Latin: which would he take ___V.___
in hand, he should, he said, undertake a thing most proper Anno 1550.
and agreeable to his place, his study, his wit, his judgment, and his ability: and that thereby he would hold
forth a great light to the commendable imitation of Demosthenes and Tully, the princes of the Greek and Latin
speech. He now also propounded to him to disperse and
communicate his pronunciation of Greek abroad in the And upon
world, that other nations might be acquainted with it: publishing
his pronun-
adding, that if he would but send him the copy, he would ciation of
the Greek
soon offer it to the view of mankind; and that he doubted language.
not but to obtain the assistance of Johannes Sturmius (the
most learned Professor of Strasburgh) to give some illus-
trations to it. Pity it was, that this suggestion prevailed
not with Cheke to set forth his learned exercitations upon
the Greek tongue, and the correct way of sounding it,
having this convenience of printing the book well, in some
printing-house abroad, and whilst Ascham, or some of his
friends, might have had the supervising of it; whether it
were our learned man's modesty, or his other cares and
business hindered. Yet the sum of his thoughts upon this
subject came to light soon after his death, in his exquisite
Latin letters to Bishop Gardiner, printed at Basil, as we
have told already. And as to the other motion made by
Ascham, of translating something of that prince of Greek
orators, that he did, either upon this advice or before. And
beside these, many other of that orator's works, as his
Philippics and Olynthiacs, he translated, and left behind
him, (though I fear now utterly perished,) as we shall be
told hereafter, when we come to mention his writings.

SECT. VI.

Cheke translates the Communion Book. His friendship
with Martyr and Bucer. Hath a son.

BUT now to look at home. It was not far from this
time that the Archbishop of Canterbury thought it neces-

E 3

CHAP.
III.

Anno 1550.

The Communion
Book put
into Latin
by Cheke.

sary that the first Communion Book should be carefully re-
vised and corrected; and that in this work foreign Divines
of the greatest learning in divinity, and best acquainted
with the ancient ecclesiastical writers, should be consulted.
There were many in England at that time, the chief
whereof were Bucer and Peter Martyr: both whose judgments the said Archbishop required, and willed them to set
down their censures in writing for his use. In this matter
our Cheke was concerned: he translated into Latin the
substance of the said Communion Book for P. Martyr,
(not understanding English,) now being at Lambeth with
the Archbishop: and from this translation Martyr made
his censures by way of annotation. And, moreover, Cheke
had conference with that learned man concerning the
amendments to be made, and concerning a meeting of the
Bishops that were to consult and deliberate about it; many
of which secretly bearing a good-will to Popery, Martyr
confessed his fears to Cheke, that the reformation of the
book would stick with them. But Cheke hinted to him,
" ᵇthat if the Bishops would not alter what was fit to be
" altered, the King would do it by himself, and when the
" Parliament met, he would interpose his own authority."

Congratu-
lates Bu-
cer's reco-
very.

Cheke was a fast friend and patron to these outlandish
learned Confessors. And as we have seen something between Peter Martyr and him this year 1550, so in the
same year there was a kind correspondence between him
and Bucer. Upon his first coming to Cambridge to be the
King's Professor there, he had been dangerously sick: and
as the fear of losing so useful a man in that public station
caused no small trouble to Cheke, and such friends of the
Reformation as he, so his recovery gave them no small
content. And Cheke, by way of congratulation and counsel, wrote thus from the Court at Greenwich to him in

Asch. Ep.
p. 433.

May: *Audio te firmiorem, &c.* i. e. " I hear you are

ᵇ Hoc non me parum recreat, quod mihi D. Cheekus indicavit, si noluerint
ipsi, ait, efficere, ut quæ mutanda sint, mutentur, Rex per seipsum id faciet, et
cum ad Parliamentum ventum fuerit, ipse suæ majestatis authoritatem inter-
poneret. *Mat. Parker's Lett. C. C. C. C.* et v. Asch. p. 438.

" grown stronger, and that all your weakness and sickness
" which had afflicted you is gone: for which I do ear-
" nestly, as I ought, give thanks to God, the Father of all
" comfort, who hath delivered you from so great a disease,
" and strengthened you to take in hand and undergo such
" an office in the Church. But pray take heed you be not
" too earnest in your beginning, and undertake more than
" the measure of your health will bear. We must so labour,
" as to think, not how soon, but how long we shall be able
" to perform our work. You know how far that of St. Paul
" reaches, *Use a little wine;* and how it may diffuse itself
" to all the actions of life. I do that to you which I could
" never induce myself to do to any else; that is, to advise
" that you be more remiss and moderate in this your al-
" most intolerable labour of mind: for the greatness of it
" stretched beyond one's strength distresses the body, and
" disables it to take care for meaner things." This was the
advice of a true friend.

Bucer had solicited Cheke in behalf of his friend and coun- Bucer soli-
cits Cheke
for Sleidan.
tryman Sleidan the historian, who had a yearly honorary
pension assigned him by King Edward the VIth, for his
excellent learning and abilities. This pension, behind and
unpaid, (for money was not very plentiful with this King,)
it was Bucer's request to Cheke to use his interest for it,
signifying what address had been made to the Archbishop
of Canterbury in this behalf. To this Cheke's answer was,
" That the Archbishop was of a benevolent disposition,
" but a slow patron of causes; and that in this business
" there was need of a Privy Counsellor, and likewise of a
" greatness of spirit, that might be fit to undertake causes
" with moderation and judgment; adding, that if the
" opportunity once slipped away, it would be more easily
" sought than found. That, for his part, he did not cease
" to put the Archbishop in mind, and that he would still
" do further what he could." Asch. Ep.
p. 434.

In the same year, the xii. of the calends of November,
there passed another letter from Bucer to Cheke, styling Bucer sends
Cheke his
him therein *his most honoured patron;* herewith sending book De
Regno.

E 4

him up his famous book that he wrote for the use of the
King in reforming religion, *De Regno Christi consti-*
tuendo; signifying that he had shewn it to none but P.
Martyr, who was, as he said, of the same opinion with
him. He added, that this book should be read by none
but such who should read it for their own and the Church's
profit. And he desired him to recommend this his labour
and pains to the King.

Cheke's
presence
desired at
Cambridge.
Asch. Ep.
p. 434.
This year Cheke was about coming to Cambridge, as
we find him afterwards to do, in a considerable capacity.
But when some doubted of his coming, Bucer entreats him
to come, because his presence would be so very necessary
for that School; he meant that University. He lastly
prayed the Lord to keep him, his most honoured wife,
and his son, who might now be about two years old.

SECT. VII.

Cheke reads *Aristotle's Ethics* in Greek to the King. Instructs him for government.

Cheke's
course in
his direc-
tion of the
King's stu-
dies.
CHEKE still plied his duty close with the King, in following him in his studies. A Cambridge friend of his (who
was wise and learned, and well understood the education
of noble youth) took occasion now to tell Cheke his judgment concerning the instruction of his royal charge, who,
being now about thirteen years of age, and endued with
an understanding beyond his years, should be let into the
reading of such books as might be proper to shew him his
duty as a Prince. And a book of that nature having been
composed by Xenophon the Grecian, for the institution of
Cyrus, he thought the King might be a double gainer in
reading of it, both by forwarding him in Greek, and also
by the noble and wise instructions proper for a Prince's
behaviour. But though Cheke approved well of this counsel, yet he thought fit first to enter him into Aristotle's
Ethics in Greek: that so his royal mind might first be
well principled in moral virtues; and when he understood
well these precepts, and had imbibed the knowledge of all

the parts of virtue and vice, he would be the better enabled   SECT.
to look into and judge of the manners and actions of men;   VII.
and thence might more properly be led into history, and Anno 1550.
be able to pass a judgment upon the matters he should
read there. Cheke had read over Tully's philosophy to
him already; and, by his pains, Latin and Greek were
become easy to him, both to write and speak elegantly
the former, and to translate into the latter.

Let us add here some few things more relating to Instructs
Cheke's care in the education of his Prince. Among other him in the
things that he instructed him in, one was about matters interest of
of the kingdom. He shewed him the general history of the king-
England, the state and interest, the laws and customs of dom.
it, and such like: and this he taught him before he was
King. Where Cheke shewed himself so well skilled in the
mysteries of this State, that it is said that King Henry
observing it, had an eye upon him for Secretary.

And that all King Edward's transactions, and the emer- Directs him
gencies of his kingdom, whether public or private, might to keep a
be the better remembered by him, (whereby his experience
might be the greater,) Cheke directed him to keep a diary
of all occurrences of weight; and to write down briefly,
under each day of every month, debates in Council, des-
patch of Ambassadors, honours conferred, and other re-
marks, as he thought good: and this, we may conclude,
produced that excellent Journal of this King preserved in
the Cotton library, and printed thence by Bishop Burnet.
And, to set forth the benefit of keeping of such a day's
book, Cheke is said to use this aphorism, " That a dark
" and imperfect reflection upon affairs floating in the me-
" mory, was like words dispersed and insignificant; where-
" as a view of them in a book, was like the same words
" digested and disposed in good order, and so made signi-
" ficant."

SECT. VIII.

Concerned about the death of Bucer, the King's Professor at Cambridge.

Cheke is afflicted at Bucer's death.

THOUGH Cheke was gone from the University, yet he bore a great share in the affairs there. The latter end of the year 1550, Martin Bucer, whom the King had sent thither to read divinity, died; which did very much affect him, considering the great loss the University sustained in being deprived of such a man, whose readings had been so beneficial to the students there, for the enlightening them about the truth of religion, and freeing their minds from the corrupt notions that had hitherto so infected the study of theology; and, as Cheke himself wrote to Peter Martyr upon this occasion, that the Cantabrigians had been in this respect happier than others, that God had sent so great a man to them, and that Christ's discipline took such deep root by him. Bucer's death was bitter to Cheke upon this public account; and not therefore only, but because of that dearness and friendship that was between them. Which Nicolas Car (one of Cheke's University friends) well knowing, could not but by a letter relate to him the sad news of his death. And that for this rea-

Carri Epist. in mort. Buc.

son, *Quis enim illo charior tibi? quem is dilexit te magis? &c.* i. e. " For who was dearer to you than he? " whom did he love more than you? for whom did he per- " form more offices of respect and love? and whom did " you embrace as you did him? So that he, methinks, was " happy, who had a value for such a man as you; and you " most happy in holding so strait a conjunction with so " holy and learned a man as he."

Writes to Martyr the news of Bucer's death.

And knowing how heavily the other pious and his fellow foreigner, and Professor at Oxford, Peter Martyr, must needs take his death, Cheke thought good, in a consolatory letter, to acquaint him with it; beginning, *Ita natura fert, &c.* And to give you a taste of his pious spirit, I shall translate some passages of his said letter: " He

" thought," he said, " that such a man as he [Peter Mar-
" tyr] was, would bear moderately and christianly the
" death of that grave and religious man; and that his na-
" ture would not shew itself so repugnant to the will of
" God, as to suffer any too vehement disturbance to enter
" into his mind in such a common and natural accident, to
" which all were subject. You know," said he, " whose
" he was when he lived; who dwelt in him; how he was
" not his own, nor at his own command, who had devoted
" himself wholly to the service of Him by whom he was re-
" deemed. And since God gave him not to us, but lent him
" for some time, shall we bear it the more bitterly that God
" hath called for him, and not rather give him thanks that
" he hath so long left him with us? That his years and
" age was such, that though he were worthy of longer life,
" yet nature could not extend it further. And when he
" had led a most constant life, and with the same con-
" stancy finished it, with how much joy ought his friends
" and acquaintance to be affected, that he was thus taken
" away by God, that malice might not pervert his mind;
" and that by the constancy of his death he might com-
" plete and crown the innocency of his life. And who is
" there that can doubt of the Divine power, wisdom, and
" goodness? Nor ought we to contend with him, but to
" submit ourselves to his greatness and power: that we
" take with a thankful mind whatsoever is offered to us
" from so great an Author, lest we be found stubborn in
" crying out against his doings, or weak in not bearing
" what he lays on us, or ingrateful in taking amiss what
" he sends. But it is a very fond thing, and unworthy of
" the spirit of Christ, to think that we can do any thing
" better than the rule of Divine Providence hath ap-
" pointed; the foolishness of which [Providence] doth far
" exceed all the reach of human understanding. But wis-
" dom can be seen by none, when nothing spiritual or
" divine can affect our understanding, in many respects
" depressed and dark, unless brought in by the light of the
" Spirit. But they that think God is good and favourable

" unto his people, (who turneth all things to good, not
" only miseries and afflictions, but even sinful and wicked
" actions,) how can they persuade their minds, that this is
" unprofitable, hurtful, and damageable to those that be-
" long to him? of whom he taketh so exact a care, that
" not a hair of their heads falls to the ground without his
" will. And when in all our prayers to God we join this,
" that *his will may be done*, how inconstant and light
" shall we be, if before we ask of God to do what he
" pleaseth, but afterwards we cannot bear that which we
" have asked: and that which we prayed for before, we
" now do pray against; not bearing that change, whereby
" God would have his people exercised and instructed to
" patience and suffering. For although we have lost a
" great ornament and pillar of integrity, religion, and doc-
" trine; yet he is not to be lamented, who is gone to his
" Father's inheritance, for which we here are labouring
" with misery; neither is the state of the Church to be
" lamented, which hath sent away so great a man to hea-
" ven. Nor ought we to lament our own afflicted (as they
" appear) and decaying affairs, who should place more
" hope and safety in the Spirit of Christ, than in the voice
" even of an Apostle. But let us," as he subjoined, " learn
" hence to draw away our thoughts unto Christ, and again
" and again to beg his saving Spirit; that the Church,
" being, as it were, devoid of all outward defence, may be
" refreshed by the inward aid of his Spirit; and while we
" are deprived of our so great a parent, may be relieved
" by the authority of his Spirit.——But why do I thus
" discourse with you? While I talk with you, I comfort
" myself; and while I meditate the ease of your sorrow, I
" seek some medicine for mine own disease: not so much
" studying what is fit for me to write to you, as what
" seems convenient to ease mine own grief." And then,
as a further means to comfort Peter Martyr, (to whom he
wrote all this,) when he should hear with what honour
and respect his funerals were celebrated by the University,
Cheke descended to shew him how he was interred in the

University church: that his corpse was attended thither by
the Vice-Chancellor, the Doctors, and others that had obtained degrees in the University, and by all the rest of the
Scholars; and likewise by the Mayor of the town, and the
townsmen, who joined themselves with the University, the
more to honour his funerals, to the number, in all, of three
thousand persons. And that after the customary prayers
were said, Haddon, Doctor of Laws, and Orator of the
University, made an excellent Latin oration, setting forth
the praises of the great man deceased; and Dr. Parker,
Head of a college, [he that was afterwards advanced to be
Archbishop of Canterbury,] made a sermon in English.
That the next day they resorted to the church again, when
Dr. Redman, another venerable man of the University,
preached a sermon upon the occasion; and the students
did their parts, in honouring his hearse with copies of
verses. And lastly, that the good Archbishop Cranmer
took care of his family; and that the University had wrote
to the King and his Council in that behalf. All this did
Cheke impart to Martyr, concerning Bucer's death, by a
letter sent to Oxford.

To which I may add another letter upon the same sub- Cheke's ad-
ject, by the same pen, sent to Cambridge to Dr. Parker vice to the University
afore-mentioned, who was Bucer's executor: it is extant, concerning
and remaining among the MSS. of Bene't college, and Bucer.
lately published in the Memorials of Archbishop Cranmer.
Therein he signified, that he had delivered the University's
letter to the King, and spoke with the Lords of the Council, and with Archbishop Cranmer, for Bucer's widow.
That he doubted not, but " she would be well and worthily
" considered. That the University had not done so great
" honour to Mr. Bucer, as credit and worship to themselves.
" The which, if they would continue in, as they ceased not
" to complain, they might be a great deal better provided
" for than they thought they were.——That if they would
" have sought either to recover or to increase the good
" opinion of men, they could not have devised wherein by
" more duty they might worthily be commended, than in

" following so notable a man with such testimony of ho-
" nour, as the child ought to do to his father, and the
" lower to his superior. And though he doubted not, but
" the King's Majesty would provide some grave, learned
" man to maintain God's true learning in his University,
" yet he thought, that of all learned men, in all points,
" they should not receive Mr. Bucer's like; whether his
" deepness of knowledge were considered, or his earnest-
" ness in religion, his fatherliness in life, or his authority
" in knowledge.——He wished that what was wanting
" now by Mr. Bucer's death, they would, by diligence and
" wisdom, fulfil in themselves; and what they praised in

Cheke de-
sires Bucer's
papers for
the King's
library.

" others, would labour to obtain themselves." Then he
prayed Dr. Parker, that Bucer's books and scrolls unwritten might be sent up, and saved for the King, that he,
choosing such as should like him best, might return the
other without delay; except Mrs. Bucer thought some
other better thing to be done with them, or that she
should have loss by them, if they should not be in her
ordering. He was tender of being in the least prejudicial
to the benefit of her whose husband he so much valued,
however desirous he was to furnish the young King's
library with the books and MSS. that once belonged to a
man of such worth and note as Bucer was.

SECT. IX.

Cheke piously writes unto Dr. Haddon, being sick.

Cheke's
consolatory
letter to
Haddon.

MENTION was made of Dr. Haddon. He was Doctor
of Laws, of King's college, and one of the topping men of
the University for piety, good learning, and especially for
a cleanly Ciceronian style, and was one of Cheke's chief
friends. At this very time he laboured under a dangerous
lingering sickness, that had brought him very low. And yet,
in the midst of it, however indisposed he was, his respects
to Bucer put him upon pronouncing an oration at his funerals, as was shewed before, when he seemed in all outward
appearance to be the very next man to follow him. Cheke

was now at Court, but was not unmindful of Haddon's
declining condition, and did the part of a true spiritual
friend, by sending him his counsel and comfort in a wise
and compassionate letter; which, having such a mixture of
piety and eloquence, and to preserve the small remainders
we have of this great man's composures, I shall translate
for the English reader's benefit, though falling far short of
the writer's elegant Latin. It began, *Ærumnæ et miseriæ
nostræ, quibus non modo quotidie jactamur, sed fluctua-
mus etiam, &c.*

" Our afflictions and miseries, wherewith we are not
" only daily tossed, but also are fluctuating up and down,
" do administer great ease to your ailments, and comforts
" in your sickness. I suppose, now you do not only look
" upon death, which is the end of life, but also upon
" Christ, who is the end of death, whose servants we are,
" whether we live or die; you have the example of a good
" and religious man, whose departure you lately most elo-
" quently bewailed, [in his funeral oration upon Bucer,]
" who hath prepared you an entrance to Christ. That if
" any must leave this light, the enjoyment whereof is wont
" to be dear to us all, he cannot be furnished with so many
" nor more noble exhortations, if he would turn over all
" the monuments of antiquity, than you have now placed
" before your eyes; *viz.* the length of the distemper, which
" by much premeditation mitigates all grief; the frequent
" and necessary thoughts of death, which take away the
" delights of this world, and diminish the childish appre-
" hensions of life and ease; the great and heavy assaults
" of a disease, which break strength, and draw you neces-
" sarily into the meditation of death; the death of Bucer,
" the worth of whose life, if it could not deliver him from
" the jaws of death, what hope may we have of others,
" whose praise, although great, yet of him there could not
" be greater and worthier; but as children, so you per-
" haps, when they see their parents going out, they la-
" ment, they take on, they pray they may go abroad with
" them. Servants, who are employed upon ordinary and
" domestic work within doors, do not ask for that which

" they cannot obtain; nor do they know what they should
" do abroad, being not accustomed to the business that
" lieth without, nor skilful how to manage it. You see
" Bucer going before you. In his departure, you, half dead,
" cry [after him;] your friend doth not hear; you go not
" where fain you would: but there is one perhaps that
" hears, and leads you after your parent; and in the mean
" time increaseth the anguish of your disease, which press-
" eth you with grief, to make you weary of your body
" as a prison; that your mind, free and at large, might
" take her flight to heaven, as your dwelling-house, and
" deliver it from these common and daily afflictions, which
" set so hard upon human life.

" Considering all this, what else may you think than
" this: My father is gone home; he calls me; I must fol-
" low: so my will, so my nature bids me; and so the wise
" and the good God will have it; whose goodness I per-
" ceive as a son, whose wisdom I perceive as a mortal
" man, and whose presence as a creature. You arm your-
" self against the rage of the flesh, which if it be not quite
" buried, yet it is broken with diseases; and it teacheth
" you, (unless the eternal Workmaster restore you,) that
" an inveterate evil cannot be mended, and that we must
" look for another house whither to go, when we see the
" imminent and tottering ruin of this. But why do I call
" it a *house*? A kingdom, and that hereditary, and a spa-
" cious territory, is prepared for you; which, when it was
" once lost, Christ purchased for his people, by redeeming
" them from their sins, and bestowing on them his Spi-
" rit.

" Here, perhaps, you will interpose, and say, Not all who
" are oppressed with these pains presently ought to de-
" spair of health. It is not of necessity indeed; but, how-
" ever, it is the part of wisdom to provide against the
" worst; and, that nothing may happen unawares, to think
" of extremities, not to be afflicted for the loss of life, and
" not to despair of a better state: for neither should we
" live without hope, nor die with care; lest either the life
" be miserable, wanting the comfort of hope, or death be

" bitter, being in a torture at the approach of it. For there
" are twelve hours in the day; which being spent, the sun
" sets; being not spent, the light diffuseth itself to mor-
" tals: nor does it set before the time prescribed by God
" come; nor doth it stay longer than the appointed end of
" its course.   Not so much as an hair falleth to the earth
" without the will of our heavenly Father, at whose com-
" mand they all fall, and without it they remain; giving
" us to understand, that life and death are governed by his
" authority and pleasure.   And we should not be afraid of
" what he provides, nor shun what he sends, nor decline
" what he commands.   But I have no time for further dis-
" course of these things, by reason of my business; nor
" have you leisure to read them, by reason of your indis-
" position. You will therefore excuse me, that here I make
" a stand.   Farewell in Christ, dear Haddon.   March 19,
" anno 1551. [*i. e.* anno 1550 *exeunte.*]"

This was the sum of Cheke's Christian as well as eloquent letter to the sick Haddon; wherein he shewed himself a true friend, in the spiritual comforts and counsels
suggested to him.   But Haddon (though at this present
low ebb of health) at length recovered, and lived to be
made use of both by King Edward and Queen Elizabeth.
To the latter whereof, after she had employed him in embassies abroad, he became Master of her Requests.   And
as he not long after this was preferred by the King, so was
Cheke: the one to be President of Magdalen college in
Oxford, anno 1552; the other, as a special mark of the
King's favour, to the honour of knighthood this ensuing
year, as we shall hear by and by.

CHAP. IV.

From the time of Cheke's knighthood, to his being made a
Privy Counsellor and Secretary of State.

SECT. I.

Cheke is knighted.

Honours
conferred by
the King
upon Cheke
and others.
For in the year 1551, and in the month of October, was a great advancement to honour granted unto certain of the nobility: Henry Grey, Marquis of Dorset, who married a daughter of the late Duke of Suffolk, (which daughter he had by Mary of the royal blood,) was created Duke of Suffolk; John Sutton, alias Dudley, Earl of Warwick, was created Duke of Northumberland; Paulet, Earl of Wilts, was created Marquis of Winchester; Sir William Herbert was made Lord Cardiff, and soon after Earl of Pembroke; and at the same time, for the greater splendour of the day, the King knighted his Secretary Cecil, his schoolmaster Cheke, and two that were chief gentlemen of his privy chamber, Nevyl and Sidney.

The King's
gift to him.
To which I add the King's gift to him about six months before, namely, in May, to enable him the better to maintain the port and honour that he was ere long to be invested with. It was a gift in fee simple to John Cheke, Esquire, (as it is set down in the warrant book,) in consideration of the surrendry of an hundred mark rent, granted him by letters patents, dated the 26th of August, in the second year of his reign for twenty-one years, if it should so long please the King, of all the manor of Stoke juxta Clare (as he had before given him the site of the college, and other lands belonging to it) in the counties of Suffolk and Essex, with divers other lands, tenements, &c. all to the yearly value of 145*l*. 19*s*. 3*d*. To hold all the premises *in capite*, by the fortieth part of a knight's fee, (except the Fuller Mill in Stoke, and the Guildhall house there,) the Pistery pasture, and other premises in Spalding, and the rec-

tory of Sandon, and other premises in Sandon; to be holden as of the manor of Greenwich by fealty only, paying yearly to the King for the manor of Stoke 4*l.* 17*s.* 7*d.*

SECT. II.

Cheke inquisitive after Dr. Redman's declaration concerning religion at his death.

NOTHING of moment passed at Cambridge, or relating to the members of it; but Sir John Cheke was inquisitive about it. Dr. Redman, Master of Trinity college, some time fellow collegian with Cheke, one of the learnedest and gravest men in that University, in the month of November, anno 1551, departed this life. A man he was of such great esteem for his deep knowledge in divinity, and acquaintance with the ecclesiastical fathers and writers, and skill in the Scriptures, that his words bore a very great weight and authority. This Doctor was reckoned rather of the Popish side, than that of the Protestants. He owned outwardly transubstantiation and justification by works; though in other matters he was more loose from the corruptions and superstitions of the Roman Church. But coming to lie on his deathbed at Westminster, the learneder sort attended him, and prayed him, as a dying man, (since the world had such a deference for his learning,) to declare impartially his thoughts of several matters then controverted in the Church, which he promised he would do most sincerely. His answers were all in favour of the Reformation, and particularly he shewed the rottenness of those distinguishing Papal doctrines before mentioned, which he seemed outwardly to have adhered to. There were then present Wilks, Master of Christ's college, Cambridge; Alexander Nowell, Master of the King's school at Westminster, and divers others; and particularly Mr. Yong, B. D. of Trinity college, none of the most earnest favourers of religion, and a great opposer of Martin Bucer, but a learned man. Cheke, desirous to know the truth of these things, sent to the said Yong, praying him

Yong's letter to Cheke concerning Redman.

F 2

CHAP.
IV.

Anno 1551.
Fox, first
edit. p. 870.

for a just account of the declaration that grave and reverend man had made. In answer to which he sent him a
large letter, the original whereof fell into the hands of John
Fox, the Martyrologist; and he printed it in his first edition of his Acts and Monuments. The translation whereof
into English remaineth in the after editions. It began,
Etsi animus mihi non mediocri dolore perculsus est, vir
amplissime, propter immaturam (nisi ita Deo visum) et
flebilem sanctissimi et eruditissimi viri D. Redmanni mor-
tem; adeo ut luctu et mærore multum stupefactus, vix
tandem semet aut ad agendum aut ad cogitandum expe-
diat; tamen cum id tuam amplitudinem me facere velle
intelligam, libenter me ipse colligo, atque quæ ab ipso pio
et docto Redmanno bonæ memoriæ viro, dum adhuc diu-
turna infirmitate contabescens certam mortem expectaret,
de religionis controversiis, quibus hodie Christi sponsa
Ecclesia misere divexatur, pronuntiata audiverim, fide-
liter et vere hisce meis literis enarrare instituo : i. e. " Al-
" though, worthy Sir, I am struck with no small grief
" at the untimely (had it not so pleased God) and deplo-
" rable death of Dr. Redman, that most holy and ex-
" cellently learned man, so that much overcome with
" mourning and sorrow, I scarce can recover myself freely
" to do or think any thing; yet since I understand it is
" your pleasure I should do it, I willingly recollect myself,
" and do resolve faithfully and truly to declare in this my
" letter, what I heard the pious and learned Redman of
" good memory speak, while he was wasting with sick-
" ness, and expected certain death, concerning the con-
" troversies of religion, with which the Church, Christ's
" spouse, is miserably vexed." Then he shewed Cheke
how Mr. Alexander Nowell, one that was always a lover
and valuer of him, accosted him once, being near his end,
to shew his mind concerning certain points to him and
the rest present; and what they should look upon, as
though it were an oracle from heaven. The points were
these: concerning his judgment of the Bishop and see of
Rome; concerning purgatory; whether the wicked eat the

body of Christ; whether Christ be present in the Sacrament, and be to be worshipped there; concerning the carrying about of the Sacrament in solemn pomps and pro-
cessions; concerning commemoration of the dead, justification by faith, and the merit of good works. To all
which, that reverend man gave his resolution the Protestant way, as Yong shewed Cheke at large in his letter,
which he thus concluded: *Atque hæc quidem sunt, quæ
ego ad questiones sibi propositas, eum respondisse audivi.
Nec vero usquam (quod memini) ab ea quam ab ipso
enuntiatam audivi sententia deflexi. D. noster Jesus
Christus has turbulentas, quibus Ecclesia jactatur, tem-
pestates compescere dignetur, miserumque suum ovile mi-
serabiliter jam dissipatum et dispersum propitius intuea-
tur et aspiciat, propter nomen sanctum suum. Amen.
Ipse tuam amplitudinem gubernare dignetur et servet.
Londini, 3 Novembr. &c.* i. e. " And these are the things
" which I heard him answer to the questions to him pro-
" pounded. Nor have I ever myself (as far as I remem-
" ber) wandered from that opinion which I heard declared
" by him. Our Lord Jesus Christ vouchsafe to allay these
" stormy tempests, with which the Church is tossed, and
" regard and look in mercy upon his poor sheepfold, mi-
" serably dispersed and scattered for his holy name sake.
" Amen. May he vouchsafe to rule and keep you. Lon-
" don, the 3d of November, &c."

SECT. III.

Cheke's disputations concerning the Sacrament.

ABOUT this time Cheke, with some others, was en- A relation
gaged in two disputations, or rather friendly conferences, of the con-
privately with Feckenham, (who was afterwards Dean of Cheke and
St. Paul's and Abbot of Westminster,) and one or two others,
about the
more of his party, in the great controversy of the real pre- Sacrament.
sence in the Sacrament. The first was held at Secretary
Cecil's house, and the latter at Sir Richard Morison's.
The auditors were but six, *viz.* the Lord Russel, Sir Tho-

mas Wroth of the Bedchamber; Sir Anthony Cooke, one of the King's instructors; Throgmorton, Chamberlain of the Exchequer; Mr. Knolles and Mr. Harrington; with whom were joined the Marquis of Northampton and the Earl of Rutland in the second conference. The disputants were Sir John Cheke, and with him Sir William Cecil, Secretary of State; Horn, Dean of Durham; Whitehead and Grindal; who were against the real presence: Feckenham, Yong, and, at the second disputation, Watson; who were for it. Some account of these disputations are still extant in Latin, in the MS. library of Bene't college in Cambridge. And to preserve what remainders we can of Cheke's, and likewise to satisfy any that are desirous to look into the Church history of England in those days, I have translated them into English, and exemplified them here: only first premising, that I suppose this conference might be occasioned from an appearance of the said

Feckenham in the Tower, brought before Cheke. Feckenham before Cheke by public order, to be examined by him; when Cheke entered into discourse with him about points of religion, and endeavoured to bring him from his Popish principles, but could not prevail, which might provoke to a more particular disputation between them upon the great master-controversy of transubstantiation.

The sum of a conference held Nov. 25, an. Dom. 1551, in the house of Cecil, the King's Secretary, concerning the Sacrament.

AUDITORS.

The Lord Russel	Mr. Throgmorton
Mr. Hales	Mr. Knolles
Mr Wroth	Mr. Harrington
Sir Anthony Cooke	

DISPUTANTS.

Sir William Cecil	Mr. Feckenham
Sir John Cheke	
Mr. Horn, Dean of Durham	and
Mr. Whitehead	
Mr. Grindal	Mr. Yonge

Mr. Cheke began to propound; but first Mr. Cecil SECT.
made a protestation, that it should be free for any one to ___ III.
produce his sentence or opinion, and that whatsoever in Anno 1551.
this discourse should be spoken, should redound to no E Biblioth.
man's harm or prejudice. C. C. C. C.

The question. *What was the true and genuine sense of
the words of the Supper,* This is my body; *whether that
which the words taken in the grammatical sense hold
forth, or some other.*

Feckenham. All the words of Christ are either ostensive
or effective: ostensive, as, *I am the good shepherd, &c.;*
effective, as to the leper, *Be clean :* Ephphata, *Be opened,
&c.* But in effective speeches, the Lord doth those things
which the words sound, and that by reason of his omnipo-
tency. Since therefore these words are effective, it followeth, &c.

Cheke to this answered; Admitting that division, it may
be answered, The Lord hath done that which he would, if
the speech be effective. But he would here institute a
sacrament; to the institution of which it is not necessarily required, that the words should be understood in a
grammatical sense.

Feckenham. The Lord would not institute a sacrament
only, but also give his body in the sacrament, according
to his promise in these words, *This is my body;* and according to that, John vi. *The bread which I will give is
my flesh, which I will give, &c.* There is *I will give*
twice; once in the Supper, and again in the cross.

Cheke. That we may therefore come, said he, briefly Questio.
to what we would have, I demand, whether the Lord
would institute here a sacrament, or not?

Feckenham answered he would; but not only a bare
figure, but a sacrament, and the matter of a sacrament.

Cheke. I ask, therefore, whether this is the true sense
of the word, *This is my body,* that is, my natural body;
or this rather, *This is the sacrament of my body?*

Feckenham answered, Both might be the sense of the
words.

Ch. But *This is the sacrament of my body* can be no
sense, unless we admit a trope in those words.

Mr. Whitehead. There can be no grammatical sense
of this place. For Christ said, *I leave the world;* which
all confess to be understood of the humanity of Christ:
but to leave the world, and to be in the world, are repugnant. *Ergo.*

Feck. He left the world as to his visible presence and
conversation; but in his invisible presence, the substance
of his body is present in the Sacrament, according to his
own words, *This is my body.*

Whiteh. To be in the world, and to be not in the
world, are terms contradictory; but God cannot make
contradictories to be true together, as Scotus said. *Ergo.*

Yong. Then Yong, when the nature of contradictories
was urged, said, They are not contradictories, but *subalterna.*

Wh. Yea, they are *singularia,* not an universal, and a
particular, *I leave the world,* and *I am in the world.*

Yong. But it may be contradicted out of the Scriptures from this place, *For I am with you always, &c.*
which seem to be understood of his humanity.

When the contrary was urged, that this is to be understood, according to the opinion of St. Augustin, of the
divine majesty and grace, then

Yong. But, said he, according to his *majesty* and *grace*
he was always present to the Fathers of the Old Testament. Therefore what greater matter seems to be promised to the Apostles than was given to the Fathers?
This must be understood of his humanity.

Then all with one mouth said, The Lord was present
with his Apostles, according to the more plentiful grace
and energy of the Holy Spirit, than he was with the Fathers, and this was asserted by all interpreters.

Yong ingeniously confessed it was so, and that he
brought this for disputation's sake.

Therefore the intermitted argument was resumed, *viz.*
Absent is not present, and the same answer was given as
above.

Cheke. Whether can this be truly spoken, Christ left
the world, therefore the substance of Christ left the world.

How Feckenham answered, he remembereth not.

That of Augustin was added, " Take away the spaces
" of places from bodies, and they will be no where." And
because they are no where, they are not. And this is the
difference between the Creator and a creature, that God
alone may be at every time every where, or in more
places; whence the ancients prove the divinity of the
Holy Ghost. But no creature can be together in more
places; therefore the body of Christ, though it be now
glorified, yet is not a spirit, and if it were a spirit it would
signify nothing; for the angels, if they are not in a place
circumscriptive, yet they are definitive, &c. therefore the
body of Christ cannot be in more places at once.

Feck. The body of Christ is in more places at once
tanquam in loco. He is in heaven *as in a place.* In the
Sacrament, although he hath quantity, quality, and other
proprieties of a true body, yet he is not in the Sacrament
secundum modum quanti, or, as the Schoolmen speak, he
is not there *quantitative* or *localiter.*

Cheke. These are monsters of words, which cannot be
comprehended by human understanding.

Feck. The thing is of faith, not reason; therefore we
ought to believe the word of God.

Cheke propounded an argument of evil men, and of unworthy receiving the Eucharist.

If this be the sense of the words, which the words hold
forth, then the evil eat the body of Christ.

But Christ saith, *He that eateth my flesh &c. shall live
for ever.*

Therefore the evil have eternal life.

Feck. The wicked receive Christ's body; but to condemnation, according to that of St. Paul, *He that eateth*

and drinketh unworthily, eateth and drinketh damna-
tion.

When it was on the contrary objected, that Christ could
not remain together with Satan in wicked men:

Yong interrupted this discourse, and said, that there
was a great variety of opinions in asserting this doctrine,
[of the wicked eating Christ's body,] many absurdities
concerning the length of the time of his tarrying, [in the
communicant,] concerning the time of his departing; and
pretending, as he seemed, that this assertion, that the
wicked eat Christ, did not sufficiently please him.

Horn said, that the circumstances of the place evince,
that Christ spake not according to the grammatical sense.
For Christ, when he said, *This is my body,* added also, τὸ
διδόμενον, *delivered.* But an adjective in speech cannot be
drawn from its substantive in grammatical sense: it followeth therefore, that the body of Christ was delivered,
when these words were spoken: and so it was delivered
[or given] before his passion.

Feck. Although it be here read, *traditum,* "delivered,"
yet it may be easily perceived, that Christ spake of the
time to come as though it were past.

Horn. I ask whether the body of Christ was a true and
natural body, and qualified with all the accidents of an
human body, or had some privileges?

Feck. When he admonished, that the question was
double, and answered both were true, *viz.* That he had all
the accidents of human nature; and yet, when it seemed
good to him, he had some privileges; then

Horn. The body of Christ before his passion was a
mortal body, and in some place; but if we admit the
grammatical sense, when he reached forth to each the Sacrament, it was in their hands to whom he gave it. And
he sat not only there, but in the Apostles' hands; he was
at once in various places: therefore Christ's body had not
the true accidents of an human body.

Feck. Therefore, because of this I said, that Christ's

body had certain privileges. For when he walked upon the water, he retained not the natural reason of a ponder-ous body. So therefore in the Supper. And if he were then mortal, yet he gave his body after an immortal manner. So also in the Mount he transfigured himself, and yielded a certain specimen of immortality; where he kept not the natural accidents of an human body, but shewed there an immortal body.

When Yong had come in with something, I know not what, as though by some other answer he would oppose the former argument;

Feckenham said, that he nothing helped the cause. For by your answer it would follow, that the body of Christ would be at the same time mortal and immortal; which is absurd: for some interpreters affirm the body of Christ in the Mount for a time was immortal, and could not in that time by any means be put to death by the Jews.

When Mr. Horn had pursued the same thing a good while by subtile reasons, Edmund Grindal was bid to propound a reason or two.

Then he; Because we ought to argue out of the Scriptures, it would be best to compare the circumstances of places, and other words of the Supper together: first, therefore, this seemeth worthy to be noted, that the Holy Ghost calleth it so often the *bread*, and Paul the *bread*, and the Holy Ghost best knoweth the names of things: therefore it is bread.

Feck. Then it was called *bread*, because it was bread; or the rod of Moses, &c. and therefore in Paul is always added, *That bread, &c.*

Grind. What did Christ take into his hand?

Feck. He answered, Bread.

Grind. What did he break?

Feck. Bread also; but, saith he, we must consider also, that he brake it before the consecration, and before these words, *This is my body.*

Grind. You differ indeed from others, that he brake it, being already consecrated; and yet the breaking was not in the body, but in those species, and that also absurdly enough; but we shall not tarry upon these things, but because it is much more plain of the other part of the Sacrament, therefore I shall produce that before us. The words are manifest enough, *I will not drink hereafter of this fruit of the vine.* Therefore there is nothing but wine.

Feck. Luke twice makes mention of the cup; once, before the mention of the Sacrament; the second time, when the Supper was over. These words of Christ seem to be referred to the cup not consecrated.

Grind. This conjecture is not a demonstration; for Matthew and Mark presently after these words, *This is my body,* (which are the words, as you say, of consecration,) join the words recited before. And although Luke twice makes mention of the cup, yet Augustin, in his book of the consent of the Gospels, thinks the same thing is twice told in Luke: but I demand whether Christ drank of the cup consecrated?

Feck. He answered, he drank of it.

Grind. What therefore did he drink? his own blood?

Feckenham acknowledged it.

Grind. But for what end did he drink of his own blood? Chrysostom writ, " That he, by drinking, did call off his " Disciples from this thought; that they should not think " or say, Behold, we drink blood," &c.

When Feckenham always urged these words of Christ, *This is my blood which is shed for you,* as clear, and therefore no man should doubt of them, it was asked him by the way (because he noted the emphasis of the words, that Christ said *hic* and *hoc.*)

What was shewn by *hic,* " this?"

Feckenham answered, The blood.

Then Grindal, What grammatical sense is this, *Hic sanguis est sanguis,* i. e. " This blood is blood."

Lastly, he propounded this argument; These words of the Supper, *This is my body,* can be by no better way searched out, whether they be spoken figuratively or properly, than

if the words of the other part of the Supper, as I said, be
viewed together; for if in the other part a trope shall manifestly appear, why not also in this?

Feckenham denied there was a trope in these words,
This cup is the new testament in my blood.

Grind. Neither the cup, nor that which was contained
in the cup, can be the new testament. For the new
testament is defined the covenant of grace between God
and the elect; therefore neither the symbol itself, nor the
blood of Christ, can properly be called the new testament, when the blood of Christ is the confirmation of the
new testament.

Feck. The blood of Christ in the cup (for this cup
hath a trope) is both a confirmation of the new testament, and also the new testament.

Grind. That which is contained in the cup, whatever it
be, is a substance. The new testament is a relation, and
so also an accident. From whence follows, (the word being rightly understood,) that a substance is an accident,
and that there is an identical predication between substance and relation or accident.

Feckenham and Yong by long fetches endeavoured to
shew, how the body of Christ might properly be said to be
the new testament, &c.

The second conference, Dec. 3, an. Dom. 1551, *in Sir
Richard Morison's house.*

PRESENT.

The Marquis of Northampton.
The Earl of Rutland.

The Lord Russel, with the rest formerly named, together with Mr. Watson on the Papist side.

Cheke. Whether the words of the Supper are to be understood according to the grammatical sense, or rather in
a figurative sense.

Watson answered the same to this, as Feckenham before; namely, that there were two kinds of speaking, the one narratory, the other operatory, &c.

Being desired of Mr. Cecil, that he would propound more contractedly what he said a little before more largely, he propounded this argument:

These words, *This is my body*, are the form of the sacrament of the Eucharist: but in every form of a sacrament God worketh that which the words signify. Therefore in these words, *This is my body*, God worketh that which his words signify.

Mr. Cheke desired him to confirm the major with reasons.

Then he brought the example of Baptism: in which these words, " I baptize thee in the name of the Father," &c. are the form of the sacrament, but God worketh that which the words signify, taken in the grammatical sense. For as the body is washed with water, so inwardly the soul is washed by the Holy Spirit. Moreover, saith he, this is a principle in divinity, *God worketh those things which the words signify in the forms of the sacraments.*

Cheke. I do not acknowledge that principle in divinity, (truly so called,) that words should be all taken according to the grammatical sense and proper meaning of speech. It is as if God worketh that which the Spirit of God would signify by his word, whether taken figuratively or properly.

Cheke propounded a new question, whether Christ in the Supper instituted any sacrament or not?

Watson. Here is an equivocation in the word *sacrament.* For a sacrament is taken both for the sign and for that very thing that is signified. So among the ancients, that which they call *the Sacrament of the body of Christ*, and *the body of Christ*, speaking of the Eucharist, is the same.

Cheke. This distinction is unseasonable; for if Christ instituted a sacrament, it is necessary that there be a sacrament and the matter of a sacrament.

Watson granted it.

Cheke. But a sacrament and the matter of a sacrament are *membra dividentia,* and so *disparata;* therefore
one thing cannot be another. And so the same thing cannot be the Sacrament and the matter of the Sacrament.

Watson. I opened before the equivocation of the word,
that we may more briefly pass it over. For in this Sacrament the body of Christ is the true matter of the Sacrament, and the Sacrament also; for it is the Sacrament of
the mystical body of Christ.

Cheke. The same thing cannot be a sacrament and
the matter of a sacrament by the definition. For the Sacrament is a visible sign of an invisible grace, and the sign
of a sacred thing, &c.

Grind. No better way can be gone for the understanding of these words, than by comparison of the sacraments,
and the circumstances of the words; which you seem
yourselves very much to approve of. Let Baptism therefore and the Eucharist be compared, whence we may collect after this manner; God doth not work that which
the words taken in the grammatical sense do signify concerning Baptism, therefore neither in the Eucharist.

Watson bade him confirm his antecedent.

Grind. Concerning Baptism it is said thus, *Unless a
man be born again of water and of the Spirit, &c.* But
according to the proper and grammatical manner of
speech, no man is born again in Baptism. Therefore the
same may be affirmed in the Eucharist.

Watson. I said, that God performs those things which
the words do signify in the forms of the sacraments; but
these words, *Unless a man be born again of water, &c.*
are not the formal words of Baptism; but these, " I bap-
" tize thee in the name of the Father," &c.

Grind. Although these are not, as the schools speak,
the form, yet these do express the true effect of Baptism,
when nevertheless they are metaphorical: but let us examine even the formal words, " I baptize thee in the
" name," &c. Is *I baptize* here taken properly or meta-
phorically?

Watson answered, Properly.

Grind. To *baptize* in the proper sense is to *wash;* but the true effect of Baptism is not the washing of the body, as Peter teacheth, but of the soul. The soul is not washed, if we speak properly : therefore neither is it baptized.

Watson. The soul properly speaking is washed.

Grind. Nothing is washed besides the body. The soul is not the body. *Ergo.*

Grind. I demand, when Christ said, *Take ye*, must we believe he spake properly?

Watson. Properly.

Grind. Eat ye; was that properly spoken?

Watson said, Yes.

Grind. Therefore the body of Christ properly speaking is eaten or chewed.

Watson. He granted that too.

Grind. To eat, if it be defined according to the propriety of the word, is to divide with the teeth, and to carry it down into the stomach; but the body of Christ properly speaking is not divided, because it suffereth not. *Ergo.*

Watson here cavilled much of I know not what *spiritual* eating; which yet was proper, and without any necessity of suffering.

Mr. Cecil would have had some demonstration propounded by somebody syllogistically, which might evince it to be a trope, that Watson might answer. Therefore this argument was offered :

A trope is to be admitted, rather than a contrariety to be suffered in the Scriptures; but these words of the Supper properly understood do bring in a contrariety in the Scriptures : therefore a trope must be admitted in them.

Watson would have the minor proved.

Grind. The Scriptures distribute to us the flesh of Christ, with all the accidents of a true body; but if in the Eucharist there be a true and natural body, to wit, longitude and latitude, whence a contrariety is brought into the Scripture.

Admitting the propriety of the words, it followeth, that the evil and the wicked do eat the body of Christ. But that brings with it a contrariety and repugnancy in the Scriptures. Therefore the propriety of the words is not to be admitted, but a trope.

Watson. That the wicked eat the body of Christ is not repugnant to the Scripture.

Grind. *He that eateth the flesh of Christ hath eternal life,* John vi. The wicked have not eternal life. Therefore they eat not the body of Christ.

Watson. The matter of the Sacrament is twofold; the *natural* body of Christ, and the *mystical* body of Christ. The wicked eat the body as to his substance, but the virtue of the Sacrament, that is, the mystical body of Christ, they eat not.

Grind. The Church is the mystical body of Christ; but who saith that the Church is eaten?

After followed a subtle kind of dispute between Cheke and Watson, of essential and accidental grace; for Watson had said, that Christ himself was the essence of grace.

Cheke. If the wicked eat Christ, they receive essential grace; but essential grace is somewhat a greater thing than accidental. But he that receiveth the greater, receiveth that which is less. Therefore the wicked in the Sacrament do receive Christ and remission of sins, or the fruit of Christ's passion, which you call *accidental* grace.

Watson eluded the argument with I know not what logical distinction.

Whitehead's argument. Transubstantiation destroys the nature of a sacrament, which ought to have some similitude with the thing itself; as Augustin in his Epistle to Boniface. And Paul brings an argument from this similitude, *We being many are one bread and one body, &c.* There is a similitude, as bread in the Sacrament is made of many corns, so we, &c. But now if there be no bread, there is no similitude.

Watson. This place very much strengtheneth my opinion; for Paul saith, *We all partake of one bread.* But

G

what is that one bread but Christ? For the bread which you take in the Sacrament one time, and I at another, is not one bread, but many. Paul saith, *We all eat of one bread, &c.*

Whiteh. It is one, because it is taken for the same end, and is used in the same mysteries. For Paul doth not speak of that which is one in number, but one *in specie.*

Then followed a new wrangling with Mr. Cheke, whether it might be truly said, that it is the same water of Baptism in which various persons are baptized at various times.

Watson said, It is one Baptism, but not one water.

Cheke added another reason, *viz.* that all that were baptized had put on Christ, and received the Spirit of Christ; for, *whosoever hath not this Spirit of Christ is none of his:* by Baptism it is effected, that we are brethren and coheirs of Christ; which cannot be, unless we do participate of his body and blood in Baptism. Therefore Paul, 1 Cor. xii. expressed by these words the same effect of Baptism and the Eucharist; *By one Spirit we are all baptized into one body, and have all drank into one Spirit:* which latter clause Chrysostom understands of the Eucharist. Therefore he attributed to Baptism incorporation with Christ; to the Eucharist the receiving of the Spirit: that from hence it may be manifestly collected, even in Baptism the same communion of Christ is conferred upon us, as is in the Eucharist. But because in Baptism there is no need of a real and natural presence of Christ, there will not be need of it also in the Eucharist.

Watson. There is a diverse reason of Baptism and the Eucharist, and different effects. For in Baptism we receive the Spirit of God to regeneration, and so by his Spirit our spirit is quickened: but in the Eucharist we receive the true substance of his flesh; from which not only our spirit, but our flesh is quickened. And so that comes to pass which is so often in Cyril; that we are *naturally* united to Christ, and that there is a *natural* union betwixt the flesh of Christ (which hath a power of quickening) and our flesh, which without it cannot have life. And to this

sense he took the words of John, chap. vi. *Unless ye eat*
the flesh of the Son of man, &c. that is, unless in the _____
Eucharist ye be partakers of his natural flesh, ye shall not
have life in you, that is, in your bodies, or in the flesh; for
" our flesh would not rise to glory without the flesh of
" Christ," as it is in Hilary.

Here the condition of infants was urged, and dying in
infancy; and of adult persons dying soon after the par-
taking of the Eucharist.

Watson did endeavour to evade by certain distinctions;
to wit, that *nisi*, " unless," makes not an absolute necessity, but if he have the Sacrament, or the desire of the Sacrament. As it is in Baptism, where it is said, *Unless one
be born again, &c.* Yet nevertheless he seemed to attribute something less to children departing before the Eucharist, than to the adult which have communicated.

Grind. If our flesh cannot rise any otherwise to life
(which you assert) but by eating the natural body of
Christ, and by that *natural union*, as you call it, we shall
indeed fall into many absurdities. For what shall we say
of the Fathers of the Old Testament? Paul saith, *They
eat the same spiritual meat*, which we do, *and drank the
same spiritual drink*, to wit, Christ: but they could not eat
the natural flesh of Christ, as being not yet born, therefore
we may together with them eat Christ, though we do not
eat his natural flesh.

Watson denied that the Fathers eat the same meat
which we do. For they eat the same spiritual meat; but
we eat not only the same spiritual meat, but real food
also.

Grind. If the Fathers had not the same communion
with Christ, and natural conjunction with him, as we have
in the Eucharist, it would follow, the Fathers should not
have life in their bodies; and so in the resurrection, the
bodies and flesh of the Patriarchs, wanting this substantial
participation, would not rise to life, which is most absurd.
Augustin saith, " Many shall come from the east and
" from the west, and shall sit down, not above Abraham,

"Isaac, and Jacob, but with Abraham, Isaac, and Jacob,
"in the kingdom of heaven."

Arguments from the Fathers.

A place of Augustin was produced from the twelfth
chapter of the book, *Contra Adamantum Manichæum.*
"Nor did the Lord doubt to say, *This is my body,* when
"he gave a sign of his body."

Feckenham confessed a sign, but not a sign only.

Another place was produced out of Augustin, in his
third book of Questions upon Leviticus, chap. lvii. where
he saith, *The seven ears of corn are seven years.* He
saith not, *they signify. The Rock was Christ;* not, lastly,
as though that were which indeed for the substance was
not, but by signification. *The Rock was Christ,* and, *This
is my body,* are of the same nature; but the first proposition is figurative, therefore the second.

Watson contended that this proposition, *The rock was
Christ,* was not figurative.

A place was brought by Watson, which is in St. Augustin, lib. i. Of the Merits and Remission of Sins. "We do
"not doubt but the blood is shed for baptized infants,
"which before it was shed, &c. So the Sacrament was
"given and commended, that it might be said, *This is my*
"*blood.*"

To which place it was answered thus; That none were
ignorant that the ancients used that form of speech, as
Christ himself, calling the sacraments by the same names
as the matters of the sacraments were. Augustin in his
Epistle to Archbishop Boniface, *numero* 23. saith, "The
"sacraments have the names of those things of which
"they are the sacraments; therefore the sacrament of
"faith is called faith," &c.

Watson. That place to Boniface makes nothing for you;
for although it may be taken according to a certain manner, yet that manner is not to be thought significative;
for otherwise it may be inquired, according to what manner the sacrament of faith is called faith?

Then he, [Grindal, I suppose,] According to whatever manner you will. Properly speaking, Baptism, or the sa- crament of faith, may not be called faith; and so neither the sacrament of the body and blood of Christ, according to that reason, is the body and blood of Christ.

The Marquis of Northampton produced a place out of Cyprian, and it is in the sermon *de Unctione.* Let the place be read.

" The Lord gave in the table bread and wine, in the " cross," &c.

In which place Watson laboured after a wonderful man- ner. The first antithesis, *viz.* " The Lord gave bread," he lightly passed over; he insisted on the following words, namely, " That Christ should teach the Apostles, that " they in like manner might teach the people, how bread " and wine is flesh and blood;" for otherwise, saith he, if bread and wine are only signs, he might easily teach this. That way he wrested that which followeth.

Cheke. He saith not how they were changed, but how they were: but bread and wine by no means can be the body and blood of Christ, unless after a sacramental and significative manner. And therefore afterward he saith, the things that signify, and the things signified, are to be reputed under the same names.

That place also of Augustin was objected, lib. iii. Of the Christian Doctrine; *Si flagitium aut facinus, &c. It is a figurative speech;* and therefore it was urged, it was a figurative speech *to eat the flesh of Christ,* John vi. and therefore the words of the Supper are figurative.

Feckenham acknowledged this place to be difficult, yet to it, it might thus be answered; Augustin saith, *Videtur præcipere facinus,* " He seemed to command a wicked " deed;" but indeed in these words no wickedness is com- manded. And Augustin in another place hath it, " It is " forbid in the law to eat the blood of living creatures; " but to us it is commanded, not to drink the blood of a " living creature, but of Christ himself."

Cheke. See therefore how you endeavour to invert St.

Augustin's opinion; for he gathereth, that it is a figure
from thence, that he seemeth to command a wicked deed,
and therefore he subjoineth, " Therefore it is a figure."

Watson said, that the speech was *proper*, as it pertain-
eth to the true eating of Christ; but *figurative*, as it be-
longeth to such things as follow in Augustin, *viz.* when it
is taken for the imitation of the passion, and remembrance
of the death of Christ.

But this answer was shewn to repugn sufficiently to
the scope of Augustin, who makes the whole speech to be
tropical; not proper, but tropical: for, saith he, "in the
" proper sense he seemeth to command a wicked deed."

Another place was produced out of the same book in
these words, " As it is the part of servile infirmity to fol-
" low the letter, and to interpret signs for things, so to
" interpret the signs unprofitably is the part of extrava-
" gant error."

Watson answered, that Augustin speaketh there of the
signs of the Old Testament; but when he had read the
place, where it speaks manifestly of Baptism and the Eucharist, he again gainsaid somewhat, I know not what.
And the most rose up, that here might be an end.

SECT. IV.

Resigns his Greek Professorship. Gets Leland's MSS.
Falls sick.

CHEKE had hitherto held the place of the Greek lecture in Cambridge, conferred upon him by his old master,
King Henry VIII. though I suppose he substituted somebody else to read in his stead, who seems to have been
Nicholas Car, Fellow of Trinity college; who now, the
12th day of October this year, being an exquisite Grecian,
was appointed to succeed Cheke in that lecture, by order
of the Privy Council, and that by procurement, as it seems,
of Cheke himself.

It was Cheke's practice (in order to the furnishing up
an excellent library for the King) to procure as many

MSS. as he could of learned men, into his possession, for SECT.
King Edward's use. Thus, as he got the papers and books of IV.
Dr. Martin Bucer, after his decease the last year, so he did Anno 1552.
those of John Leland, the antiquarian, this, upon his death,
which happened in April 1552. And all the MSS. and collections, (as we are told by a late author,) with many Procures
other matters of moment belonging to Leland, by virtue Leland's pa-
pers for the
of a commandment from the King, were brought into Sir King,
John Cheke's custody, for the use of that King's library; Athen.
Oxon. p.
and which the King seemed to have a right and title to, 69, 70.
since Leland had been employed by the King's father to
make those collections out of the libraries of the dissolved
monasteries and elsewhere, and had a salary allowed him
for that purpose, and other preferments granted him.
That author adds, that not long after, our Cheke (it must
rather be his son Henry, who was Secretary to the Council in the north under Queen Elizabeth) gave four volumes
of these collections to Humphrey Purefoy, Esq. one of the
said Council, whose son, Thomas Purefoy of Barwel in
Leicestershire, gave them to the antiquarian Will. Burton
of Lindley in the same county, anno 1612, who made use
of them in his description of Leicestershire. And many
years after by his gift they came at last to be safely
lodged in the public library at Oxford. Lastly, the same
author tells us, that some other of these collections, after
Cheke's death, came into the hands of William Lord
Paget and Sir William Cecil.

Now we are speaking of the King's library, it may not Keepers of
be amiss to note here, that the keeper of it was the the King's
library.
learned and ingenious Roger Ascham, preferred to it by
Cheke's means, with an honourable salary: and after him
Bartholomew Traheron, preferred afterwards in this reign
to be Dean of Chichester. For Ascham being now abroad,
as was shewed before, Cheke thought good he should resign
this place to some other that could daily attend; and recommended the said Traheron to Ascham, who shewed himself
willing he should succeed him, whom, he said, he loved
upon many accounts; and that he should the more easily

CHAP. suffer himself to be shut out of that library, [however
IV.   highly he esteemed the place,] for the sake of so worthy
Anno 1552. a man to be let into it. This was in January 1550.

Cheke falls   It had been a very crazy time in England by reason of
dangerously the sweating sickness that raged the last year, and by fe-
sick.
vers before and after that, whereby very many persons
were cut off, and some escaped very hardly, after that
they had been brought even to the gates of death: and as
Haddon, Cheke's dear friend, was one of these the last
year, so Cheke himself must have his turn this. His distemper (under which he laboured in May) brought him
exceeding low. The King and all good men were extra-
ordinarily concerned for him, knowing how useful a man
the nation was in danger of losing; the King inquired of
the physicians every day how he did, who, not able to
conquer the malignancy of the distemper, at last told the
King the heavy news, that there was no hope of his life,
and that they had given him over as a man for another
world. But the pious King had not only recommended
his schoolmaster to the care of his physicians, but also
to the heavenly Physician, whom in his devotions he earnestly implored to spare his life; and upon his prayers
such a strange assurance was impressed in his mind that
Cheke would recover, that when the doctors (as was said)
despaired of him, the King made this surprising reply to
them; " No," said he, " Cheke will not die this time; for
" this morning I begged his life in my prayer, and ob-
Recovers. " tained it." And so it came to pass; for towards the
latter end of the month of May he recovered. This was
attested (saith Fuller) by the old Earl of Huntingdon,
bred up with the King in his young years; who told it
to Cheke's grandchild, Sir Thomas Cheke of Pyrgo, aged
near eighty years, anno 1654, who then, it seems, made a
relation of it to the said Fuller. His recovery was looked
upon as a public blessing, and all good men rejoiced at it.
Bishop Rid- Bishop Ridley, in a letter to the Secretary, speaking of
ley and
Lever, their him, added, " in whose recovery God be blessed." Mr.
Joy at it.   Lever, a very learned and pious preacher, wrote to Ascham,

(of whom we have spoke before,) now at Villacho in Carin-
thia, and in his letter prayed to God, that England might
be thankful for restoring such a man again to the King.
" And I am firmly persuaded," said he, " that God wist
" and would we should be thankful, and therefore be-
" stowed this gift upon us. He trusted," as he went on,
" that God's wrath was satisfied in punishing divers or-
" ders of the realm for their misorder, having taken away
" many singular ornaments from them, as learning by the
" death of Bucer, counsel by Denny, nobility by the two
" young Dukes [of Suffolk, who died very shortly after
" one another of the sweating sickness,] courtship by gen-
" tle Blage, St. John's college by good Eland; but if
" learning, counsel, nobility, Court, and Cambridge, should
" have been all punished at once by taking away Mr.
" Cheke, then I should have thought our wickedness had
" been so great, as cried to God for a general plague, in
" depriving us of such a general and only man as he."

SECT. V.

*Cheke at Cambridge. Departs thence to the King. Places
conferred on him.*

I FIND him this year at Cambridge, gone thither, I suppose, to enjoy his native and beloved air after his sickness ;
and taking perhaps the opportunity of the King's progress
this summer, to go to his residence upon his Provostship
in King's college. Now at a Commencement, (as we are Cheke dis-
told,) Sir John Cheke did the University the honour to putes at a
Commence-
make himself a part in the learned exercises then per- ment,
formed; for when one Christopher Carlile, whose office it Athen.
Oxon. p.
was to keep a divinity act, maintained the tenet of Christ's 111.
local descent into hell, our learned man in disputation opposed him. This seems to have been done by consulta-
tion, and the argument resolved on, on purpose to meet
with the Popish doctrine of the *limbus patrum ;* that is,
an apartment of hell, where, they say, the ancient patriarchs and good men before Christ were detained, and

The question disputed.

whither Christ descended to deliver them thence. For Carlile's question was, that our Saviour went into no other hell but the very lowest, that is, that of the damned. This disputation making some noise, Dr. Richard Smith, sometime Professor of Divinity at Oxford, wrote a pretended confutation of it; which was after printed, anno 1562, at Louvain, as it seems, where he now resided.

Places and favours granted him by the King.

Soon after the Commencement, Cheke seems to have departed from Cambridge, and to have gone after the King, then in progress in the south-west parts. And as the King, his gracious master, had the last year honoured him with knighthood; so he thought it fit now to add some farther royal testimonies of his favour to him, and to qualify him the better to bear that post: therefore this summer he granted him certain places of honour, and some of benefit too. First, he granted him a patent, bearing date July 23, that one of his household servants, at all times, might shoot in the crossbow, hand-gun, hack-butt, or demy-hack, at certain fowl and deer expressed in the patent, notwithstanding the statute made to the contrary in 33 Henry VIII. This was dated at the honour of Petworth in Sussex, the seat of Sir Anthony Brown, late Master of the Horse, where the King now was in the way of his progress. Again, August the 25th following, a patent was granted him to be one of the Chamberlains of the Exchequer, or of the Receipt of the King's Exchequer, which was once Sir Anthony Wyngfield's office, now dead; and also to appoint the keeper of the door of the said Receipt, when his room should fall, and the appointing of all other officers belonging to the same, *pro termino vitæ*. This was dated at Sarum, where the King was now gotten. Also, as a further token of his interest and favour with the King, he obtained the wardship and marriage of Thomas Barnardiston, son and heir of Sir Thomas Barnardiston, Knight, in the counties of Bedford and Suffolk, and the annuity of 30*l*. per ann. But his last and highest steps were to be a Privy Counsellor, and Secretary of State. Of which we shall hear more in the ensuing chapter.

Made Chamberlain of the Exchequer.

CHAP. V.

*From Sir John Cheke's highest advancements to his exile;
and from thence to his surprise, imprisonment, recantation, repentance, and death.*

SECT. I.

*Cheke's highest advancements. A Privy Counsellor. Se-
cretary of State. Stands for the Lady Jane.*

WE come now to the thirty-ninth year, or thereabouts, Anno 1553.
of Sir John Cheke's age, a year that saw him advanced
very high, and soon after pulled down as low, stripped of
all his honour and wealth, and first made a prisoner, and
then an exile; for as this year concluded the life of that
dear person his royal scholar, so with him of all his temporal felicity.

He was now Clerk of the Council, and so he is entitled He is Clerk
in one of the books of the Office of Heralds, under the of the Council,
Chekes of Hampshire. And in May anno 1553, the King
bestowed on him and his heirs male, Clare in Suffolk, with
divers other lands, (as he had given him the manor of
Stoke juxta Clare a year or two ago,) to the yearly value
of 100*l.* But this clerkship was but in order to an higher
advancement, namely, to that of one of the principal Se- and Secre-
cretaries of State, which he was called to in June, and tary of
made a Privy Counsellor. For to me it seems that in State.
this juncture one of the Secretaries was intended to be
laid aside, and he perhaps was Cecil, who cared not to go
along with the purposes of the ambitious Duke of Northumberland, to advance his daughter-in-law, married to
Guilford Dudley his son, to the crown, and so to bring the
kingly dignity into his blood; though the attempt proved
to his own and his children's ruin. Cecil was now absent
from Court, sick in mind as well as in body. But Cheke's
zeal for religion made him willing to side with Northum-

CHAP.
IV.
Anno 1553.
berland and his party, who put the sick King upon settling the kingdom upon the Lady Jane, eldest daughter of
Grey Duke of Suffolk, excluding the next legal heirs, his
two sisters. And it must be placed among the slips of the
loose pen of the author of the State Worthies, when he
writes that Cheke was against this will of King Edward,
and puts this sentence in his mouth thereupon, " That he
" would never distrust God so far in the preservation of
" true religion, as to disinherit the orphans to keep up
" Protestantism."

His inclina-
tion to Jane
Grey.
It swayed him, while he foresaw what a persecution was
like to ensue, and what an overthrow of that reformed religion, that had been so carefully planted by good King
Edward. For though some secular and ambitious ends
drove on the Duke in these lofty and dangerous projects,
yet the fears of the return of Popery, and miserable times
consequent thereupon, both to the nation and to the state
of true religion, were the arguments that prevailed with
Cheke to countenance that interest; and his inclination
perhaps to this party made the way for him to be Secretary. To which office he was sworn and admitted June
the 2d, and the two other Secretaries were yet continued,
and all three Secretaries appeared in Council together.
And this appears from the Council Book. So that a cer-
State Wor-
thies.
tain observator, that tells the world that Cheke enjoyed
this place three years, imposes upon his readers, since in
truth he enjoyed it little above four weeks: to which we
may add the nine days of the Lady Jane Grey's reign.

Ascham
congratu-
lates his
high place
he was ad-
vanced to.
Ep. III. 9.
Now we may look upon him employed in the public affairs of state, and advanced into a high and honourable
station. On occasion of which, Ascham, being now at
Brussels [a] with Morison the King's Ambassador, begged
his pardon for detaining him with his letters, forgetting
the authority he had, and the momentous businesses with
Ep. III. 11.
which he was now taken up. And in another letter congratulated the high place he was advanced to; adding,
" that this was an honour long before due to his learning,

a Augsburg.

" his prudence, and integrity, by the voice of all; and that
" he did not so much congratulate him alone, as those to
" whom, in his opinion, it was a greater commendation of
" their prudence in choosing him, than a part of his hap-
" piness in ascending to this promotion. He congratulated
" therefore," he said, " the whole British name, and first,
" and chiefly indeed, the Prince; that as his childhood en-
" joyed Cheke, a most excellent preceptor, so his youth,
" and hereafter his elder age, should make use of him as a
" most prudent and faithful Counsellor for many long
" years to come;" [but alas! that could not be, the good
King was dead just a day before Ascham wrote this letter.]
He proceeded; " I extremely congratulate our civil state,
" our.land, and our Christian state; the safety of all which
" three was always so dear to you, that the single tran-
" quillity of each man, the desired name of studies, the
" quiet of purer religion must henceforth abide in your
" authority alone, in your excellent learning, and in your
" ardent love of God. I heartily congratulate Cambridge,
" which brought you forth; but above all, St. John's col-
" lege, which taught you: of the one you were a native,
" of the other a most flourishing scholar; both see you
" now their best and ablest patron." But alas! all these
congratulations, which came to Cheke's hands not many
days after his master the King's death, were to him but
like the joy of Jephthah's daughter to Jephthah, when she
came out to him with her timbrels and dances, congratu-
lating his victory; it was but a trouble and unspeakable
grief to him to hear and see it.

King Edward being dead, and the Lady Jane set up and
proclaimed Queen, letters at this time were sent from the
Council to the gentry, and other state letters were written
by Cheke as Secretary. He checked his brother Cecil,
who would not be induced to meddle in this matter, but
endeavoured to be absent; and to the very utmost day of
Queen Jane's reign, viz. to July the 19th, he acted as Secretary to her and her Council. On which day, upon in-
formation from the Lord Rich, Lord Lieutenant of the

CHAP.
V.

Anno 1553.

county of Essex, that the Earl of Oxford (who lived in that county,) had gone over to the Lady Mary, a letter signed by the Lords of Queen Jane's Council, sitting in the Tower, to excite that Lord to stand firm, was drawn up by Cheke's own pen, and by him signed with the rest: which letter he thus worded; " requiring him like a noble " man to remain in that promise and stedfastness to our " sovereign Lady Queen Jane, as ye shall find us ready " and firm with all our force to maintain the same: which " neither with honour, nor with safety, nor yet with duty, " we may now forsake."

SECT. II.

Committed, indicted, pardoned. Travels abroad. Sojourns at Strasburg.

Cheke committed to the Tower.

Fox's Acts.

Indicted.

Cranmer's concern for him. Fox, Epist. MS. penes me.

IT was but the next day that the Lords that signed this letter turned about, proclaimed Mary Queen, and wrote their letters to her, owning her their Sovereign; and thus was poor Sir John Cheke left in the lurch, (for he could not do as they did,) and on a sudden thrown down from his worldly greatness, which indeed he never affected; and within eight or nine days after, *viz.* July the 28th, together with the Duke of Suffolk, committed to the Tower as a traitor. And whereas the rest that acted as Queen Jane's Counsellors, being either Papists or indifferent in religion, were easily pardoned, Cheke and some few others (as the Archbishop of Canterbury and the Lord Russel) were sent to the Tower, or kept under harder and longer restraint. An indictment was drawn against him the 12th or 13th day of August; and his friends feared it would go hard with him. Archbishop Cranmer, who valued him highly for his learning and goodness, privately sent to Cecil to know " whereupon " he was indicted; and signifying withal, that he had " great cause to hope that he should be one of them that " should feel the Queen's pardon, as one who had been " none of the great doers in this matter against her, [as

" was Northumberland, and those that were actually in
" arms:] and that his trust was not yet gone, except it
" were for his earnestness in religion. For which, " said
the good Archbishop, " if he suffer, blessed is he of God,
" that suffereth for his sake, however the world judge of
" him:" adding, out of his dear respect for him, and his
usefulness to be continued in the world, " Alas! if any
" means could be made for him and my Lord Russel, it
" were not to be omitted, nor in any wise to be neg-
" lected."

Sir John, (together with some others,) the next year, Pardoned.
being almost spoiled of all his substance, obtained the fa- Is licensed
vour of the Queen's pardon. But being not able to satisfy to go abroad.
his conscience in the religion that was setting up, and
foreseeing the evil times that were drawing on, obtained a
licence from the Queen for some time to travel into foreign
parts; but intending a voluntary exile, with many other
noble and reverend personages, who fled their own country upon this change, and sojourned in divers places in
Germany and Switzerland, or elsewhere, where they might
enjoy their religion with safety. Such were Sir Anthony
Cooke, Sir Thomas Wroth, Mr. Knolles, Mr. Hales, the
Duchess of Suffolk and her husband Mr. Bertue, Mr. Rogers, and many of the best and eminentest sort of divines,
as Barlow, Scory, Bale, and Ponet, Bishops; Cox, Grindal,
Horne, Parkhurst, Jewel, Sandys, Pilkington, Nowell,
Whittingham, Fox, Lever, and many more. And some
took this opportunity to travel into Italy, and to see the
countries: and of these were Sir Anthony Cooke, and our
Sir John Cheke, who passed into Italy through Basil; Comes to
where staying some time, (for there were divers English Basil.
Protestants here,) he came acquainted with Cælius Secundus Curio, a learned man, father-in-law to Hieronymus
Zanchius. With this man he happened in their learned
conferences to discourse of the pronunciation of the Greek
tongue, and communicated to him at length the letters of
that argument that passed between himself and the Bishop of Winchester. But because Cælius could not read

CHAP.
V.
Anno 1554.

Reads Greek
at Padua.

Wylson sets
forth De-
mosthenes'
Orations in
English
from
Cheke's
Latin.

Settles at
Strasburg.

them over suddenly, Cheke, at his request, left them with
him, till he should call for them again, and so pursued his
journey into Italy.

And being come to Padua, where was a famed University, he met with Dr. Thomas Wylson, sometime Fellow
of King's college in Cambridge, (afterwards Secretary of
State to Queen Elizabeth,) and other English youth also,
students there. To whom Cheke in an obliging way addressed, and exhorted them to follow their books, and directed them in their studies; and for the time he stayed
there, read to Wylson and others certain orations of Demosthenes out of the Greek; the interpretation whereof
they had from his mouth. And Wylson made his use of
this afterwards, when being in England, and preferred for
his learning to be Master of St. Katharine's near the
Tower, he looked among his writings for Cheke's translation of those orations; and some he found, though not all,
which he turned out of his Latin into proper English, and
printed anno 1570, *viz.* three Orations in favour of the
Olynthians, and four against King Philip of Macedon; dedicating the book to Sir William Cecil, Cheke's brother-
in-law and most dear friend; taking occasion there to
speak largely of the great skill and learning of the said
Sir John Cheke.

When he returned from Italy, he cared not to go into
England, observing how rigorously things went there, and
what a dark and dismal cloud hung over his own country,
but chose rather to settle himself at Strasburg, where the
English service was kept up, and a great many of his
learned and pious friends resided. This was taken hold of
at home, and his back-friends aggravated matters against
him; of whom his old antagonist Bishop Gardiner, now
Lord Chancellor, may be reckoned none of the least. He
had been chief instructor of King Edward, in his principles of religion, to which he stuck so fast: he was one of
the great stays of evangelical doctrine, and had complete
learning to maintain it against the gainsayers: and therefore, whatsoever his innocence and merits otherwise were,

it was concluded by these Popish politicians, that he was
to be dealt severely withal. And this advantage in not
coming home at the expiration of his travel was to be
taken against him.

So first Cheke's demeans, lands, and estate were con- His estate
fiscated to the Queen's use, whatsoever was left him. Nor seized.
would this suffice, till by an inhuman piece of craft, and
insidious way-laying, they got his person too, as we shall
hear in the process of our story.

SECT. III.

Some letters of his printed. Writes to Cecil. His condi-
tion become mean. Reads a Greek lecture at Stras-
burg. Taken prisoner, and brought to England.

IT was shewed before how our learned exile had left his Anno 1555.
papers concerning the true pronouncing of Greek, at Basil, His letters
about pro-
in Curio's hands; who, after he had them a year or better, nouncing
the Greek
and by perusing them understood the excellent learning printed at
and use of them, put them into the press without the au- Basil.
thor's knowledge, setting only his own dedication before
the book to Sir Anthony Cooke; wherein he prayed him,
that in case Sir John Cheke should take amiss what he
had done, that Sir Anthony would appease him; considering that he thought he might take the boldness to do that,
which would neither be injurious to Cheke's name, and
would serve so much to the profit of others. The book
was printed at Basil in octavo, bearing this title, *Joannis*
Cheki Angli de Pronuntiatione Græcæ potissimum Lin-
guæ, Disputationes cum Stephano Wintoniensi Episcopo,
septem contrariis Epistolis comprehensæ, magna quadam
et elegantia et eruditione refertæ. In these elegant, copious, and learned epistles, both the Bishop and Cheke
shewed so great learning, parts, and reading, that they
seemed not epistles, but rather the antagonistical orations
of the best orators, as the publisher wrote. And it was a
token of the constancy and presence of Cheke's mind, in a
good cause, and a cause of truth, that he was not afraid of

H

CHAP.
V.

Anno 1555.

the power of so great a man as he contended with, and so much then above him: nor would forsake the cause he had undertaken, but stedfastly persisted in it; having this in his thought, that nothing is stronger than *truth*.

Cheke at
Strasburg.

In this year 1555 he was at Strasburg, among the rest of the godly exiles there, where he enjoyed indeed his liberty and his religion; but his lands and livings were seized, and the stock he brought out of England in effect spent; so that now was the time come for him to exercise his philosophy and religion, to uphold him under such a change of fortune: but this mean condition he willingly chose, rather than to swim in his former plenty and grandeur; which undoubtedly had been restored him, if he would have returned into England, and renounced his for-

Writes to
Cecil.

mer good principles. In this juncture he wrote a letter to Sir William Cecil, advising him most piously to stedfastness in religion, knowing how sharp the persecution now grew, and what severity was commonly exercised to all that would not go to mass, and believe transubstantiation. But Cecil had the favour and connivance of Cardinal Pole, and other great friends, that he made a shift to rub out the reign, and was reserved for better times.

Cheke sick.

And in this year of his exile he fell into an ill state of body, and was oppressed with a fit of sickness: for which cause he excused his omission of writing to his friends in England. He and the rest of the good men abroad, in their pilgrimage for the sake of religion, had often made their inquiries after the state of affairs in their own coun-

Pleased with
the news of
Cecil's be-
haviour in
Parliament.

try, and particularly concerning religion. In a Parliament this year, Sir William Cecil, however Popery now carried all before it, had the courage to speak boldly in the Parliament House against some abuses and intrusions of the Pope upon the ancient liberties of this imperial crown and kingdom; whereby the said Cecil did not a little endanger his own peace and safety. The fame of which speech, as it made a great noise in the realm, so coming abroad as far as Cheke, created in him a satisfaction: and when he first heard that Cecil was a member of that Parliament, he

was glad, expecting some service to be done by him there; SECT.
supposing, as he told his friends, that such fruits of ho- III.
nesty were left in him, as would and should serve for the Anno 1555.
good of the commonwealth. And his expectation, as he
said, was not deceived in him, being glad to hear tell of his
well-doing, to his praise, and others' profit.

He had a great eye upon this man, remaining still in Cheke's
England, whom he seemed to foresee like to prove after- counsel to Cecil.
ward one by whom great things would be brought to pass,
being also his brother-in-law, and sometime his pupil;
who made a shift, by a wary behaviour and some great
friends, (as was shewed before,) to continue these hard
times in the realm. Cheke heard now and then of him;
and was sorry sometimes on his account, lest he should go
too far in straining of his conscience to secure his peace.
And therefore in the latter end of this year, he took upon
him to be his monitor, and by an excellent letter to him
to remind him, " a that he had much to do in this brittle His letter to him.

---

c This letter of Cheke's to Cecil, transcribed from the original, exactly word for word, (according to his way of reforming the spelling of English,) was as followeth:

If I received a letter from you, & maad noo answear to the saam, ye think peradventure I wold much lesse hav written unto you unprovoaked, I wold heerin excus miself, if my staat of helth weer or hav been unknown unto mi frende; but bicaus it is known unto them, as I diverslie do perceive, I presum it not unknown unto you, and therfoar think mi lettres do not maak mi excus, but confirm them maad.

I was verie glad to heer of your being in the parl. h. supposing to be left in you such fruits of honestee as wold and shold serv for the C. W. [commonwealth.] Mi looking was not utterlie deceived in you, and was and am as glad to heer tell of your wel doing, to your prais and others profit; as I am sorie many tyms, when I heer the contrarie.

You hav much adoe in this britil staat of lyf, as everie good examiner of his lyf hath, to content God quietlie, & to satisfie an unhardened conscience, wherin bicause you be wys inough your self, & habil to giv others counsil in such a cas, I need not sai much unto you. On thing I wold wish whatsoever multitud of men, the dazed zel of the ignorant, the commun allowans in order doth approv, deceiv not your self in judgment: whatsoever ye know to be evil indeed, so judg it, & taak it alwais, and let nother your own doings whatsoever, nor commun usadg, nor favour of anie freendship carrie you away to deceiv your self in error, that yee may avoid the extreem curs of the Prophet that crieth again them that cal gud bad, & bad gud. For thoos who of frailtie do

" state of life, as every good examiner of his life had, to " content God quietly, and to satisfy an unhardened con- " science. Wherein, because he was wise enough himself,

amiss, & rejoiss in their evel as gud, but acknowledg bi fauting theer week-nes, hav so much the greeter degree to amendment, that thear own knowledg praieth on them to amend; rebuketh inward thear doings, & striveth again wilfulness of affection. And therefoar Christ said wel of the divers sorts of men, that tollers [publicans] & harlots whoos fautes nother was nor could be unknown to them, shold enter into the kingdom of heaven, before the Phari-sees, whoas herts were so blinded, that seeing & heering they nought saw nor herd.

Yee know in philosophie what difference is between ἀκρασία [intemperantia] and ἀκολασία [petulantia,] and what the wys philosophers hav disputed of the comparison of thoos vices, & what a man in his own lyf may judge of them. I had rather for my part have you corrupted in the lower part of your mind, then heer of you that both your parts weer utterly rotted away from that soundnes that common opinion of just causes hath had of you. So long as a man hath sparks left in himself, he may be assured, as in a fire wel raked up, to light a candle or make a fyr in a convenient tym. If because things be usually don in others commonly, or els of a few, or of yourself, they shold be taaken to be gud, it should follow that either use shold make gud & bad, & not Gods commandment, or els mens judgments shold cause gudnes or badnes in things, & not Scripture. But you think not, I dare say, that because things be don theerfoar they be gud; but rather bicause they be gud, therefore they shold be don. Plato saith wel, that bi plesure and grief gud may be judged from evel. Not that whosoever followeth plesure, he is gud, but bicause who-soever applieth to delight in gud things and to be grieved with evel, he is gud & honest. That plesure ruled & seasoned might shew gudness; unruled & wandring might declaar the evel. Even so the opinion in judgment, as the other in choise, to be no rule, but ruled. And then a man to be judged bi his opinion wys, when he yeeldeth in agreement to truth, & his disagreement to falshood. And so not to judg simplie by liking, but bi liking truly. Wherin in manies reasoning standeth the whole doubt, what should be thought truth. Ye doubt & theer in reason have not doubted. And theerfoar do not now. If science cannot be removed nor altered, which hath had not onely a fair shew of liklihood, but also a necessary caus of assent, & I think verily, yee doubt not, having given to you of God as much understanding as hath been not onely needful for judgment, but also praisable for lyf.

Thus much I have said for this end, that yee do not, as divers others every wheer do, whatsoever they do either in privat matters, or common causes, to allow it, when they have don it, & to stand to the saam as gud and lawful. And theerfoar either convenient to be don or sufferable. Ye ask me, what find I in you that I talk thus long? I answer, I desyr to find noon; nor had been no great examiner of other mens doings; and you know that mi wit is θετικὸν in writing. And theerfoar spend out my paper as ye see. I mean my freends thus much gud, that if they wil corrupt theer own doings, as I can say nothing

53818

" and able to give others counsel in such a cause, he SECT.
" needed not say much unto him.   One thing he wished, III.
" that whatsoever the multitude, the dazzled zeal of the Anno 1555.
" ignorant, and the common allowance in the order of reli-
" gion approved, that he deceived not himself in judg-
" ment: that whatsoever he knew to be evil indeed, so
" to judge and take it always; and that neither his own
" doings whatsoever, nor common usage, nor favour, or
" any friendship, carried him away to deceive himself in
" error; that so he might avoid the extreme curse of the
" Prophet, that cried against them that called good evil,
" and evil good.   That as for those that of mere frailty
" did amiss, and rejoiced not in their evil as good, but ac-
" knowledged their weakness, they came up so much the
" more to amendment, as their own knowledge called al-

of yours; yet where I fear that I knew, I was thavoiding that I fear; if they
wold keep theer judgments sound, & not so lov theer own doings, that they
wil make them the rul of theer judgment.   But of this enough.

Ye intended in K. Edwards time two things.   The one an order of the po-
licie & officers of the realm, their order and duties.   Another, the setting forth
of Bracton, the Lawier, that he might be seen & read of al men.   Then ye
lacked leisur, & in much busines ye sought to add that labour.   Now ye have
more leisur, ye shold not have les will.   Seek to profit with your leisur your
native countree · · · · · not only of furnishment but of saftie.   Let your wisdom appeer in leisur, as your honestie [in busines.]   I wold be glad to se
some fruit made of an evel tym, if not for the remedie of an outgrown evel,
yet for the forwardness of some common gud.

I am learning how to liv, & imagining by what occupation I shal be able
to feed myself.   For if when licenced to go, be shut out when they be gon, &
cannot tarrie without displesur, whither they were licenced with favour, nor return without danger whither they be by extremity called, what is thear left,
but in this old ending of lyf, to begin a new living, & learn at length how to
some way, while death end lyf & living.   And bicaus necessity maaketh it desirable, desyr maketh it ungrievous; & doth daily learn us hope of better, de-
cayeth to content himself with present staat offered, and bicaus he feeleth no
better to judg it verie gud.

But I must leav, mi paper biddeth me so.   And thus I commend to you &
to my ladie, and you boath to God; wishing you that stedfastnes of truth, &
that chois of doing wel, that I do desyr of God for myself.   Fare ye wel, &
bring up your son in the true fear of God.   From Strousborough, the 18 of
Feb. 1556.

Your assured br
JOAN. CHEEK.

H 3

" ways on them to amend, and rebuked inwardly their do-
" ings, and strove against wilfulness of affection. And
" that therefore Christ said well of the different sort of
" sinners, that *tollers and harlots* (whose fault neither
" was nor could be unknown to them) *should enter into*
" *the kingdom of heaven before the Pharisees;* whose
" hearts were so blinded, that seeing and hearing, they
" neither saw nor heard. That he knew in philosophy
" what difference was between ἀκρασία [i. e. *intempe-*
" *rance*] and ἀκολασία, [as one would say, custom and
" wilfulness in that vice,] and what the wise philosophers
" have disputed of those vices, and what a man in his own
" life may judge of them. That for his part, he had ra-
" ther to have him corrupted in the lower part of his
" mind, than hear of him, that both his parts were utterly
" rotted away from that soundness which common opin-
" ion for just causes had of him. So long," added he, " as
" a man hath sparks left in himself, he may be assured, as
" in a fire raked up, to light a candle, or make a fire in a
" convenient time."

He went on; " If because things be usually done, either
" commonly, or else of a few, or of yourself, they should
" be taken to be good; it should follow, that either use
" should make good and bad, and not God's command-
" ments, or else men's judgments should cause goodness
" and badness in things, and not Scripture: but he dared
" to say, that Cecil thought not, that because things were
" done, therefore they were good; but rather, because they
" were good, therefore they should be done. He alleged
" Plato, who said, that ' by pleasure and grief good men
" were judged from evil.' Not, that whosoever followed
" pleasure, he was good; but because whosoever applied
" to delight in good things, and to be grieved with evil,
" he was good and honest. That pleasure ruled and sea-
" soned, might shew goodness; unruled and wandering,
" might declare the evil. That even so was opinion in
" judgment, as the other in choice, to be no rule, but
" ruled. And then a man was to be judged by his opinion

" wise, when he yielded agreement to truth, and his dis-
" agreement to falsehood, and so, not to judge simply by
" liking, but by liking truly.

" That he [*viz.* Cecil, to whom he was writing]
" doubted not, nor had doubted, what should be thought
" truth; and therefore advised him not to doubt of it now,
" if science could not be removed nor altered; which had
" not only a fair shew of likelihood in it, but also a ne-
" cessary cause of assent. That he thought verily, he
" [Cecil] doubted not; so much understanding having been
" given him of God, as had been not only needful for judg-
" ment, but always praisable for life. That he had said
" thus much for this end, that he did not as divers others
" every where did; that whatsoever they did in private
" matters or common causes, to allow it when they had
" done it, and to stand to the defence of the same as good
" and lawful: and therefore convenient to be done or suf-
" ferable." Thus bravely and wisely did this Christian
philosopher argue.

But it was not Cheke's meaning in all this, to charge
this his friend with absolute guilt of some sinful compliance against his conscience: for he excused himself from
being so understood; " since he was no great examiner of
" other men's doings; and that his wit was θετικὸν in writ-
" ing; and therefore, that he spent out his paper in that
" manner as he did. And that he meant his friends so
" much good, that if they would corrupt their own doings,
" (as he could say nothing of this his friend,) that where
" he feared that he knew, he wished the avoiding of that
" he feared. Yet that they would keep their judgments
" sound; and not so to love their own doings, that they
" should make them the rule of their judgment."

Cheke took this opportunity to put on Cecil to be bene- Moves Ce-
ficial to his country, by despatching certain useful things cil to publish certain
for the view of the public, that he had formerly in his books.
mind to do, but wanted that leisure which now he had.
And they were the setting forth *an Order of the Policy
and Officers of the Realm*, their order and duties; and the

H 4

publishing of Bracton the Lawyer, that then was but in MS. that he might be seen and read of all men. And to excite him to this, Cheke used such words as these to him: " that in King Edward's time in much business, he " desired to take that labour upon him; and that now " he had more leisure, he should not have less will: that he " should seek to profit with his leisure his native country, " which had not only [need] of furnishment, but of safety: " that his wisdom would appear in leisure, as his honesty " had done in business : that he [Cheke] would be glad to " see some fruit made of an evil time, if not for the reme- " dying of an overgrown evil, yet for the forwarding of " some common good." But as this advice shewed Cheke's generous principle towards the promoting of the public good, so probably the reason the other thought not convenient to do this now, was to avoid the hazard of this ticklish time, and to keep himself as private and as untaken notice of as possible.

This good Knight began now to be reduced to narrow circumstances; insomuch, that he was put upon devising ways to live in this his exile condition, and imagining by what occupation he should be able to feed himself. He complained, " that he was licensed indeed to go abroad, " but he was in effect shut out, when he was gone; and " that yet he could not tarry where he was without dis- " pleasure, nor return without danger, where he had been " by extremity called. So that now," he said, " nothing was " left for this old ending of life, but to begin a new living; " and learn at length how to live some way, while death " ended both his life and living." And this he seemed cheerfully to submit to; " because," as he said, " neces- " sity made it desirable, and desire made it ungrievous; " and did daily learn us hope of better, and to content a " man's self with the present state offered; and because " he felt no better, to judge it very good." Thus long did he play the part of a steady Christian, if he could but
have persisted, when the greatest shock of all came. Some tell us he read a Greek lecture now at Strasburg :

which might be the way he took for a present subsist-
ence.

It was not long after this, the poor gentleman met with
harder sufferings; and the sadder share by far of his afflic- His person
tions is behind. His enemies are resolved to have him seized, and brought
one way or other, and to bring him into England, there to prisoner to England:
put him to death or to shame. In the country where he
thought himself secure, even there he was caught in the
high way, together with Sir Peter Carew, (who had been
in Wyat's business,) and both brought prisoners to England after a strange and barbarous manner, which we shall
relate by and by. The reason that was pretended for this And why.
usage was, that he having obtained leave to travel, and
licensed thereupon to go out of the realm, had transgressed in not returning again, but abiding abroad without
leave, and settling himself out of the Queen's dominions:
though his being a Gospeller was the chief, if not the only
true cause, as indeed was told him, when he was a prisoner in England.

We are now therefore drawing near to the most deplor- Cheke con-
able conclusion of this gentleman's life: to which his too fiding on astrology
much confidence in that uncertain art of astrology contri- goes to Brussels.
buted in part. For together with his knowledge in other
sciences, he was not unskilful in astrology. And doubtful
of his own safety in an intended journey to Brussels, he
consulted with this art, to know whether he might go
without danger. And according to the satisfaction he gathered thence to himself, being about the spring of the
year 1556, he went, (being now in the Low Countries,
come thither to fetch his wife.) His going to the said town
of Brussels was occasioned by an earnest invitation given
him by the Lord Paget and Sir John Mason, two of his
former learned acquaintance, but who had complied with
Queen Mary's religion, and were come in great honour
and reputation with her, and now arrived in those parts;
the former in a more private capacity to use the baths, the
latter in quality of her Ambassador at the Court of Brussels. These had made the motion to Sir John Cheke to

take that opportunity to come and see them; and for his better security, Mason had assured him of safe-conduct thither in King Philip's and his own name. He went with Sir Peter Carew in his company, and enjoyed his friends, Paget and Mason, (if they might now be called his *friends*, and not his betrayers;) whom after he had attended towards the sea, as he was coming back, he fell into a fatal snare between Brussels and Antwerp: for intelligence and order having been sent from King Philip,

Seized in the way by the Provost Marshal. he being there waylaid, was on a sudden, May 15, seized on by the Provost Marshal, with his fellow-traveller, unhorsed, blindfolded, bound, and thrown into a waggon, and so conveyed on shipboard, and brought over sea unto the Tower of London. " Being taken as it were with " whirlwind," (as he was taught to word it in his recantation,) " from the place he was in, and brought over sea, " and never knew whither he went, till he found himself " in the Tower of London." And this chiefly out of charity to his soul, as he was told at his examination, " out " of compassion," forsooth, " to his soul, to bring him " from his false religion." An excellent way, no question, to do it. Thus are the foulest actions of princes coloured over by their favourites with the most specious pretences, and their malice goes for religion and charity.

The seizing of Story somewhat parallel. Seldom hath such an act been heard of, or read in history, unless perhaps the seizing of Dr. Story in the year 1569 may have some resemblance of it; who was surprised also in Flanders, and brought to the Tower by a wile. But Story had been a most bloody persecutor of religion under Queen Mary, and ever an implacable enemy to Queen Elizabeth. This man fled abroad to Antwerp under this Queen, and was much favoured by the Spaniards, the Queen's enemies, and appointed by the Duke d'Alva searcher of all ships that came thither, for English goods and heretical books: by which means he still continued his former practice of persecution. One Parker, master of a small vessel, employed by certain persons, (to which Secretary Cecil, brother to Cheke, was thought to

be privy,) arriving at Antwerp, repaired to Story, and in- SECT.
III.
formed him of a little ship come from England. Where-
upon, in pursuance of his office, he presently went aboard, Anno 1556.
and according to his wont searched about, and then going
down into the hatches, they in the ship presently clapped
them down, and the wind proving favourable, brought him
away, and lodged him safely in the Tower. And in the
year 1571, being found guilty of treason, he was executed.
Whether this were to make some atonement for the treacherous apprehension of Cheke, I leave others to conjecture.

But sure it is, that Cheke upon this seizure was appre- His friends'
hended by his friends to be in great danger. And so Bale apprehen-
sions for
writes in the first edition of his Centuries, which came out him.
about this time, that he fell in the hands of those who Centur.8va.
Joan.
always hated him; and subjoins this prayer, " The Lord Cheke, 97.
2 Thess. ii.
" direct his heart into the love of God, and the patience
" of Christ, and let him be delivered from absurd and
" wicked men."

SECT. IV.

*Too credulous to astrology. Betrayed. Complies. Sub-
scribes. Recants.*

HERE then we leave Sir John Cheke a disconsolate Cheke de-
prisoner in the Tower, now the second time under Queen ceived by
astrology.
Mary, to repent his credulity to the words and promises
of Romanists, and his too much confidence in astrology,
whereby he is imposed upon to his destruction. He went
safe indeed to Brussels, but was far from returning safe
back again. This art of conjecturing at or foreknowing Astrology
things and events by the position of the stars, was about much stu-
died in
these times exceedingly studied by both nobility and gen- these days.
try; insomuch, that Dr. Lawrence Humfrey, (who lived
in these days, and was afterwards a learned Professor of
Divinity at Oxford,) in a book which he wrote for the use De Nobilit.
and instruction of the gentry, exhorting them to the study lib. iii. p.
347.
of divers sciences, observed how this science, above the

CHAP.
V.

Anno 1556.

rest, was " ^c so snatched at, so beloved, and even devoured
" by most persons of honour and worship," that they
needed no enticements to this, but a bridle rather; not a
trumpeter to set them on, but a reprover to take them off
from their heat. And that many had so trusted to this,
that they almost distrusted God, and partook of such
events as proved unhappy, not in truth foretold by the
stars, nor expected by themselves: yet as he would not
wholly condemn the art, so should not the nobility have
him a persuader nor an applauder of it; for that there
were enow of them already. So he. But return we to
Cheke's misfortunes.

Cheke be-
trayed by
his friends.

There was a person then living, and he of considerable
quality and knowledge of the intrigues of those times, that
makes this to have been a base laid plot of the Lord Paget
and Sir John Mason, great acquaintance and friends of
Cheke and Carew under King Edward, but now under
Queen Mary strong Papists. Though I will not charge
the memory of these two great men with so treacherous
an act, yet I will relate it as I find it. " By Mason's

Ponet's
treatise of
Politic
Power.

" working," saith my author, " and Paget's devising, Sir
" Peter Carew went into Flanders, (who was before in
" France,) Mason pledging for his safeguard King Philip's
" fidelity and his own honesty. Afterwards he and Sir
" John Cheke, being enticed both to come to Brussels to
" see the Queen's Ambassadors, and having brought Paget
" on the way toward England, both in their return were
" taken by the Provost Marshal, spoiled of their horses,
" and clapped into a cart, their legs, arms, and bodies tied
" with halters to the body of the cart, and so carried to
" the seaside, and from thence into the Tower of London.
" And before Paget came to Calais, Sir Peter's man com-
" ing out of England meeteth him, and asketh for his
" master; Paget smileth, and said nothing, but that his
" master was in health. But how cometh this to pass?
" Mark well; the Queen thought Paget a meet man for
" her in all things, seeing that without cause she sus-

^c Sic rapi, sic adamari, et devorari a plerisque nobilibus.

" pected his religion. And at his ^d coming over she like a SECT.
" woman uttereth to him what she thought of him, and IV.
" promiseth, if she may perceive his heart and mouth to Anno 1556.
" agree together, she would set him aloft. He assureth
" her, that whatsoever she should will him should be
" done; yea, he would do more than she should require
" him."———And a little after, " coming over he bruited,
" that he liked not the state in England, (for he is one of
" them that hangeth now on prophecies, but of a wrong
" thing,) and therefore would be out of the way in the
" height of the mad month of May, [when insurrections
" frequently used to be in the city of London,] and pre-
" tendeth to come to the bains to ^eAcon; but indeed the
" intent was to see if he could practise with some of the
" Duke of Cleves's men, to betray the poor Duchess of
" Suffolk, (who was fled abroad for her religion,) and some
" of the English congregation at Wesel; that he, to per-
" form his promise, might send them to the Queen. But
" when he saw his purpose failed, (God had better pro-
" vided for the Duchess, to keep her from traitor's hands,)
" he cometh not to the bains, he needeth them not at that
" time. But then he caused Carew and Cheke, whom
" Mason had prepared ready to serve his turn, to be taken
" and carried away, as before ye have heard. And at his
" return had great thanks, and the Queen's favour in-
" creased towards him." Thus that relator. And sure
enough there was some truth in this matter, if you lay to
this what Mr. John Fox relates, namely, that Sir William Fox's Acts
Paget was set craftily to catch Mr. Bertie and the Duchess and Mon.
p. 1886.
of Suffolk, newly come to Wesel: of which, (when they
thought themselves happily settled there,) a watchword
came from Sir John Mason, the Queen's Ambassador in
the Netherlands, that my Lord Paget had feigned an er-
rand to the baths that way: and whereas the Duke of
Brunswick was shortly with ten ensigns to pass to Wesel,
for service of the House of Austria against the French
King, the said Duchess and her husband should be with

^d turning Papist. ^e Aix.

the same charge and company intercepted. To prevent
which, Mr. Bertie and his Duchess fled away hastily from
Wesel, and came to Wineheim in High Dutchland; and
in April 1557 they hastened to Poland.

But howsoever it was, Cheke being now fast, found
there was no way for him, but either to forsake those doctrines, which he had upon the best and strongest grounds
embraced himself, and recommended to others, or else to
be put to a cruel death as an heretic.

For when he was first examined, he understood it was
the matter of religion that was the great quarrel against
him. Confused indeed he was at first to be so used; and
seeing it was for his religion he suffered this, he very re-
solutely chose in his own mind to die any death, rather
than to renounce it. Soon after, two of the Queen's Chaplains came to the Tower to confer with him, to try to
change him, pretending much good-will and charity to
him. Whereupon he received them with the like civility,
and communicated to them his doubts that hindered his
compliance with the corporeal presence, and other Popish
doctrines; and desired to be better informed by them.
But Cheke's doubts were too hard for them to solve, and
their endeavours gave him little or no satisfaction; nor
could they move him any thing, and so left him, as giving
little hope of being *reconciled to the unity of the Church,*
as they called his turning Papist. But the desire of gain-
ing over so great a man, whereby such a glory might redound to their Church, caused the Queen to try once
again, and to send to him Feckenham, Dean of St. Paul's,
a man of more learning, it seems, than the two former,
and of whose abilities the Queen had a great opinion.
This man was of a moderate and obliging temper, and
with whom Cheke had been acquainted in the late King's
reign; and to whom, being then in the Tower, Cheke was
sent to confer with him, in order to reduce him to the religion then established, but could not. He was now to
perform the same office to Cheke, and in the same place,
and was furnished with one great argument to use to

Cheke, which Cheke had not to use to Feckenham, *viz.*
compliance or death.

By this time, by hard imprisonment, and seeing nothing
but burning to follow, if he persisted in his resolutions,
his courage began to quail; and so the coming and communication of Feckenham made some impression upon
him.   Cheke had a mind to speak with Cardinal Pole, for
some satisfaction and favour; and he had his desire.   For
by his order, Feckenham brought him out of the Tower to
him: who, when he came, gravely advised him to depart Brought be-
from the variety of Doctors to the unity of the Church. fore Cardinal Pole.
In fine, Cheke cannot, nor durst hold out any longer, and
Feckenham has the credit to prevail with him to " commit
" his sense and reason to the doctrine of the Church," as it
was worded for him in one of his recantations.   And this
being done, he is fain to submit his person, to be ordered
as it should be thought best for his soul's wealth, to them
that had authority in the Church upon such offenders.

The matter being thus far effected, the poor gentleman Writes his
was put upon making a writing; therein to signify his opinion for
the carnal
sentence for the carnal presence; to which, and to this presence.
conclusion, *in hac causa et in reliquis omnibus idem me*
profiteor dicere et sentire, quod Sancta Christi, et Catho-
lica tenet Ecclesia, he subscribed his own name.   The
writing consisted of certain allegations out of Hilary,
Chrysostom, Cyril, and Augustin, which seemed to favour
that doctrine; hoping that this writing might have suf-
ficed to obtain his liberty, without more confessions and
public declarations of his change.   This paper, written and Writes to
subscribed by himself, he sent by the Dean of St. Paul's the Cardinal.
to the Cardinal, with his letter from the Tower, dated
July the 15th, praying him that this might put an end to
any further question concerning him, and that he would
favourably grant certain petitions, that were then by the
Dean put into his hand; the chief of which seems to be,
that he would have so much compassion of his frailty, as
to spare him from making an open recantation.   But that
would not be granted him; and it required some time be-

CHAP.
V.

Anno 1556.

And to the
Queen.

His letter
to the
Queen. Int.
Epist. vol.
C.C.C.C.

fore he would be brought to do that; but after a double communication with him in one day, he was fain to yield to Pole's order, and dissemble a willingness too, *viz.* to recant and to recant again, and that in the most public manner, that they might make the greater triumph of him. Cheke likewise sends a letter to the Queen of the same date, and brought by the same messenger, the Dean; who, as he wrote, should shew her his mind now, as to the matters of religion, trusting, that as it was truly minded of him, so she would agreeably receive it. He promised all obedience to her laws, and to her orders in religion. The letter ran in this tenor:

" Pleaseth it your Majesty to understand, that in mat-
" ters of religion I have declared my mind unto your Ma-
" jesty by your virtuous and learned Chaplain, Mr. Dean
" of Paul's; trusting, that as it is truly minded of me,
" so your Highness will agreeably receive it. I beseech
" your Majesty therefore, as I have been and am your
" faithful subject, whom I do as God's minister faithfully
" honour and serve, that your Majesty will have the same
" opinion present of me, that my faithfulness, I trust, and
" duty hereafter, shall shew unto you. And I trust, among
" many obedient and quiet subjects, which God storeth
" your Highness with, I shall be found, though not in abi-
" lity of other qualities, yet in will and readiness, and obe-
" dience of your laws, and other orders of religion, as glad
" to serve and obey as any other, desiring your Majesty
" most humbly to favour such poor suits for my liberty, as
" Mr. Dean shall make to your Majesty in my behalf. Al-
" mighty God prosper and increase your Majesty in all
" honour and godliness. From your Majesty's Tower of
" London, the 15th of July, 1556.

" Your Majesty's most humble
" and obedient subject,
" JOHN CHEKE."

SECT. V.

His submission to the Cardinal as the Pope's Legate; and his recantations.

AFTER this, to declare his repentance for his rejection _{Anno 1556.} of the Pope, he was to do as the Parliament and the ^{Absolved} Clergy, and other apostates, had done before upon their ^{and admit-} ^{ted by the} knees, in order to their reconcilement; namely, to make ^{Cardinal.} his solemn submission before the Cardinal, suing to be absolved, and received into the Church: which he did; and so was graciously admitted a member of the Roman Catholic Church.

But notwithstanding these supplications and submis- ^{The order} sions, he was kept in prison two months and better, after ^{and manner} ^{of his re-} all this hard service, before he was admitted to his public ^{cantation.} shame; I mean, to make his recantation: which was done by him October the 4th, in a most public manner before the Queen; and for the greater formality ushered in by an oration of Dr. Feckenham, his ghostly father and converter, made by him to the Queen, as it were, in favour of Sir John Cheke, standing by him: which ran in these words:

" Virtuous, good Queen, Lady, Mistress; whereas it ^{Fecken-} " hath pleased your Highness, among other of your learn- ^{ham's ora-} ^{tion to the} " ed Chaplains to send me unto this man, Mr. Cheke, ^{Queen be-} " your Highness's subject, for his conversion and reconci- ^{fore Cheke's} ^{recantation.} " liation to the unity of Christ's Church, from his most ^{Int. MSS.} ^{Guil. Petyt.} " dangerous error and wicked heresy of Berengary, the ^{Armig.} " first denier of Christ's very true real presence in the " most blessed Sacrament of the Altar; I am by so much " the more bolder here, openly to put myself in place with " him, and, by humble suit unto your Highness here, to " open my mouth for him. Forasmuch as he is at present " a very sorrowful and penitent man for the same; and, " with the Apostle St. Peter, hath shed bitter tears for the " denial of Christ; and, with St. Paul, did presently make " his humble submissions, saying, *Domine, quid me vis fa-*

I

" *cere?* and, with the Apostle St. Thomas, is at this present
" so certified and established in the Catholic faith of Christ,
" as, with him, forced to wonder at the marvellous works
" of God, and to say, *Dominus meus, et Deus meus.* Most
" humbly, therefore, good gracious Lady and Mistress, I
" beseech your Highness now mercifully to receive him
" into your favour and mercy, which, with so much loyalty
" and obeisance of heart and mind, doth yield himself
" wholly unto your mercy; and let him taste now of that
" your Highness's great mercy, accustomed to all converts
" and penitent offenders, which doth here so openly crave
" and beg for the same; most humbly suing, with the lost
" child in the Gospel, *Peccavi in cœlum, et coram te, et*
" *jam non sum dignus vocari filius tuus. Fac me sicut*
" *unum de mercenariis tuis.* And by so much the more as
" he sheweth, at the least wise here openly in this place,
" more repentance than any other man hath done hereto-
" fore, more sorrow and detestation of his offence, more to
" the pacifying of God's wrath and displeasure, more to
" the contentation and satisfying of the world for his slan-
" der given in the same; (whereof so many of your High-
" ness's subjects, which, without number, within this latter
" storm and trial of faith made in this realm, were carried
" away into no small errors and horrible heresies;) this
" only man, Mr. Cheke, is now the first that here openly
" hath given the example of true Christian penance; where
" he only is content openly to acknowledge his error, and
" confess his heresy; and he only here present doth sub-
" mit himself to recant the same. This man, Mr. Cheke,
" doth, in plucking off the visor of all feigned and counter-
" feit penance, stand here openly to beg for the remission
" of his offence at the hand of God, forgiveness of the
" whole world, and pardon of your Highness's laws. And
" therefore, most gracious Queen, think him only in re-
" spect of the rest most worthy the same: most humbly
" beseeching your Highness to take him to your mercy,
" and bow down your most gracious and most merciful
" ears to hear him."

And then the afflicted gentleman began his palinode, as SECT.
follows : " The acknowledging of an error is the right entry   V.
" into a truth.   For even as in life, the first degree [of Anno 1556.
" goodness] is to avoid evil, and then to do good; so in Cheke's recantation,
" faith errors must be avoided, that the right religion may before the
" take place.   Wherefore, as before I made my humble Queen.
" submission unto my Lord Cardinal's good Grace, who first
" accepted the same well, and so received me as a member
" of Christ's Catholic Church; so now, before your Majesty,
" whom God hath marvellously brought unto your noble
" and due place of government under him, I do profess and
" protest, that whatsoever mine opinion of the blessed Sa-
" crament of Christ's body and blood, and of the sense of
"Christ's words spoken of the same, hath been hereto-
" fore ; I do now, after conference had with certain learned
" men, your Majesty's Chaplains, and especially the right
" worshipful Master Dean of Paul's, believe firmly the
" real presence of Christ's very body and blood in the Sa-
" crament, and none other substance there remaining :
" moved thereunto by invincible reasons of the Catholic
" Doctors against the Arians, of Christ's very true and
" natural being in us, and also by the consent of Christ's
" Catholic Church.   Unto the which, both in these and in
" all other matters of my faith, I most humbly submit
" myself.   Wherein, [as] for the success, [so] I do most
" humbly thank God for the manner and the clemency
" thereof, shewed in drawing me with mercy thereunto.
" I do most humbly give thanks unto the ministers of
" mercy in Christ's Church, whereof I do acknowledge the
" Pope's Holiness to be head; and especially my Lord
" Cardinal's good Grace, Legate of England from the
" Pope's Holiness, and Primate of the same.   Unto whom
" I made my submission ; not moved by policy and worldly
" respects, but persuaded by learning and conscience, when
" otherwise I could have been contented to yield myself to
" the contrary.   And also I do give most humble thanks
" to your Majesty for your great mercifulness towards me :

" who as in other excellencies do follow your heavenly
" Father, so in this precise quality of mercifulness do ex-
" press his holiness, that commandeth you to be merciful.
" Your Majesty herein hath great cause to give God
" thanks, as in all other your princely gifts, that ye need
" not under God to seek no example of mercifulness to
" follow, but yourself : who, daily inclining to follow God
" in mercy, shew great evidence whose heavenly child
" your Majesty is.

" And, as I beseech God, your Majesty do continue the
" same grace to others that have need of mercy, so I trust
" God our Saviour will work the like in others, that he by
" your Majesty hath wrought in me.　For as they may
" well learn of me to beware of singularity, and trusting
" unto certain sayings of Doctors, rather than to the
" Church, and preferring private judgments before the
" Catholic consent of Christ's Church ; so shall they easier
" be led from error to truth, when they see them drawn
" by your Highness's mercy, and not plucked by extre-
" mity ; and that their life and mendment is sought, not
" their [death] and shame.　In the which lesson they shall
" find, I doubt not, as I do, much contentation of mind
" and quietness of conscience.　Which I trust, for my part,
" continually to keep in all matters pertaining to the Ca-
" tholic faith of Christ's Church : and hope to shew
" myself, in the residue, so faithful a subject to your
" Highness, as my bounden duty serveth me for ; and in
" matters of religion so obedient, as becometh a Christian
" man.

" According unto the which my doings, I most humbly
" beseech your Highness to shew your clemency and fa-
" vour ; none otherwise.　And I shall pray unto God, ac-
" cording to mine humble duty, that as he hath trodden
" down errors, and set your Highness marvellously in this
" your high state of your most lawful kingdom, so he will
" preserve your Majesty with the same providence, to the
" increase of his glory, and honour both of your Highness

" and of the noble King and Prince, King Philip, your SECT.
" Majesty's dear husband; and the quietness of your Ma- V.
" jesty's subjects."   Anno 1556.

Besides this recantation, I meet with another, framed Another re-
for Sir John Cheke's mouth by Cardinal Pole's pen or cantation of Cheke,
direction: the above written recantation, spoken before spoken be-
the Queen, being, in the Cardinal's judgment, not enough; fore the Court.
but, since he had lived long in the Court, and had been
instrumental to sow the doctrine of the Gospel in the
hearts of many there, it was thought convenient, that he
should recant likewise in the face and hearing also of the
Court. And this also the poor man was forced to do. This
form of recantation is long, according to the usual tedious
style of the Cardinal: however, I shall here exemplify it.

" I am come hither afore this most honourable and E Foxii
" gracious audience, to accuse myself, and to give thanks MSS.
" to Almighty God, especially for this cause, that he hath
" given me the grace to accuse myself: which, without
" his great special grace, I could never have done, being
" so far gone in mine own conceit, and so much delighting
" in the same. So that being now brought from the same,
" and willingly to confess my error, I count one the great-
" est grace that ever came unto me; and such, without
" this, no other gift of God (of whose grace cometh all the
" good that I have ever had, or can be in me) may do me
" any good. But the more his gifts have been towards
" me aforetime, the more they be to my condemnation,
" without this grace that God hath given me now, which
" is willingly and gladly to accuse myself. And the same,
" for to be called a *grace*, must bring with it a knowledge
" and detestation of my most grievous and horrible offence,
" with desire of mercy of that is past, and submitting
" myself most humbly to that order that it shall please
" them to set, whom God, the Lord of mercy, hath made
" governors in his Church, of like offenders as I have
" been.

" And all this having pleased the goodness of God to
" work in the secret of my heart, I am come now to utter

" the same openly before you, to the praise of his mercy,
" and, as I trust, to the edification of some other; which I
" do, following the order which hath been given unto me
" by them whom in such case I am most bound to obey.
" Wherein also I do knowledge the goodness of God, that
" hath put in their mind to enjoin me to make the confes-
" sion of my grievous error, in that place where I did most
" grievously offend, both to the ruin of myself, and of other
" that were conversant with me, which are here in the
" Court; where I had more occasion to do hurt, for the
" place of schoolmaster I had with young King Edward,
" and with all the youth of the nobility, than any other
" had. And albeit mine office was not to teach him the
" matters of religion, which was committed to others; yet
" I confess, touching my pestilent error, I peradventure
" did no less to confirm and set forward the same in his
" mind, and all the rest of the youth, than any other.

" And what mine error was, though it be not unknown,
" I think, to any in this honourable assembly, yet coming
" to confess the same, which I myself, a little before, took
" for no error, it may please you to understand the quality
" thereof: which was a blasphemy of the holy name of
" God, under colour to glorify the same; and a persecution
" of the name of Christ, more grievous than ever were
" they, that, deceived by others, crucified Christ, or af-
" terward did persecute those that were his disciples; I
" having a greater cause than ever St. Paul had to say so,
" when he went from town to town, having obtained au-
" thority of the chief heads of the Priests, to imprison
" those that professed the name of Christ. But that per-
" secution I made was not so open as his was, as my blas-
" phemy also was more hid; and so hid to myself, that I
" thought all were blasphemers that held contrary opinion.
" Wherefore I may well say in this part with St. Paul,
" *Misericordiam consecutus sum, quia ignorans feci.*

" Albeit mine ignorance was not such, but that it did
" rather aggravate mine offence than excuse it; being
" much more excusable the ignorance of the Jews that

" killed Christ, and also of St. Paul, that did persecute
" his servants; both following the motive of those whom
" the law of God gave authority to be judges in all such
" matters, as were *principes sacerdotum;* of whom St.
" Paul had letters to persecute Christ's servants; and by
" their motion the people were set up to cry against Christ,
" *Crucifige eum:* for whom Christ did pray to his Father,
" *Ignosce illis, quia nesciunt quid faciunt.* And St. Paul
" might well ask Christ, *Quis es Domine?* having no
" knowledge of him by the doctrine of his superiors, that
" it was Christ he did persecute. But mine ignorance was
" not such; for if I would have believed my superiors, all
" told me contrary to that I did; all did forbid me to do
" as I did, and curse me if I did attempt the same. Which
" they did, following the rule and knowledge of their fore-
" fathers, that were counted most to have lived in the
" grace of God. So that mine ignorance can have no
" colour of excuse, but all to aggravate my greater damna-
" tion; entering into the same by mine own election, and
" prosecuting the same by mine own authority, when I
" would be wiser than all other: and by the justice of
" God was made more ignorant than all other, as the
" effect did shew. For what an arrogant blindness was
" this, what great madness, to think I saw more touching
" the Sacrament of the Altar, than first all the Prelates of
" the Church in this realm, since the time the faith was
" received! For if it were true that I took for true, that
" the sacrifice of the Mass was idolatry, never-ceasing
" Mass to be said in that manner it is now, and never no
" fault to be found therein; either this must be a deep
" ignorance in them that brought in the faith, that saw
" not this, or in me the most execrable, that condemned
" both them and the rest of the world in the same. Which
" is the most blasphemy that could be said against the
" providence of God, and against the love that Christ
" beareth to his Church: making him more benevolent to
" the old Synagogue than to the Church, *quam acquisivit*
" *sanguine suo;* letting them never to fall into idolatry,

" but they had warners thereof, and great chastisements
" therefore ; and we to have no warner in this long space of
" so many years living in idolatry. What would blaspheme
" more the providence of God towards his Church, from
" the which he promiseth never to be absent.

" And whenas we know the old people could not fall
" in carnal vices, but they had Priests and Prophets to
" warn them ; and if they did not of themselves, then God
" himself warneth them, and reproveth them for their si-
" lence, calling them sometimes *canes mutos non valentes*
" *latrare*. But what reproof were worthy our Priests and
" Prophets, if, when such idolatry crept into the Church,
" there was not found the space of so many hundred years
" as passed from the primitive Church to Berengarius's
" time, that did reprove men of this idolatry ?

" So that here, when I consider myself, I cannot so
" much marvel at mine own blindness, that I saw not in
" this point how I blasphemed Christ, and condemned the
" Church, taking that for idolatry, that the Church conti-
" nually had used, and was never condemned. But yet
" here I cannot say I was so blind, but I saw somewhat
" this inconvenience, what a thing it was thus to go
" against the whole consent of the Church. But to avoid
" that, and to amend it, I fell into another ; which was, to
" displace the Church where Christ had set it, as I had
" displaced the body of Christ in the Sacrament. So that
" the congregation of all Christian men, which was com-
" monly called *the Church*, I took not for the Church ; but
" sometime I made the Church a spiritual congregation
" without a body, invisible as the spirit is ; and yet, seeing
" some inconvenience in that, I began to belie the Church,
" and say it was visible, and seen on earth, but most seen
" in the Apostles' time, which was the primitive Church.
" And those I took to be of mine opinion, and divers
" Doctors that followed, whose sentence I did interpretate
" as to agree with mine. Wherein I went from error to
" error, mending the first with a second, and so increasing
" in blindness, which I took for light, and did what I could

" to bring the whole realm into blindness; as it was as
" much as man's wit and malice could do, by them that
" had highest authority in the realm.   But *non est consi-*
" *lium contra Dominum: et potestati ejus quis resistet?*

" This God having ever shewed most notable, hath now
" also shewed it in this realm, preserving a virgin to shew
" the marvellous work of his presence, his true doctrine,
" in all the time of that tempestuous world, as it were a
" lamp-light in the midst of a stormy wind in a maiden's
" hand; whom no learning, no persuasion, no fear could
" turn, no power oppress; but made her oppress them
" that had all the power of the realm in their hand : which
" was a great miracle to all them that had grace to see it.
" But here, alas! I was so far from grace to see it, and to
" receive it as all the rest did, that I began to think how I
" might flee it, and judged it most wisdom so to do.   And
" so I did, fleeing from that place, where true religion,
" being trod under foot afore, began to spring again; and
" went thither, where I had more occasion to be confirmed
" in my corrupt opinion.   But in my case I may say also,
" *non est consilium contra Dominum:* which, when I
" thought least, subverted all my counsel, and, as it were
" with a hurle-wind, took me from the place I was in, and
" brought me over the sea, and never knew whither I went,
" afore I found myself in the Tower of London, which of
" all places I abhorred most.

" And yet at last I came to have that comfort, that I
" confess now I never came into place where I had more
" cause to thank God.   But at the beginning I was so
" confused with this strange chance, that when I knew at
" mine examination the cause of my sudden bringing,
" which was chiefly for religion, there was no death but I
" had liever suffered it, than to change that opinion I
" brought with me.   Albeit, after a few days that I was
" first examined, being sent unto me two learned men, as
" they shewed full of charity, I shewed myself to hear
" them not unwillingly; and gladly to confer my doubts
" with them, and desired to be better informed.   Yet the

" conclusion was such with them, that in very deed they
" moved me nothing, and so left me as desperate to be
" reconciled as their desire was; and so continued, until
" it pleased God to put in the Queen's Majesty's mind, of
" her grace, mercy, and charity, to prove me yet better.
" And her Grace, not knowing, sent unto me one, who, in
" King Edward's time, being in prison in that same place
" where I was now, by order that was given then, was
" fetched out to be examined afore me. To whom I shewed
" that courtesy the case could require; but I could not
" bring him to mine opinion. And the selfsame man now
" was the mean to bring me utterly unto his; and fetched
" me out of the Tower to come afore my Lord Legate;
" which in truth I did desire.

" Beginning now to incline to the Catholic sentence;
" but not so far as to make any manner of confession of
" mine error, or open recantation, (wherein I desired my
" Lord Legate to have compassion of my frailty;) but after
" twice communication in one day of the same matter, at
" last, God of his mercy was stronger in me, and made
" me, as I did in the doctrine, submit my reason and sense
" to the doctrine of the Church: so also my person I sub-
" mitted to be ordered, as it should be thought best for
" my soul's wealth, of them whom God had given autho-
" rity in the Church upon such offenders. And this being
" my Lord Legate's order, that I should appear in this
" place to confess and retract my pernicious sentence, in
" this I thank Almighty God, first, with an humble and
" contrite heart, that it hath pleased him to use this mercy
" with me; and afterwards the Queen's Highness, that
" she vouchsafed first to bear with my infinite offences, and
" to send unto me such men as she did, to direct me, and
" confirm me in the right way; and finally, to be content
" to let me come to her presence; and so withal to my
" Lord Legate that gave the order, and all that have been
" ministers therein.

" And for an assured token, that I say with my mouth
" that which I think with my heart, being fallen into the

" error which Berengarius fell into, I make the selfsame SECT.
" recantation that he did, only changing the name.   V.

   " I, Sir John Cheke, Knight," &c. The tenor of which Anno 1556.
was, that he pretended with heart and mouth to profess, Decret. iii.
that he acknowledged the true catholic and apostolical Distinct. ii.
faith, and did execrate all heresy, and namely that wherewith he lately had been infamed, as holding that the bread
and wine upon the altar, after the consecration of the
Priest, remained only a sacrament, and were not the very
body and blood of our Lord Jesus Christ, neither could be
handled or broken by the Priest's hands, or chewed with
the teeth of the faithful, otherwise than only in manner of a
sacrament. That he consented now to the holy and apostolical Church of Rome, and professed with mouth and heart
to hold the same faith touching the sacrament of the Lord's
Mass, which Pope Nicolas, with his Synod* at Rome * Met
anno 1058, did hold, and commanded to be held by his chiefly a-
evangelical and apostolical authority: that is, that the rengarius.
bread and wine upon the altar, after consecration, are not
only a sacrament, but also are the very true and selfsame
body and blood of our Lord Jesus Christ, felt and broken
with hands, and chewed with teeth: swearing by the holy
Evangelists, that whosoever should hold or say to the contrary, he should hold them perpetually accursed; and that
if he himself should hereafter presume to teach against the
same, he should be content to abide the severity and rigour
of the Canons, &c.

   " Thus you have heard mine open and plain confession:
" which it may please Almighty God so to accept, that not
" only it be to the wealth of my soul, but of as many as
" hear it. Upon which trust I came the gladlier hither;
" nothing more desiring at this time, than that it may
" please the goodness of God to give me time and grace,
" that, as mine example, holding my perverse opinion, hath
" been cause of ruin and slander of many, that either, by
" my occasion, or by another, be fallen in the like error, or
" yet be in any wavering in their opinion of the blessed
" Sacrament: which, that it may be better eschewed, I

" shall adjoin (pleasing you to hear it) the very beginning
" of my fall; which is none other than the same beginning
" that bringeth men to all kind of heresy. And that was
" pride, which stood in confidence of mine own wit,
" making myself a master and judge of the doctrine of the
" Church: whereas I was not come to the perfectness to
" be a good scholar. But when I heard other men begin
" to put a doubt in this article of the Sacrament, and also
" afore I heard them doubt, I began myself to make doubt
" to myself, seeing that doctrine so far beyond all reason
" and sense, whether this were a figurative speaking, as
" many other be in Scripture like, or else a plain literal
" sense, as the words sounded; and seeing divers places,
" both in Scripture, and in some other Doctors that
" seemed to favour the opinion of a figurative speaking;
" seeing also that, taking it in that sense, it should not be
" so much abhorred commonly of men, of what religion
" soever they were, nay, of the Jews themselves; which,
" if they did take the thing, that Christ made himself
" *victima paschalis* for us, would never abhor this manner
" of sacrifice to be a figure of that. Upon this ground,
" hearing and reading what was written at this time of
" learned men in Germany, and what a great number were
" fallen into this opinion, this confirmed me utterly in the
" same: especially seeing (as I took it) the providence of
" God had wrought, that also it was accepted in the whole
" realm, all masses cast away, and condemned as a sacri-
" fice of idolaters; whereby I was so confirmed. Seeing
" withal, that many places of Scripture, being more illus-
" trate than they were in our fathers' days; and the whole
" Scripture more read, and the intelligence of it more
" sought, than it was these years past, when this opinion
" was less doubted of; I thought this was one greater
" light given to the world, which by the more study of the
" word of God was more revealed; and that the other was
" brought in when men began to fall from studies of Scrip-
" tures, and gave them to their own inventions: which
" was after the Apostles' times and the primitive Church,

" which I took utterly to be of mine opinion. And that
" when men were more deceived, as they relented from
" the life and doctrine of the primitive Church, which
" I took most of all to be in our days, when the Clergy
" were so far gone from the ensample of life of their first
" fathers, and gave themselves more to all kind of studies
" than to the Scriptures. Which experience greatly con-
" firmed me to think that God had blinded them, and with
" the study of Scriptures had brought in more light; and
" especially in this article of the Sacrament of the Altar:
" wherein I judged them utterly blinded, that had not so
" well boulted the Scriptures as they have done in Ger-
" many, which hold most this opinion that I was in.

" So that you see now how I fell: which I counted no
" fall; but that all other fell, that held the contrary opin-
" ion; I standing in the true faith of the primitive Church:
" thinking withal, that Lanfrancus, Archbishop of Canter- Lanfrank,
" bury, which was one of the first writers that set forth Archbishop of Canter-
" the opinion of the real presence of the body and blood of bury.
" Christ, impugning the contrary, did defend his own opin-
" ion, and not that of the Church; and that opinion which
" he defended began with him, when all true knowledge
" was much obscured, and the life of the Clergy more de-
" formed.

" Thus far I was gone: which was not only to go *in*
" *consilio impiorum, et stare in via peccatorum*, but to
" firm my seat *in cathedra irrisorum et pestilentiæ*. Which
" I did, making myself judge of the catholic doctrine and
" the Doctors; scorning the same in the greatest article
" of all, touching the Sacrament; and infecting with my
" pestilent opinion as many as I was conversant withal.
" In the which chair I was so fixed, that no power, but
" only God, could subvert the same, to make me know
" myself. Which so now the hand of God, by his mira-
" culous power, as I do knowledge it, hath done of his
" high mercy, both for mine own self, and, as I trust, for
" the edification of many, whom I had afore ruinate, sitting
" in my chair of pestilence. In which hope standeth now

" all the joy of my life. And this is that tempereth the
" sorrow of my mind, that I take for mine horrible offence;
" trusting that God will turn all the more to his glory.
" Without the which trust, now that I know my fault, I
" were not able surely to bear myself. But if I have any
" part of contentation in this life, all standeth in this, as I
" may see God glorified by my sin, giving me true repent-
" ance thereof, that the good may be confirmed in their
" good faith, and the ill returned to the same; as I trust
" this day the same grace that hath worked in me shall
" work in many.

" This only I will warn all that have been tempted with
" the same false doctrine that I have been, and now shew
" themselves outwardly to refuse the same, that they be
" well ware of another great temptation, and a pernicious
" counsel, which to follow is more odious to God, than to
" profess openly the false opinion; that is, if they should,
" for policy sake, shew themselves to follow the Prince's
" opinion, which is catholic; and to think otherwise in
" their mind of God: which we have seen hath lighted
" upon some already: for *nihil est occultum, quod non*
" *revelabitur*. And this is a more mocking of Christ, and
" more dishonouring, than when the Jews saluted him,
" saying, *Ave Rex Judæorum!* with their mouth, the same
" time they brought him to be crucified as a malefactor.
" Wherefore let all men beware of this; whereof I do the
" more earnestly warn you, because there hath not lacked
" that would have given like counsel to me: from the
" which the mercy of God hath utterly delivered me, and
" maketh me the more earnestly warn you of the same.

" Now having none other thing to say at this present,
" but to desire you all, upon my knees prostrate, and
" especially my noble Mistress, that it will please her to
" give thanks for me to God, for recovering a servant of
" hers that was utterly lost. And though I am not worthy
" of myself to be remembered, yet if the angels in heaven
" make more joy of one sinner converted, than of so many
" just men, my conversion, being to the glory of God, is

" not unworthy to be remembered on earth, with due
" thanks to the goodness of God, by whose grace I am
" returned.   In the rest, submitting myself with all humi-
" lity to all the order of penance and satisfaction, that it
" will please my Lord Legate to put unto me : which can-
" not be so sore, as I trust God shall give me grace and
" will to fulfil it to the uttermost.

    " And thus Almighty God, that hath begun to shew his
" mercy on me, of the same his infinite mercy, may do the
" like upon all the rest that be either contrary or waver-
" ing. *Amen.*"

SECT. VI.

Observations upon Cheke's recantations. The Queen grants
him lands in exchange.

    I SHALL not make observations upon these foregoing Popish ri-
recantations, though many might be made ; only I cannot gors to-
but observe two or three things *en passant*.   As, how ri- Cheke.
gorously these Popish masters dealt with Cheke, now they
had got him into their power, in putting him to make one
long recantation after another : and in them prescribing
him words and sentences, so grievous and grating upon
his very heart ; whereby he was fain so to belie and be-
spatter himself, as in effect to accuse himself to be one of
the vilest wretches on earth : *viz.* " That he blasphemed
" the name of God, and persecuted the name of Christ,
" and that more than they that crucified him ; and that
" the ignorance of the Jews that killed Christ was more
" excusable than his.   That he did what he could to bring
" the whole realm into blindness.   That since he came
" into the Tower, he never came into place where he had
" more cause to thank God.   And that for an assured
" token to the auditors, that what he said with his mouth
" he thought with his heart, they put the very words of
" Berengarius's recantation into his mouth, to own all the
" absurdities of transubstantiation ; and divers such like
" expressions."

CHAP.
V.

Anno 1556.

A reason of
this malice
against
him.

Cheke's an-
guish and
perplexity.

Submits to
penances.

The Queen
exchanges
lands with
him.

I observe also, by a clause of the recantation, upon what reason their anger and malice against Cheke was chiefly grounded; namely, because he had been the great instrument of good religion unto King Edward, and other noble youth of the Court, more than any other; whenas his office, as he was instructed to say, was not to teach him matters of religion, an employment committed to others.

And, lastly, I make one remark with great commiseration; and that is, in what a deplorable anguish and perplexity, not to be expressed, this poor gentleman was, whilst he was thus constrained to speak matters so utterly against his knowledge and conscience; and what a woful fall this good man made to save a poor life. Such weak frail creatures the best are, considered in themselves. Which makes me think what Archbishop Parker writ on the margin of the copy of one of these recantations, *Homines sumus*, i. e. " We are but men."

Nor yet was this all the penance that Sir John Cheke was to do, (though one would think this had been enough of all conscience;) but further, after all this, he was to undergo penances, whatsoever they should be, (and he promised it,) that should be enjoined him by the Pope's Legate, the Cardinal.

And now, having done all this drudgery, and undergone all these hardships for his life, (wherein the Romanists were to triumph and glory,) he makes all his interest to obtain his lands of the Queen again, which in his absence she had taken possession of. And his lands at length he had restored to him; but upon condition of an exchange with the Queen for others. And so he was required to make a surrender to her of all his lands and manors that he had obtained under his late royal master, King Edward. Which having been the revenues of religious houses or chauntries, the Queen thought fit to take into her hands, perhaps with an intention, in due time, to resettle them upon the old foundations, and restore them to their first purposes; yet granting him other Church lands at a greater distance from London, as in Devonshire and Somerset-

shire: which it may be afterwards, means should have
been made to dispose also to their original constitutions.
Which required surrender, Cheke complying with the
Queen, granted him a patent, (which I have seen in the
hands of my honoured friend, John Conyers, Esq.) dated
April the 12th, in the 3d and 4th of King Philip and Queen
Mary: wherein mention is made of the manor of Brampton Abbot in Devonshire, given by King Henry VIII. to
Sir Hugh Stukely, Knight; and of the customary lands
and reversions in Freshford and Woodwick in Somersetshire, given by King Edward VI. to Philip Juys, one of
the said King's gardeners, &c. All these lands and manors
Sir John obtained of the Queen, in consideration, as the
patent runs, of a certain recognizance of the town of Clare,
and the site of the college of Stoke; and of the manors of
Stoke, Clare, Hundon, Ashton, and Pitley, alias Pightley,
with the appurtenances in the county of Essex; and of
the advowsons of the churches of Clare, Hunden, and
Ashton; and also of the office of Feodary of the honour of
Clare, and the hundred of Chilton, Chibel, &c. in the
county of Cambridge; and of the manors of Preston, Beck-
wel, &c. in Sussex; and of the priory of Spalding, &c. in
Lincolnshire; and other demeans in Norfolk; and of divers other manors and tenements; levied and done by Sir
John Cheke, and Mary his wife, to the Queen and her
heirs, at Westminster, in Hilary term, in the 3d and 4th
of the said King and Queen. For which and other causes
their Majesties moving, they of their special grace granted
to the said Cheke and Peter Osborn, Esq. the reversion of
the said manor of Brampton Abbot in Devon, belonging
formerly to the monastery of Clive; and the annual rents
of 37l. 2s. 6ob.; and the reversion of the customary lands
of Freshford and Woodwick in Somersetshire. They granted also to him and the said Osborn the manor of More in
Devon; and the capital messuage of Batokysborough, and
the manor of Aisshetote, alias Ayscote, in Somersetshire;
and the manor of Northlode, parcel of the possessions of

K

the monastery of Glascon; together with some other things granted to the said Sir John Cheke and Mary his wife, and Peter Osborn.

SECT. VII.

What happened to Cheke after his recantation. Troubled.
Repents. Dies.

Cheke made
to consort
with Pa-
pists.

BUT all these temporal accessions could not heal the wounds he had given his mind by his apostasy or hypocrisy; which so excessively dejected him, that within less than a year after it ended his life, as we shall be told by and by. But the Papists now outwardly made much of their convert; had him frequently in their companies, at their tables, to eat with them; and on their benches, when the pretended heretics were summoned before them, and examined; to shew him openly, no doubt, as an example to them, what a leading and learned man had forsaken their party; and for him to exhort them to do as he had done. Which were but so many fresh stings to him.

Cheke re-
pents.

The Protestants extenuated as much as they could his dismal fall, making it not so foul as was at first represented. An Englishman in exile, sojourning at Strasburg, (and seems to be Grindal,) wrote to Peter Martyr, then at Zurich, March 15 anno 1556, informing him, that Cheke had given significations of his repentance and sorrow for his fall. Which gave such satisfaction to that reverend Father, that he wrote back to his friend that gave him this intelligence, that it was very acceptable to hear what he had wrote concerning Cheke, because Cheke had now de-

Int. P. Mar-
tyr. Epist.
p. 784. col.
2. edit.
Genev.

clared, " that his faith was rather bent, than broke and " quite extinguished, however reports might be carried of " him." But Martyr added, that he thought it almost past belief, that he should persevere while he tarried in England; and subjoined his earnest prayer, " that God, " the Father of our Lord Jesus Christ, would so by his " Spirit repair his shipwreck, that, with as little loss as

" might be, he might at last arrive at the haven of salva-
" tion." And God heard his prayer : for it was not long
after that Cheke made his exit.

And pining away with the shame and regret of what he Dies.
had done, he died Sept. 13, 1557, aged 43, at his friend
Mr. Peter Osborn's house, in Wood-street, London; and
wa̡ buried in St. Alban's church there, in the north chapel
of the quire, Sept. 16. On whose grave were engraven
these verses, made by his learned acquaintance, Dr. Walter MSS. D. H.
Haddon; which I shall here set down, as I have them Kt. Garter.
transcribed from the monumental stone, taken by Charles
Lancaster, herald, anno 1611, rather than as they are
varied in Cheke's life, composed by H. Holland, and from
him by Dr. Gerard Langbain. On the stone, on the right
side of the inscription, is engraven the coat of arms of him
and his wife; being three crescents, and a crescent in the
midst for distinction. The woman's coat, a salteir vaire,
with a martlet in the nombril point, between five martlets.
The epitaph as follows :

Doctrinæ lumen CHECUS *vitæque magister,*
   Aurea naturæ fabrica, morte jacet.
Non erat e multis unus, sed præstitit unus
   Omnibus et patriæ flos erat ille suæ.
Gemma Britanna fuit, tam magnum nulla tulerunt
   Tempora thesaurum, tempora nulla ferent.

Where one may observe, that neither his religion, his fall,
nor his repentance, are in the least touched, those times
not suffering it.

To which I will add the verses that Sir Thomas Chaloner, a gentleman and excellent scholar that lived in those
times, in his miscellanies made of him :

Epitaphium D. Joannis Checi.

Tu nunc exuvias liquisti corporis hujus,
   CHEKE, *Deo vivens, lux nova juncto polo.*
Fulsisti inter nos lumen radiantius ; et nunc
   Astra tuo exortu languidiora micant.

SECT. VIII.

*His circumstances at his death. His arms. His person.
His lady. Her fortune. Mac Williams her second
husband. Some account of him. Her death.*

**Dies in
debt.**

HE left Henry, his son and heir, but in bad circumstances, dying a thousand marks and more in debt. He
left behind him, in land, to the value of three hundred
marks a year; his wife being joint purchaser with him for
two hundred marks thereof, and Peter Osborn (at whose

**Peter Os-
born's
kindness.**
house he died) for the third. But that true friend of Sir
John, though he had an estate in that land for the term of
his life, and might have taken all the profits thereof to his
own use, was contented to forbear it, of very kindness to
the Lady Cheke his widow, and to Henry Cheke and his
brothers: as in divers other respects he had shewn himself
kind to that family, and discharged Sir John's debts, and
maintained Henry at school during his minority, and fully
answered such debts as his father owed him; and, when
he came to full age, he released him the commodities aris-
ing of the land, and suffered him to receive them to his
own use during his life.

**His arms
and crest.**
Sir John's paternal coat of arms was argent, three crescents gules. There be two crests shewn in the Heralds'
Office for his crest. The one is a leopard seiant, with a
collar and chain: the other a crescent of the colour of the
crescents in the coat, with a cross *patee fitche* placed
within the horns of it, of the same: which was that he
commonly bore; and seems to have relinquished the other
for this. Which very aptly denoted (as it were by some
prophetic spirit in him or the herald) that great cross and
affliction that befell him for the sake of Christ.

**His person
described.**
All that I can describe of his person is from a picture of
him yet remaining at Pyrgo, in the long gallery there:
where he is represented with a round cap on his head,
and a letter and other papers in his right hand, as Clerk
of the Council, or principal Secretary. A book lying upon

the table before him, signifying either his own learning, or SECT.
his place and charge of instructing the King. A full comely VIII.
countenance, somewhat red; with a yellow large beard, Anno 1557.
covering his upper lip, and hanging below his chin, somewhat forked. A visage portending wisdom and careful-
ness.

His lady (who no question suffered deeply with him) Lady Cheke
yet lived to see better days, and enjoyed a long life. For gain to Mac
she married again to Henry Mac Williams, of Irish extract, Williams.
Esquire, a gentleman of the Court, and of considerable
quality. But a match that proved unhappy for the children
she had by Sir John Cheke; her estate (which was considerable) going to her second husband, and the children by
him.

Her fortune brought to this gentleman was, in western The estate
lands, by year, 132*l.* 3*s.* 4*d.* The fines and casualties to him.
thereof was worth the first year 300*l.*; the yearly casualties afterwards were, *communibus annis,* 66*l.* 13*s.* 4*d.*
She had in plate 1000 marks, in jewels 800 marks; gowns,
five; kirtles, nineteen; partlets, sleeves, and other linen,
to the value of above 300*l.*; household stuff that cost
above 400*l.* For her service of her Majesty she had a
lease in Wales, which, first and last, was worth 1000*l.*;
she had moreover in sheep 360*l.* she had Barnardiston, a
ward, worth 500 marks; more, two leases for the provision
of her house, that, to be sold, were worth 200*l.* Such a fortune was she to her second husband, and such an injury her
second marriage did to her children by the former husband,
leaving them in the mean time very bare and needy.

This Henry Mac Williams was a person of valour and This Mac
chivalry, being one of those that were chosen by the Earl man of chi-
of Leicester, in a great exercise of tilts and tournaments, valry.
anno 1565, before Queen Elizabeth, (wherein he met with
a remarkable accident,) at the marriage of Ambrose Dudley, Earl of Warwick, with a daughter of Francis Russel,
Earl of Bedford, solemnized before the said Queen, at her
palace at Westminster, Sunday, 11th of November, the Ex Officio
Armor.

year above-said. For the greater magnificency, on the said Sunday, and two days after, were holden justs, tourneys, and barriers, at Westminster, by four gentlemen challengers against all comers, viz. Sir Henry Knoles, son and heir to Sir Francis Knoles, Vice-Chamberlain; Thomas Leighton, Christopher Hatton, and Robert Colshill.

Robert, Earl of Leicester, being chief defendant, with twenty-two other noblemen and gentlemen in his company; namely, Henry L. Herbert, son and heir to William Herbert, Earl of Pembroke; Arthur L. Grey, of Wilton; Walter Winsor, Henry Norrys, and, among the rest, Henry Mac Williams. The third day, being Tuesday, Henry Mac Williams ran with Henry Knoles at the tourney, who overthrew both Mac Williams and his horse. Whereupon the said horse and armour became a due droit to the officers at arms; who, according to their right, and according to the judgment of the Lord Judge there present, seized upon the same. But being put in question, whether it were a droit to them, the Duke of Norfolk, Earl Marshal, called before him the Kings of Arms and Heralds, willing them to bring to him, and shew him such precedents as they had for their right therein: which they did accordingly. Upon the sight of which precedents, the said Duke awarded unto the said officers, in consideration of the premises, the sum of 20l. Which sum, for redemption of the said horse and armour, was paid to the said company by the Earl of Leicester; and so discharged the said Mac Williams.

Her children by Mac Williams.

This Mac Williams, by the Lady Cheke, had Henry Mac Williams, (who died without issue,) and five daughters; viz. Margaret, wife of John L. Stanhope; Susan, wife of Edward Sandeys, Esq. married again to Goddard Pemberton, Knight, and after to Thomas Ireland, Knight; Ambrosia, wife to William Kingswel, Knight; Cassandra, wife of George Cotton, Knight; Cicilia, wife to Thomas Ridgeway, Knight, Treasurer of Ireland. In short, this gentleman, Mr. Mac Williams, was a Justice of Peace in

Essex, and died in December anno 1586. And so the
Lady Cheke was a widow a second time. But for some
description of her.

She was a comely courtly lady, bred up in the Court
from her childhood. In Queen Elizabeth's time was much
at Court, being one of the Ladies of the Privy Chamber, an
honourable station in those days. Nor was she backward
in taking her place of the other Court Ladies; insomuch
that once, *viz.* in the year 1591, complaint was made of
the Lady Cheke by a Viscount's daughter (or, at least, so
valuing herself) to the Lord Burghley, (that then held the
Earl Marshal's place by commission from the Queen,) for
that the Lady Cheke went before her at Court. This lady
complainant was the Lady Frances Cooke, wife to William, a son of Sir Anthony Cooke, Knight, and daughter of
the Lord John Grey, brother to the Duke of Suffolk. She,
by a letter, dated from Charing Cross the year aforesaid,
" humbly beseeched him, as he was honourable himself,
" so it might please his Lordship to vouchsafe his honour-
" able favour towards the house she was come of; which,
" as his Lordship best knew, was once not least honourable,
" though, by misfortune, brought low; whereof, it seem-
" eth," as she proceeded, " my Lady Cheke, to whom I
" never gave cause of just offence, taketh great advantage.
" For she doth not only offer me all the wrong and dis-
" grace that she can in Court, in taking place afore me,
" where it becometh not me, in modesty, to strive for it;
" but she openly publisheth to every body, that I have no
" place at all. Truly, my Lord, I should think my fortune
" hard, and my deserts ill, if my hap fall out to be put
" down by a woman of no greater birth than I take my
" Lady Cheke to be. I hope her Majesty and your Lord-
" ship will make some difference between our two births.
" And I trust, never having offended her Majesty, that I
" shall receive that gracious favour from her, that I may
" still possess the place I did in my Lord my father's
" time, and ever since his death, till of late; which place
" I took as a younger Viscount's daughter."

Anno 1557.

What pre-
cedency due
to the Lady
Frances
Cooke.

Ladies are apt to value themselves, and affect precedency; and so, it seems, did these two: the Lady Cheke,
as she was the relict of a Knight, sometime Secretary of
State, and a Privy Counsellor; and the Lady Frances
Cooke, as being the daughter of a son of a Marquis, *viz.*
Marquis of Dorset, and younger brother of a Duke, *viz.*
Duke of Suffolk. Whereupon she gave her father the
title of a younger Viscount; though, according to the laws
of heraldry, she could not take place upon any of these
accounts: and therefore I am afraid the Lord Marshal's
decision went not for her, and the Knight's Lady had the
right of taking place; though, out of courtesy and respect
to her father, she had precedency in his life-time.

Yet, as she was daughter (and eldest daughter) to a son
and heir male of a Marquis, (his elder brothers being
dead,) as he claimed by bearing a label of three points in
his arms, and as he is styled in the inscription upon his
monument in the chapel at Pyrgo, I leave to the Office of
Arms to determine what place she was to have on that
account.

Lady
Cheke's
death and
monument-
al inscrip-
tion.

But so much shall suffice for the Lady Cheke, after I
shall have brought her to her end. She was buried in the
chancel of the church of St. Martin's in the Fields, about
the year 1616; (that is, about sixty years after her first
husband's death, and twenty years after her second:)
where she hath still a very fair monument against the
north wall; with a marble figure of her lying along, of
excellent work, and an inscription, wherein both her hus-
bands are mentioned, with their issue by her, and the
former with the title of Secretary of State to King Edward
VI. Which inscription is as follows; declaring her birth,
marriage, children, and quality.

Hic jacet Maria Domina Cheke, filia R. Hill, Armig.
Fœmina pia et prudens, et quæ fuit ad obitum una Domi-
narum in Privata Camera Reginæ Elizabethæ (quæ fuit
tunc dignitas in præcipuo honore.) Nupta fuit primo
Johanni Cheke, Militi, Magistro, et Principali Secretario

Regis Edwardi VI. viro optimo et eruditissimo. Cui pe- SECT.
perit Henricum, hæredem paternæ virtutis et Regiæ Ma- VIII.
jestati a Secretis in Concilio Eboracensi ; Johannem Cheke, Anno 1557.
virum egregium et magnanimum ; et Edwardum Cheke.

Secundo nupta Henrico Mackwilliams, Armigero, viro
ex nobilissima familia Hibernorum. Cui peperit, &c.
Vixit circiter 84 *annis. Obiit Novemb.* 30, 1616.

Now to turn our eyes again to Sir John, the husband of
her youth.

CHAP. VI.

Sir John Cheke's posterity.

SECT. I.

Cheke's sons, three: Henry Cheke, eldest son; John Cheke, the second; Edward, the third.

Cheke's posterity yet flourish. THUS died Cheke in a cloud; and his name, once most honoured, much eclipsed by his infirmity. But his repentance (which would have shewed itself more, had he lived longer) must reconcile him to men of the like frail nature; and his former singular merits will undoubtedly preserve his memory fair and in credit with all candid men. And the name of Cheke hath still lived in a posterity of men of worth, sprung from him; the family flourishing to this day in wealth and reputation at Pyrgo, a noble seat in the county of Essex, belonging to it; purchased by Sir Thomas Cheke, Knight, grandson to Sir John; and now possessed by Edward Cheke, Esq.

His sons. His sons were three: (for Dr. Langbain mistook much when he wrote that he left no issue but one son, bearing his father's name:) their names were, Henry, John, and Edward; the first and the last probably so called from his two royal masters, in grateful remembrance of their favours. The continuation of his posterity depended upon his eldest son, Henry; John and Edward dying without issue, at least as far as I could ever by search and inquiry find.

John Cheke. John was a youth of great hopes, comely and learned, and of a gentleman-like and very obliging deportment: of whom also his uncle, the Lord Treasurer Burghley, took particular care, making him one of his own family. And upon his parting thence, in some employment abroad, he wrote a very courteous letter to Mr. Hickes, Secretary to the said Lord Treasurer, as sensible of some kindnesses done him by the said Hickes. Among his other qualities, he was courageous and brave; which spirit carried him to the wars in Ireland, to serve the Queen his mistress; where, in the year 1579 or 1580, he was unfortunately slain in an engagement against some Italians and Spaniards that had invaded that country for King Philip; and was the only man that fell by those Popish hands, as his father and namesake before him had his days shortened by men of like principles.

For this gentleman had remained six years at least in the retinue of his uncle, whom on that account he called *his master;* and being impatient to remain in this unactive life, he resolved to push on his own fortunes, choosing the life of a soldier. But his own mean circumstances hindered him; so that, having not wherewith to furnish himself out with a horse, he was fain to embolden himself to ask for one of his Lordship; which he did in a modest letter, dated from London, in July 1578, thus bespeaking him: " That he found at that time nature and duty strove " very much within him: the one, to procure importu- " nately that which might secure it safe; the other, willing " him to forbear to offend in craving, where he honoured, " served, and feared: but that his Lordship had much en- " couraged him, because he had not acquainted him with " denials. He begged, therefore, for the safety of his life, " and the increase of his reputation, to bestow his dun " horse on him; a horse which he chiefly desired, be- " cause, as he said, he was wedded to him for his gentle " nature, and trust in him, knowing his goodness, and " would most willingly hazard his life on him. That ne- " cessity forced him, and life willingly spoke for itself. " He prayed his Lordship to favour him, and to forget " that duty which he owed him that forbade him this; " since nature swayed more with him than reason, though " he feared more to offend his Lordship than any: but " chiefly that his excuse might be, because he wanted." This was his style, and this his awful behaviour towards his uncle: and thus he set out like a soldier of fortune: and pity it was so hopeful a gentleman had not better success.

SECT. I.

His end.

His letter to the Lord Burghley his uncle.

Edward
Cheke.

Of Edward Cheke, Sir John's youngest son, I know little, but that Henry, his eldest brother, was, by his father's will, to pay him an annuity of ten pounds a year. I reckon he died young also: for I find the payment of his annuity ceased after his brother had payed it him six years.

SECT. II.

Henry Cheke, Sir John's eldest son.

Henry
Cheke.

HENRY, the eldest, (who was nine years old at his father's death,) was bred up to learning also, by the care of Mr. Osborn, his father's friend; and afterwards, for improvement of his studies, was removed to King's college in Cambridge, where his father was sometime Provost. Here Bartholomew Clerke, LL. D. (afterward that officiated Dean of the Arches,) an exquisite scholar, took great care of his education; under whom he made a good progress. But to go a little back to the times before. In the year 1563 (when he must have been but young, that is, about fifteen) he wrote a Greek epistle to Cecil, his uncle: wherein he mentioned the ancient friendship that was between his father and him; and that, for his sake, he was a friend to those that were his father's friends; and whereby he hoped also to ingratiate himself with him: shewing him withal, that his estate was but small, and that his dependance must be upon his learning: and, lastly, devoting himself to his service, and avowing that he honoured him as his father, and hoped in him as the stay and pillar of his family. And accordingly Sir William Cecil took care of him also, and admonished him, that in any need he should apply himself to him for his aid, and promised that he would be ever ready at hand to do any thing for him that might redound to his benefit. And when he was at the University, he had a special eye over him.

The character of Henry Cheke.

By the characters that were given of him to his uncle and patron, he did *patrizare;* treading in his excellent father's steps, and, in respect of his probity and learning, surpassing others.   Bartholomew Doddington, the Greek Professor, who was his companion, and, as it seems, his fellow collegian, gave this character of him, that he was a youth *summæ probitatis, ingenii, studii, suavissimorum morum;* i. e. of notable goodness of nature, wit, studiousness, and of the sweetest disposition. Dr. Clark, his tutor, wrote frequent letters to Cecil concerning his nephew's good proficiency in his studies. The University, out of a singular love they bore to him, as well as their honourable respect to Cecil, (who was their High Chancellor,) soon gave him his grace for Master of Arts, and adopted him into the rank of their senators in the year 1568, being then scarce twenty years old, and that without any petition or suit of his made for it. Of this Dr. Clerk informed the said Cecil, and withal prayed him to allow Henry to accept it, and to enjoy an honour the University had voted him; since, by his friends' advice, he was purposed neither to accept nor refuse it, till he had the assent and counsel of him, his said uncle. He took this occasion to commend this young student for his parts[a], spake well of his religion and piety, of his stayedness and modesty, his learning and prudence; in all which respects, he said, one might behold in him the express image of his best and most holy parent; and, that those his abilities might appear to all, the University had appointed him to dispute in the next Commencement. And, lastly, that they had done this as a testimony of their reverence to his excellent father, and knowing the young gentleman to be the beneficiary and candidate of the most wise Cecil. Thus was he made acquainted with all proceedings relating to Mr. Cheke.

To trace this gentleman further.   About the year 1569 Marries or 1570 he marries; falling in love with Frances, daughter Frances Ratcliff. of the Lady Ratcliff, who was wife to Sir Humphry Radcliff, of Elstow, Knight, whose son Edward was Earl of

[a] Sive enim religionem et pietatem seu gravitatem et modestiam, sive literas et prudentiam spectes, omni ex parte videbis in eo expressam patris optimi ac religiosissimi effigiem.

Sussex. Of this his affection he acquainted his uncle Cecil, to whom he confessed his love, but, notwithstanding, without his advice he would not proceed. And his consent and furtherance he seems to have obtained; for he married her, and had children by her.

In the year 1572 he wrote his uncle a Greek epistle congratulatory, upon his being made Lord High Treasurer, dated from Elnest in Bedfordshire.

Henry Cheke's condition was somewhat strait, and his incomes scarcely sufficient for his expenses. It appears, those lands that Queen Mary made over to Sir John Cheke were still held fast, either by the crown or private hands, and not yet possessed by his heir: for, in one of his letters to Cecil, he shewed him, that he had indeed some estate, but not to be enjoyed without much trouble and expense for the recovery, being gotten into other men's possessions, and his houses upon his farms much out of repair. He petitioned the Queen for his estate, and Sir William Cecil presented and forwarded his suit. It was for the manor of Hunden, in the county of Suffolk. The fee simple was in his father, but now in the Queen, and she had promised his mother to restore such things as were his father's. He set forth in his petition, that it was no prejudice to the Queen, but only losing the fine: for as to the parks, they were more charges to her than she received commodity by them. By this it seems to appear, that the exchange before mentioned, between Queen Mary and Sir John, was not completed at his death, or at least was not enjoyed by him, though that Queen detained and enjoyed his lands so exchanged. Certain it is, that his circumstances were at this time but short, and annuities went out of his estate. He paid 10l. a year to his youngest brother, and 10l. a year to his schoolmaster; a gratuity common in those times from gentlemen to their instructors. The remainder was 746l. 6s. 8d. which came yearly into his purse. He was fain to make some benefit of his lands by fines; but yet, notwithstanding, he went behindhand, whatever his good husbandry was: so that he acquitted himself of housekeeping, and paying for his board, by the courtesy of some of his friends; otherwise he must have fallen into extreme debt, and sold his land, as he signified his case to his uncle Cecil: notwithstanding a lease also, which he had of the Bishop of Winchester, obtained by means of his said uncle, and Mr. Vice-Chamberlain.

For two or three years he and his wife and children Sojourns with friends. resided in the country with some of his friends there, *viz.* in the year 1574 at Wintney in Hantshire, and in 1575 at Bear, in Bear Forest, in the same county.

The Queen was acquainted with his circumstances, and He travels. intended to take him into her service; but she would have him first to travel, the better to fit him for it, which he forthwith undertook. And to fit himself out, he sold so much land as yielded him 400*l.* the which yet served not to maintain all his charge and expense abroad. In the year 1576 he went abroad, being now about eight and twenty years of age. In this year I find him at Antwerp, hastening towards Italy, and comes to Genoa. In the beginning of the next year he was at Florence, where he was in dan- His danger. ger of his life or liberty; means being used to entrap him, by laying in wait to catch him, with intention perhaps to serve him as they had done his father, out of a hatred conceived to his name. He was advised of this by a certain English gentleman, who coming into the company of one Stewkely, from Genoa to Siena, gave him warning to seek some other place, and to look carefully to himself, as one greatly noted by some of his countrymen, who had spoken such words in his hearing, he said, as he might not declare unto him the particulars. Upon which Mr. Cheke thought fit to ask the counsel of an Italian friend, Seignior Lorenzo Guicciardini, brother unto Vincenzo Guicciardini of London; a grave wise gentleman, and very friendly unto him, and of great credit with the great Duke of Tuscany. By his advice he resolved for Padua. So in the beginning of April he took himself to Ferrara, and found great difficulty to enter into the Duke's estate; forasmuch

CHAP.
VI.

as being a neighbour unto the Venetians, (where the plague then was,) he kept the passages of his territories very strait. From thence he travelled to Padua about the end of the spring.

His observation in these countries.

His endeavour was (among the pleasures of his travels through this brave country) to attain to speak the language truly and readily, which he hoped to do by Michaelmas; and then he should think he had spent that year profitably: as he wrote to the Lord Treasurer. He noted various things, and made his observations in his travels here. But in the whole he made this remark, "That he had seen " many notable cities, much rich soil, and great variety of " states; but in his opinion he had not seen any city so " beautiful as Florence, any soil so rich as that of Lom- " bardy, nor any state so happy as the state of Eng- " land."

Comes home.

He is at home in the year 1579. How much sooner he returned I find not. Now he resided with his family at

Attends the Court.

Occham in Surrey. He daily attended the Court, though with little or no salary, yet in expectation of some place or preferment; for which he ceased not, as he might with modesty, to solicit his uncle, the Lord Treasurer, being his highest friend, at whose hand he looked for his greatest comfort in his necessity: for he had again lately sold some more of his land. He prayed that honourable person to bestow upon him some office in possession or reversion, whereby he might reap some yearly commodity, to the increase of his living. He was forced now, not by his unthriftiness, but by need, to sell a manor, amounting in yearly rent to the sum of 37l. 15s. 10d. as well to pay his debts with part of the money, as to employ the rest in use to the best advantage. His debts were contracted by his late travel, and afterwards by his attendance at Court without fee, and other extraordinary expenses.

Made Secretary of the Council in the north.

But some time after, viz. in the year 1581, (when he almost now despaired of succeeding at Court,) by the interest of the Lord Treasurer, he was made Secretary to the Council in the north, in the room of one Blyth, a very ho-

nest able man, deceased. The Earl of Huntingdon, Pre- SECT.
II.
sident of that Council, wrote to the said Lord for Henry's
speedy repair to the north; saying, that he was right glad
of his promotion to that place: for though a worthy man
were taken away, yet he hoped a good one should succeed;
so as the want of Mr. Blyth there was not like to be
missed, as else it would. But, he added, that he needed
not to commend him to his Lordship, who better knew
him, and could judge better of such than he. Besides this
office, he obtained the honour of knighthood also of the And
knighted.
Queen his mistress.

How long Sir Henry lived, I cannot tell: but I find one His death.
Thomas Cheke, (by which name Sir Henry's eldest son
was called,) in the year 1586, writing a Greek letter and
Latin verses to the Lord Treasurer; therein calling himself
an orphan, and speaking of his father being gone to the
joys of heaven. And he prays his Lordship, that as he
was always an help and a sanctuary unto his father, so he
would be to him. And this I conclude to be Sir Henry's
eldest son, who might now be of the age of fifteen or six-
teen: and if so, then at this year we must fix the period
of his life.

SECT. III.

*Sir Thomas Cheke, son of Sir Henry. His honourable
posterity.*

SIR HENRY CHEKE'S issue by his before-said wife Sir Henry's
children.
Frances, was Thomas, his eldest; Hatton, who followed
the wars in Flanders, and was slain in a duel by Sir Thomas Dutton, Knight, near the town of Calais, (whose
corpse was brought over, and buried at Dover;) and
Henry, his third son, who died without issue, and was also
buried at Dover, near his brother Hatton.

Thomas being thus left a minor, was bred in a school Sir Thomas
Cheke.
at York: where he had two memorable schoolfellows,
though of different inclinations and reputations. The one
was Morton, afterwards Bishop of Durham; an excellent

L.

and most learned Prelate, that wrote much and well against the Papists: the other, Guy Faux, infamous to posterity for his unparalleled Popish zeal and villainy. Thomas was knighted by King James I. and was then styled Sir Thomas Cheke of the county of Lincoln, in respect perhaps of his estate at Spalding in that county. After styled Sir Thomas Cheke of Pyrgo, in the liberty of Havering in Essex; being an estate which he purchased of the Grays, and where he lived anno 1634.

His wives. He married, first, a daughter of Peter Osborn, Esq. a very beautiful woman; as her picture shews, preserved in the long gallery of Pyrgo. To her he was married near twenty years, and had no issue. Afterwards he married Essex, daughter of Robert Lord Rich, Earl of Warwick. By whom he had three sons, Robert, Thomas, Charles; and five daughters, Frances, Essex, Anne, Isabel, and Elizabeth. And living to a great age, was buried, March 25, 1659, in St. Alban's church in Wood-street, (according to his desire and will,) near his grandfather, in the north chapel, without the furthest pillar, as appears by the register of the said parish. Upon the rebuilding of this church, in clearing the rubbish, the labourers thereabouts met with a grave bricked up, which probably was wrought about his corpse. Of whose progeny, and the honourable intermarriages thereof, partly Dugdale's Baronage, and partly the visitation books in the Office of Arms, (in one book whereof is Sir Thomas Cheke's own testimonial,) give this relation:

His sons. Robert Cheke was born in the year 1625. He was crooked, but a man of exquisite parts, and very dear to the Lord Cranborn, eldest son of the Earl of Salisbury, and sometime governor of one of King Charles the Second's natural children.

Thomas, who inherited the estate, called Colonel Cheke, was Lieutenant of the Tower under King Charles II. and King James II. He married, first, Dorothy, a daughter of Philip Sydney, Lord Viscount Lisle, afterwards Earl of Leicester; by whom he had no issue. He afterwards married Lætitia, daughter of Edward Russel, second son to Francis, Earl of Bedford; by whom he had issue Henry, who, living to the age of eight or nine years, died, and was buried in the chapel at Pyrgo, besides other children dying young. He had by his said wife a son named Edward, the only son surviving, and now enjoying the seat of Pyrgo in honour and reputation : who married a daughter of Sir William Ellis, of Nocton in the county of Lincoln, Bart. The daughters of the said Thomas and Lætitia are, Essex, unmarried, and Anne, wife of Sir Thomas Tipping, of Oxfordshire, Bart. This is the posterity male of Sir Thomas Cheke, grandson to our Sir John.

The daughters of the said Sir Thomas were five, all ho- nourably matched : 1. Frances, the eldest, was married to Sir Lancelot Lake, of Canons, in the county of Middlesex, Knight. 2. Essex, the second daughter, was wife of Sir Robert Bevyl, of Chesterton, in the county of Huntingdon, Knight of the Bath; afterward of Edward, Earl of Manchester, Lord Chamberlain of the Household to King Charles II. by whom he had six sons and two daughters. 3. Anne, the third daughter, married to Richard Rogers, of the county of Dorset, Esq. and after to Robert Lord Rich, Earl of Warwick. 4. Isabel, the fourth daughter, married to Sir Francis Gerard, of Harrow-the-hill in Middlesex, Bart. And 5. Elizabeth, to Sir Richard Franklin, of More Park, in the county of Hertford, Bart.

Thus may we see the offspring of the righteous to flourish, and our good and religious Cheke signally blessed in a very honourable house and a flourishing descent now for above an hundred and fifty years ; and his family spreading in much noble blood to this day.

CHAP. VII.

Observations upon Sir John Cheke.

SECT. I.

His natural disposition, and the endowments of his mind.

His qualifi-
cations.

I HAVE finished the history of this eminent man, as to the external appearances and events of his life. There seems one thing yet wanting to be done, *viz.* to give the world a true *idea* of him in his inward qualifications, and the disposition of his mind: which may indeed in a great part be gathered from what hath been already said of him; yet, for the giving farther satisfaction in this matter, I shall add a few things more to all I have writ.

Some learn-
ed men's
characters
of him.

We must then, in the first place, declare him to be one of the learnedest and best men of that age; and one of the most extraordinary wits: such as Providence raiseth up now and then, (but very sparingly,) for great ends, to be public documents and examples, and to do some extra-ordinary service in the world. A very learned man in those times, contemporary with Cheke, and one that knew him well, speaking of these singular men, particularly men-

Asch.
Schoolmast.

tions him to be one; attributing unto him, " a wit quick " without lightness, sharp without brittleness, desirous of " good things without newfangleness, diligent in painful " things without wearisomeness, and constant in good-will " to do all things well." And this, he said, he knew well

Dr. Wyl-
son's trans-
lat. of De-
most. Orat.

was in Sir John Cheke. And another in those times, as great a judge of learning as he, sometime Secretary of State to Queen Elizabeth, styles Cheke, " that rare learned " man, and singular ornament of this land."

To make up the triumvirate to give their judgment of our excellent man; Nicolas Car, of Trinity college, Greek Professor after Cheke, one of the best scholars in Cam-

bridge, styled him, " ᵃ One that did not exceed many in SECT.
" age, but all in learning, and was esteemed the very top   I.
" of Cambridge men in every respect."

He had a mind, even from his tender years, much dis- His early
posed to virtue and study. And as a great advantage and disposition towards vir-
spur to both, he was educated under pious and wise pa- tue and learning.
rents; who perceiving the natural genius of the lad,
spared for no care nor pains to cultivate his nature, and
encourage his good inclinations. Therefore, if we may be- State Wor-
lieve one of our historians, they appointed a German scho- thies, p.191.
lar to take care of his younger studies, and a Frenchman
of his behaviour; the godly matron his mother following
him with good precepts; and this among the rest, that
" he should take care of three things, his God, his soul,
" and his company."

He was earnestly inquisitive after truth, and sagacious Inquisitive
to find it. And this appeared both in the choice of his after truth.
religion and of his learning; both being then overrun
with error and corruption: which his clear and searching
reason and parts soon discovered to him.

SECT. II.

His learning.

UNDER the topic of his learning, several things deserve His dili-
remark, as first, his *diligence.* He stood upon no pains gence.
to inform his understanding, and improve his knowledge,
and to find out errors, and overcome them, and to restore
learning, and advance it higher than it ordinarily shewed
itself in the Universities, and among such as went in
those times for learned men. We are told, that King Ed- State Wor-
ward said to Cardan, the learned foreigner that came to thies.
wait upon him, " that he had two masters, Diligence and
" Moderation;" meaning Cheke for the former, and Cox
for the latter.

He sat not down contented in the present learning of Studies
Greek, and
ᵃ Qui ætate non multis, doctrina antecellis omnibus, quique princeps no- why.
strorum hominum in omni genere putaris. *In Epist. ad Chæc. de mort. Bucer.*

CHAP.
VII.
the Schoolmen, but had a mind to know what learning was, when the Greeks and Romans flourished, so celebrated for their learning. And therefore to compass that, he sedulously applied himself to know the Greek language, that he might the more thoroughly read and understand the books of the learned Greek philosophers, historians, orators, and poets. Which was an hidden sort of learning then, and very rare. And herein he found a strain of learning and language far beyond the present, which was all barbarous and corrupt in comparison with it. A learning proper to instruct, and excite to live virtuously, and to love and do just and worthy actions; and also to enable men to speak properly and persuasively in any argument.

Especially he loves Demosthenes.
And of all the Greek writers, he was most a lover of Demosthenes, the Greek orator; whose writings were so noble, and his spirit and ratiocination so inimitable, that he thought it pity none should be able to read him, but such as could read Greek. This put him upon translating him (which he did many of his orations) into Latin, for the greater numbers to read, learn, and improve by.

His judgment of him.
And here I will set down his judgment of that orator, and what skill he had in him, and why he judged him so fit to be read and studied. And all this in the words of a learned man in those days contemporary with him, viz. Dr. Thomas Wilson, the learned civilian before-mentioned.

Preface to his translat. of Demosthenes.
" The enterprise," saith he, " of translating De-
" mosthenes into English, if any might have been bold to
" have taken upon him, Sir John Cheke was the man of
" all that ever I knew, or do yet know in England : such
" acquaintance had he with this notable orator; so gladly
" did he read him, and so often, that I think there was
" never old priest more perfect in his *porteise*, nor super-
" stitious monk in our Lady's Psalter, as they call it, nor
" yet good preacher in the Bible and Testament, than this
" man was in Demosthenes. And great cause moved him
" so to be. For that he saw him to be the perfectest
" orator that ever wrote for this two thousand years al-
" most by-past, (for so long it was since he was,) and also

" for that he perceived him to have before his eyes in all
" his orations the advancement of virtue, as a thing chiefly
" to be sought for, together with the honour and welfare of
" his country.———Moreover, he was moved greatly to
" like Demosthenes above all other, for that he saw him
" so familiarly applying himself to the sense and under-
" standing of the common people, that he sticked not to
" say, that ' none ever was more fit to make an English-
" man tell his tale, praiseworthily in an open hearing,
" either in Parliament or pulpit, or otherwise, than this
" only orator was.' " These were the things Cheke looked
for from learning, that it might become truly useful to
human life, and this was the reason he so valued this
Greek author.

Another branch of his *diligence*, was his ingenuous His emula-
emulation to be as learned as the best. A good quality in tion.
a scholar, when the great proficiency of others beyond
him provokes him to follow hard after, to arrive unto the
same perfections. Cheke's first application of himself to
good learning was occasioned by John Redman of St.
John's college, (afterwards Dr. Redman, and Dean of
Westminster,) who had lived and studied in the University of Paris, and came over very accomplished in the two
learned languages : and by conversing much in the books
of Tully, became both an excellent philosopher and orator.
Redman's learning made him admired and much esteemed
by all : which Cheke and his fellow Smith well observed ;
and being themselves truly addicted to their studies, took
occasion hence to pursue that sort of learning which Redman was become so eminent for. And thenceforth forsook
the common course of studies in the Universities then
used, which consisted in the barbarous terms and idle
disputations of the modern schools and schoolmen, and be-
took themselves to the reading of good Latin and Greek Life of Sir
authors, as I have observed elsewhere. Thomas
Smith.

SECT. III.

Cheke considered as a critic.

NOW to look farther, and more closely into Cheke's learning, we may consider him both as a *critic* and an *author*.

First, he was a good critic, and judge of learning, and particularly of classic authors. To give you his judgment of two or three of them. Being asked his opinion of Sallust, the Latin historian, he shewed his piercing judgment of him by this censure: for after he had said, " that he " was not very fit for young men to learn out of him the " purity of the Latin tongue, he gave these reasons, *viz.* " because he was not the purest in propriety of words, nor " choicest in aptness of phrases, nor the best in framing of " sentences. And therefore, that his writing was neither " plain for the matter, nor sensible for men's understand- " ing." And when Ascham, to whom he spoke this, asked him what was the cause thereof, " Verily," said he, " be- " cause Sallust's writing is more art than nature, and " more labour than art. And in his labour also too much " toil, as it were with an uncontented care to write better " than he could: a fault common to very many men. And " therefore that he did not express the matter lively and " naturally with common speech, as Xenophon did in " Greek, but it was carried and driven forth artificially, " after too learned a sort."

His judg-
ment of
Sallust.

Asch.
Schoolmast.
p. 646.

Hence also we may see his approbation of that Greek historian before mentioned; and upon what reason, *viz.* because his style is so natural, and flowing with easy language, accommodated without any great labour to every reader, and whatever art he wrote with, concealing it.

And Xeno-
phon.

He was a great admirer of Demosthenes, another Greek author, esteeming him the perfectest orator that ever wrote; and that for this reason among others, that he applied himself so closely to the understanding of the common people, and could so raise their affections; and that

And De-
mosthenes.

he drove mainly at the promoting of virtuous undertak-
ings, and inspired men with a great honour and love to
their country, as was told before.

So that these books, with some few more, (and it was
no great matter if all the rest were laid aside,) were sufficient, in his judgment, to make a substantial learned man;
and withal to make him wise and good; which indeed is
the true end of learning. For Ascham, who conversed
much with Cheke, reports, that he often heard him say,
" I would have a good student pass rejoicing through all
" authors, both Greek and Latin; but he that will dwell
" in these few books only, first, in God's holy Bible, and
" then join with it Tully in Latin, Plato, Aristotle, Xe-
" nophon, Isocrates, and Demosthenes in Greek, must
" needs prove an excellent man."

Another part of Cheke's criticism consisted in his exquisite skill in *imitation;* as a great part of scholarship is
seen in imitating well the good authors one reads. For
this is one of the great ends and benefits of reading, to attain to those peculiar excellences of writing and speaking
that our authors were noted for; an art not so easy to be
obtained; for there is great difference between *aping* and
sound imitation. Cheke made great attainments herein,
and that partly by a curious observing how Tully imitated
Demosthenes: how he retained thus much of the matter,
these sentences, these words. Again, how this and that
he left out, which he did willingly to a certain end and
purpose: how he added in one place, and diminished in
another: how one thing he ordered one way, by placing
it here, not there; and how he altered and changed either
in property of words, in form of sentence, in substance of
the matter, or in one or other convenient circumstance of
the author's present purpose. By these critical observations of his, which he discovered and explained to Mr.
Ascham, he was enabled to lay down certain rules for imitation, which he did in his *Scholarcha,* or " Schoolmaster:"
in which he wrapt up all the necessary tools and instruments, wherewith true imitation is right wrought withal

in any tongue. " Which tools," he confessed, " were not
" his own forging, but partly borrowed out of the shop of
" John Sturmius, a learned foreigner, and partly left unto
" him by the cunningest master, and one of the worthiest
" gentlemen that ever England bred," [meaning Sir John
Cheke.] " These rules," Ascham said, " he left to his
" children; and as they used them right, he should be
" more glad," he said, " than if he were able to leave
" them a great quantity of land."

His judg-
ment in
translation.
Cheke had also an excellent judgment in *translation*,
and a notable faculty that way; a good and useful piece of
learning; to translate properly out of Greek into Latin,
and Greek or Latin into our mother tongue. To the
doing of which there must be a thorough skill in the languages, and a treasure of proper words and phrases and
idioms of speech. He had a practice relating hereunto,
which some of his hearers made a remark upon; that
when he was reading Latin or Greek, he would often
English his matter upon a sudden, by looking on the book
only; without reading or construing any thing at all. A

Dr. Wylson. usage, saith the remarker, very profitable for all men, as
well for the understanding of the book, as also for the
aptness of framing the author's meaning, and bettering
thereby their judgments, and therewithal perfecting their
tongues and utterance.

Wylson's
commenda-
tion of
Cheke's
transla-
tions.
Cheke's translations of divers select pieces of some of
the best Greek authors into Latin, shew his skill this way.
And Dr. Wylson in some critical observations upon the
Latin translators of Demosthenes, (as namely, Hieron.
Wolfius, Christopherus Hegendorphius, Melancthon, Joa-
chim Camerarius, Petrus Clobardus, Nicolas Car,) gives
this character of Cheke; " Mr. Cheke, whom I dare match
" with any other before-named, for his knowledge in the
" Greek tongue, having travailed in Demosthenes as much
" as any of them all, and famous for his learning through-
" out Europe: yet [for I will not conceal what Wylson
" thinks fit to add] was he never so passing in this trans-
" lation, that no exception could be made against him."

He was a critic also in the *pronunciation* and *orthogra-* SECT.
phy of the learned languages. As to the former, *viz.* his ___III.___

endeavour to make a reformation in the University, of a Corrects the
very bad and false way of sounding and uttering the Greek pronuncia-
language, stirred up a great deal of dust, (as we heard learned lan-
partly before in the history,) and had not a few adversaries, guages.
who generally were of the elder sort, or favourers of Popery; and so dreaded any thing that looked like innovation. The chief of these was Dr. Caius, who asserted,
that neither France, Germany, nor Italy owned any such
pronunciation. Cheke could not endure that noble language, the Greek, to be so ignorantly read: whereby the
gracefulness of the sound of it was much impeached, besides the palpable falseness of pronouncing, in confounding the vowels and diphthongs one with another. But
the Bishop of Winton, Chancellor of Cambridge, sided
with Cheke's adversaries, and made a peremptory decree
for the continuance of the bad way of pronouncing the
Greek. Hereupon a great controversy was begun between the said Bishop and Cheke; who, out of his love to
Greek, and the useful learning attainable by the study of
it, could not away with this decree. And seeing that all Expostu-
his pains, in instructing the sholars his auditors in this Gardiner
particular, was like to come to nothing, thought con- about
venient to take up his pen, and in an eloquent letter to Greek.
expostulate this matter freely with the Chancellor; yet
with all due deference to a person of his quality, and so
much advanced above him. The Chancellor in another
letter shewed all his art and learning, for the confirming
of his former order, and for the persuading and convincing
of Cheke, if he could.

Whereupon they entered into an epistolary conflict to- An episto-
gether concerning this argument. Winchester contended lary con-
to have the old way of reading Greek kept upon the au- tween Win-
thority of custom. Cheke on the contrary urged the chester and
amendment of the sounds, because the old were certainly
false. Winchester warned Cheke, that he should not be- Winches-
come an author to the youth, to frame any sounds, either ments.

of the Latin or Greek language by his own conjectures, other than what they had received from their ancestors, or which the learned then retained.——That he would not be too much a Stoic in weighing of sounds; and to remember, that as words, so also sounds, receive their authority from use and from reason. *Utere,* added he, *antiquis moribus, verbis vero præsentibus, et multo magis sonis;* i. e. " Use ancient manners, but present words, and " much more sounds." That he feared, if Cheke proceeded in these new matters, that he would turn Cambridge into Babylon by a woful metamorphosis, or, if any thing, be more confused than Babylon.

Cheke had objected, that letters and sounds were changed and defiled in the last barbarous age, which it was better to cleanse and restore, than to imitate. And for this he appealed to Erasmus, and other learned men that had taken notice of these errors. But the Bishop said, " they did not shew a contamination in the sounds of let-
" ters, but a mutation only : which he acknowledged there
" was in the present sounds; but yet affirmed, that every
" change was not to be disproved; and that the sounds of
" letters were more likely to be changed by the learned,
" [than the illiterate common sort,] since the learned were
" wont to take heed to *euphony,* [that is, agreeable and
" grateful sound,] whereas the vulgar regarded it not so
" much. And that Cheke being persuaded by a ridiculous
" collection concerning the use of writing, supposed all to
" be uttered that was written; and so brought in upon
" the ears of the present age, that absurd and ill sound,
" which by fallacious conjectures he thought he had
" found to be that which the ancients used. He insisted
" upon that argument, that it was convenient and decent
" to pronounce according to the custom and mode of the
" present age, a new way of pronouncing words being so
" surprising, and the reducing it to the use of the an-
" cients, offensive to people's ears." Thus when Cheke would have the Greek Υ not pronounced like ἰῶτα [as they then used to do,] but like the letter U, the Bishop, for ex-

ample, brought the word KYSS, which he said no man would pronounce KUSS, the old rude way of sounding that word, instead of KYSS the modern way: when people for the more handsomeness of speech had mollified the U into I. And so Winchester would have had the way of pronouncing the Greek U by I, to have been done, not ignorantly, but by judgment, and for the sake of urbanity. The Bishop added a verse made by one Nic. Rowle, an old contemporary of his at the University, who, being a witty man, made a difference between a *foul* and a *fair* maid, only by the sound of the same word, *virgo.*

Si pulchra est VIRGO, *sin turpis* VULGO *vocetur.*

But that Cheke had no regard to this, whereby he made himself ridiculous. Therefore where Cheke urged that the way he endeavoured to bring in, was the reducing sounds to their first and original truth, Winchester answered, " [a] Let all things have their age and their youth, and as " words do words, so let us allow sounds to succeed " sounds."

Besides this, he laid to his charge arrogance and rashness; and added, " that it were much better, that the " Greek language itself with its sounds were wholly ba- " nished, than that youth by his teaching should imbibe " rashness, arrogance, and vanity, most pernicious pests " to all the rest of the life. And he complained, that now " by his means the young men insulted over the old; and " being guilty of an exotic way of pronunciation, made it " a kind of delight, that they were not understood of their " seniors. And all that he would allow the Greek Pro- " fessor was, that in reading his Greek lectures, he might " instruct his auditors, as concerning old words, so con- " cerning the old sounds; that they might know them, " but not use them; that they became not ridiculous to " all. In short, he charged him, that he were not the " cause *malum bene positum de loco movendi,* i. e. 'of re-

---

[a] Sit rebus omnibus suum senium, sua juventus, et ut verba verbis, sic etiam sonis sonos suos succedere permittamus.

" moving an evil well placed :' especially when that which
" he called *evil* being taken away, he had nothing that-was
" *good* to put in the place of it."

Cheke's ar-
guments
against
Winchester.
This was the substance of the arguments, ingenious
enough, that the Chancellor of the University used.   But
Cheke, with a due deference, and yet with a scholarlike
freedom, learnedly asserted his reasons and refutation of
what the said Chancellor had writ with so much plausibi-
lity against all reforming of abuses in learning, as well as
in religion.   His business was to shew, how evidently
false the present way of sounding many of the letters and
vowels was.   And then he thought no scruple could be
made, but that they ought to be rectified; and whatsoever
was amiss ought to be amended, and not to persist in a
known error.   And for example he shewed how in one
word, consisting but of three syllables, there were as
many evident errors in the pronouncing.   As in the word
κυβέρνω, which was commonly then pronounced *chiverno ;*
to wit, by mispronouncing all the three first letters.   Likewise in pronouncing οι the diphthong as the letter ἰῶτα,
whereby no manner of difference was made between two
different words in Greek, *viz.* λοιμὸς *pestis,* and λιμὸς
fames.   And the diphthong that consisted of two vowels
was sounded but as one.   At length he brought all these
on his side, *viz.* the authority of the ancients, the perpetual consent of the old grammarians, the benefit of learning, sweetness in speaking, perspicuity and clearness in
pronouncing.

" That he could not be convicted neither of rashness,
" boldness, nor arrogance, though the Bishop had laid it
" to his charge.   Not of rashness, because he was ready
" to acquiesce in the judgment of the most learned and
" most ancient men.   Not of confident boldness, in that
" he approved of the consent of almost all ages : nor of
" arrogance, if he refuted such things as were crept in un-
" justly and unprofitably, by the authority of eminent and
" knowing men.

" That therefore he thought he should be rather che-

" rished and encouraged by him, their learned Chancellor,
" for his endeavour to reduce the Greek language to its
" true antiquity; and that he should have been assisted
" by his authority in the whole matter of antiquity; since
" it appeared, that he was himself studious of all anti-
" quity, and did with all his heart and will dislike and ab-
" hor all the innovation of later memory.   For it was not
" novelty, to discover this way of pronouncing Greek
" words according to the truth; since it was only inter-
" mitted and laid away for a time.   Nor was this to inno-
" vate any thing, to introduce that which was ancient and
" profitable."

He added moreover, " that such was his success, when
" he first propounded this reformation in the language,
" that it was received with much applause and commenda-
" tion; and, except a few, that would rather seem to be
" Grecians than were so indeed, all that either read or
" understood the language, were so convinced and well
" pleased with this true way, that they all used it.   And
" the benefit of reading Greek this way was, that they
" that learnt it profited more in the knowledge of it in a
" year, than they did before in two; and arrived much
" sooner to an ability of speaking and writing it; which
" took up a very long time before.   And this the experi-
" ence of some years shewed.   That there was so much de-
" light and sweetness now perceived in Homer's or So-
" phocles's verses, by reason of the variety of sounds and
" modulation of the numbers, that no music, no lute could
" be more pleasant.   Further, that this that he [Cheke]
" did now in the Greek, was no more in effect than his
" Lordship himself had done, when he resided at Cam-
" bridge, and was Reader of the Civil Law there; at
" which time he endeavoured commendably to purge that
" study; and turned the minds of the students thereof
" from the Glossematarians: and thereby he ran into great
" offence of some, and had great contention about it.

" That this opposition by many in the University, to
" the right sounding of the Greek, seemed to spring from

"a dislike of the language itself. As some in the ages
"past were jealous of all the learned languages, Latin,
"Greek, and Hebrew; and affecting ignorance rather.
"When the Latin tongue began to be replaced, it was
"received not without great commotion, and indignation
"of men's minds. The Greek language was odious to
"many, and yet it is; and some there were that dis-
"couraged youth from the knowledge of it. The Hebrew
"hath its reprovers, that the study of it puts the learner's
"fame and reputation into danger. That it was but a few
"years ago, but he that spake better Latin than the rest
"was esteemed as arrogant, was derided as rude. When
"in truth this came to pass, not by the fault of the
"speaker, but the fault of the hearers. Nor was it any
"such misery, to be laughed at by such, who indeed are
"themselves chiefly to be laughed at; because they know
"not what it is they deride: and as usually naughty per-
"sons seek occasion in the best things to make sport, so
"wise men do not regard so much to accommodate them-
"selves to the opinion of the multitude."

I have been large upon this point; and that partly because this reforming the Greek pronunciation is one of the
chief things redounds to the honour of Cheke's memory;
and partly, that the reader may be entertained a little with
the fine spirit that ran through Cheke's discourses.

Here I may subjoin a merry story, that Richard Cheny
(afterwards Bishop of Glocester) told to Sir William
Cecil, concerning this ill pronouncing of Greek, which
Cheke, as we heard, laboured to reform. That he, the
said Cheny, had lately been at Oxford, (it was about the
beginning of Queen Elizabeth's reign,) where this controversy of pronouncing Greek had flown from Cambridge to
that other University. There he had some conversation
with certain learned men: among whom were Dr. Babington, Dr. Wright, Archdeacon of Oxford, and the Provost
of Oriel college. Discourse happening concerning the
true way of pronouncing Greek, and they stiffly defending
the usual manner of pronouncing it; Cheny replied, "Be-

" ware, my masters, that whilst you wilfully go about to
" defend an untruth in this matter, you fall not into such
" an inconvenience as I once knew a Bishop do." And
when they would know how and where, he said, he sat
once at table with a Bishop that did as you do, defend the
untrue pronunciation of the letter ἦτα, [that is, as ἰῶτα,]
and that after he had declared many absurdities that followed thereon, he desired him to read a few words written
in the xxviith of Matthew : the Bishop immediately called
for the Testament in Greek : Cheny appointed him a line or
two. Where among other words he read these, Ἡλὶ, ἠλὶ,
λαμὰ σαβαχθανὶ, " Making false Greek," saith Cheny, " but
" true English ; pronouncing plainly, *I ly*, *I ly*." Whereupon, not without mirth, Dr. Babington presented Cheny
with Cheke's book of that argument.

Another piece of that exactness that was in Cheke ap- His care
peared in his care about orthography, that is, for true and about the orthogra-
right writing, as well as pronouncing. And here both the phy of La-
Latin and our mother tongue fell under his correction. As tin.
for the Latin, that it might be spoken truly, and the syllables in reading pronounced long or short, according to
their nature, he devised a way to write the vowels according to their quantity. As the long vowel O, after this
manner, ω, like a Greek *omega*, as in *uxωrem, liberωs*. And
the long I with two tittles over it, as in *divinitus*. And as
for the long E, especially the diphthong, which before was
commonly writ as the ordinary E, he put a tail to it, as in
le)tor : and so I find he wrote in some of his letters ; yet
I observe in his writings after, he did not so much regard
it, excepting the E diphthong.

And whereas the writing and spelling of our English And of
tongue was in those times very bad, even scholars them- English.
selves taking little heed how they spelt, (as appears
both by the MSS. and books then printed,) he endeavoured the correcting and regulating thereof, in these respects following : 1. He would have none of the letter E
put to the end of words, as needless and unexpressive of
any sounds ; as in these words, *excus, giv, deceiv, prais,*

VII.
commun : unless where it is sounded, and then to be writ
with a double E, as in *necessitee.* 2. Where the letter A
was sounded long, he would have it writ with a double A,
in distinction from A short; as in *maad, straat, daar.* 3.
Where the letter I was sounded long, to be writ with a
double I, as in *desiir, liif.* 4. He wholly threw out the
letter Y out of the alphabet, as useless, and supplied it
ever with I, as *mi, sai, awai.* 5. U long he wrote with a
long stroke over it, as in *presūm.* 6. The rest of the long
vowels he would have to be written with double letters, as
weer, theer, (and sometimes *thear,*) *noo, noon, adoo, thoos,
loov,* to avoid an E at the end. 7. Letters without sound
he threw out; as in these words, *frutes, wold, faut, dout,
again* for *against, hole, meen* for *mean.* And 8. changed
the spelling in some words, to make them the better expressive of the sounds; as in *gud, britil, praisabil, suffer-
abil.*

The Eng-
lish lan-
guage im-
proved by
him.
And here I must add, that he laboured much in the restoration of our English language. Dr. Wylson before-
mentioned asserted, that he had better skill in our English speech, to judge of the phrases and properties of
words, and to divide sentences, than any else had that he
knew; and that he was thought, by some judicious men,
greatly to have improved the language by a practice he
had, when he read his Greek lectures, to take the book,
and only looking upon the Greek, to read it into English:
whereby he did not only give a clearer understanding of
the author, but enabled his hearers the better to judge of
the things, and to perfect their tongue and utterance, as
was remembered before.

What he did further for the English language was, that
he brought in a short and expressive way of writing,
Allowed not
of foreign
words in the
English
tongue.
without long and intricate periods. And moreover, in
writing any discourse, he would allow no words but such
as were true English, or of Saxon original; suffering no
adoption of any foreign word into the English speech,
which he thought was copious enough of itself, without
borrowing words from other countries. Thus in his own

translations into English he would not use any but pure SECT.
III.
English phrase and expression: which indeed made his
style here and there a little affected and hard; and forced
him to use sometimes odd and uncouth words, as *de-*
siirful, ungrevous, tollers for *publicans, &c.*; which perhaps might occasion that rude character Sir John Hayward gave of him, " allowing his eloquence in the Latin Hayward's
" and Greek tongues; but for other sufficiencies, so far as censure of
Cheke cen-
" it appears by his books, pedantic enough." A censure sured.
too rash upon a man of such fame and learning, and indeed Life of Ed-
ward VI.
bespake Hayward to be but little acquainted with him or
his books; being far otherwise thought on by those
learned men his contemporaries that well knew him, and
wanted not for skill to judge of men. But to return where
we were, that indeed was Cheke's conceit, that in writing
English none but English words should be used, thinking
it a dishonour to our mother tongue, to be beholden to
other nations for their words and phrases to express our
minds.

Upon this account Cheke seemed to dislike the English Goes about
translation of the Bible, because in it there were so many a new trans-
lation of the
foreign words: which made him once attempt a new New Testa-
translation of the New Testament; and he completed the ment.,
Miscellan.
Gospel of St. Matthew, and made an entrance into St. D. C.C.C.
Mark; wherein all along he laboured to use only true C.
English Saxon words. The original under his own hand
still remains in the MS. library at Bene't college, Cambridge. A specimen whereof, for the reader's diversion, I
shall here set down.

The common translation.	*Cheke's translation.*
MATT. I.	MATT. I.
17. So all the generations from Abraham to David are fourteen generations; and from David until the carrying away into Babylon are	17. Therefor from Abraham unto David there wer fourteen degrees; and from David unto the out-peopling to Babylon, fourteen de-

fourteen generations, and from the carrying away into Babylon unto Christ are fourteen generations.

18. Now the birth of Jesus Christ was on this wise. When as his mother Mary was espoused to Joseph (before they came together) she was found with child of the Holy Ghost.

19. Then Joseph her husband, being a just man, and not willing to make her a public example, was minded to put her away privily.

20. But when he thought on these things, behold, the angel of the Lord appeared unto him in a dream, &c.

grees; and from the outpeopling to Babylon unto Christ, fourteen degrees.

18. And Jesus Christs birth was after this sort. After his mother Mari was ensured to Joseph, before thei weer cupled together, she was preived to be with child; and it was indeed by the Holi Ghoost.

19. But Joseph her husband, being a just man, and loth to use extremitee toward her, entended privili to divorse himself from her.

20. And being in this mind, lo the angel of the Lord appeired bi dream, &c.

CHAP. II.

16. Then Herod, when he saw that he was mocked of the wise men, &c.

CHAP. II.

16. Then Herod seeing that he was plaid withal by the wise-heards, &c.

Yet one may observe in this so over-laboured a translation, (as I may term it,) he is forced to make use of several words of foreign derivation.

Fair writing improved by Cheke. Add this lastly to the rest of the regulations Cheke made of the English, that he brought in fair and graceful writing by the pen, as he wrote an excellent, accurate hand himself. And all the best scholars in those times practised to write well. So did Smith and Cecil, and especially Ascham; who, for his exquisite hand, was the person appointed to teach the Lady Elizabeth to write. So that fair writing and good learning seemed to commence together.

SECT. IV.

Cheke an author. His writings.

AND as our learned man was furnished with all good learning, so he occasionally wrote upon several, both learned and pious subjects for the general good; namely, in divinity, as well as other human learning. The catalogue of his books and writings, printed or unprinted, is given us by the author of the *Heroologia;* and Dr. Langbain follows him; but taken by both (or at least by the former) out of Bale's Centuries; and that imperfectly, and erroneously in some things, and withal displacing the order of them. I shall present them as they lie in Bale, and add some cursory conjectures and observations upon some of them.

1. *De Pronuntiatione Græca.* This was writ in Latin, and afterwards printed; and was nothing else but the learned letters that passed between Cheke and the Bishop of Winton, concerning the pronouncing of Greek; which being printed at Basil, were entitled, *De recta Linguæ Græcæ Pronuntiatione.*

2. *Damna ex Seditione,* i. e. "The Losses by Sedition." This was writ and printed in English, for the public service of the kingdom in a rebellion anno 1549; and the book (which is well enough known) is entitled, *The faithful Subject to the Rebel.*

3. *In quosdam Psalmos.*

4. *In Psalmum, Domine probasti.* These, I suppose, were nothing but some pious meditations of his.

5. *De Fide justificante.* Against the Papists, no question.

6. *De Eucharistiæ Sacramento.* Whether this were his disputations with Feckenham against transubstantiation, or something else, it is uncertain to me.

7. *In Obitum D. Anthonii Dennei;* beginning, *Cum claras hominum vitas.* This Sir Anthony Denny was bred at St. John's college, an excellent scholar, and a person of

great worth, whose merits raised him to be one of the bedchamber to Henry VIII. and one of his Privy Council. The deserved esteem Cheke had for him, as well as ancient acquaintance with him, made him honour his memory with an heroic poem : which shall follow by and by.

8. *Super Mortem Buceri.* This perhaps is his epistle to Peter Martyr, Bucer's dear friend, consolatory concerning his death. It is printed in Bucer's *Scripta Anglicana,* and elsewhere. Unless it should rather mean the *Epicedium,* which Cheke bestowed upon that most learned divine; which shall be set down among his epitaphs, to preserve as much as we can of the worthy man we are giving the history of.

9. *Epitaphiorum lib. 1.* This one book of epitaphs, or inscriptions and verses upon persons deceased, means no more, but according to Bale's way, that these epitaphs, if they were all collected, might be sufficient to make one book. Of this sort, besides his verses upon Denny and Bucer, were probably the monumental inscriptions upon his patron, Dr. Butts, in Fulham church, and upon Richard Hills, his wife's father, buried in the church of Queenhith, mentioned before. And hitherto may be reduced an English elegy, wherein the sickness of King Edward, together with the circumstances of time and place, and his death, is described, (if we may believe it,) and was printed, anno
Heroologia. 1610, by H. Holland, as he tells us himself.

His poetry. For he was no stranger to poetry. What his abilities were in this art, may be seen by these funeral verses upon some of his friends; which I have retrieved, and think not amiss to preserve, as some further remains of his studies.

MARIÆ CICELLÆ Sororis Checi, Uxoris D. Guil. Cicelli, Epitaphium. Quæ obiit Mense Februario, an. Dom. 1554.

Ὀστέα τῆς Μαρίας Σισέλλης ἔνθαδε κεῖται,
Πνεῦμα τελευτώσης κύριος αὐτὸς ἔχει.
Ἡ πατρὸς μητρός τ᾽ ἀγαθοῖν, ἀνδρός τ᾽ ἀγαθοῖο
Οὖσα, καλῷ θανατὸν καλὸν ἔθηκε βίῳ.

In Obitum D. Martini Buceri.

Vita gravis misero, gravior mors ; sed tibi tanto
　Mors nec vita potest esse, Bucere, gravis.
Vita fuit Christus, mors lucrum ; vivere cessas
　Naturæ, ac Christo vita perennis adest.
Alma fides Christi, quam tu super astra ferebas,
　Te super astra eadem sustulit alma fides.
Cumque tui mores, pietas, doctrina probentur,
　Mors tua non gravis est, et gravis est eadem.
Mors gravis est nobis, orbatis lumine tanto,
　Non gravis est tibi, quæ vita beata tibi est.
Doctrinæ studium, vitæ constantia, mortis
　Exitus, O! idem sit mihi, Christe, precor.

In Antonium Deneium clarissimum virum.
Carmen heroicum.

Cum claras hominum vitas modulata Thalia,
Gloria quos celebreis altum in subvexit Olympum :
Aptaret digitis numeros ad carmina suavis,
Certaretque alias cantando vincere Musas ;
Interpres subito divum Cyllenius alis
Præpetibus venit, in medium seque ingerit agmen :
Atque inter medias illas est deinde locutus.

Nata Jovis, medium tu nunc abrumpito carmen,
Argutos nunc linque sonos numerosque fluentes,
Te vocat omnipotens Genitor divumque hominumque,
Te manet ad citharam doctus crinitus Apollo,
Te manet et reliquum cælestis turba Deorum.
Desine nunc laudem veterum, et clarorum heroum.
Sunt molienda tibi nova carmina, plena laborum,
Queis poteris veterum laudes superare canendo.
Materiam nacta es claram, te pulcher Apollo
Invitat, vireisque suas in carmine jactat :
Alternis tecum contendet versibus. Ergo
Sume animum, depone metum, præstantia quanta
Sit tibi, declara : poteris vicisse canendo.
Deneius venit ad superos mortalia linquens,
Britannos inter clarus (laus maxima quorum est,

Omnes quod veræ sint relligionis amantes,
Et pia vota Deo faciunt, Christique sequantur
Doctrinam, Sanctis longe lateque patentem
Scripturis, parvo totamque volumine clausam.)
Quis dignam illius factis vocem, quis promere verba.
Possit, et excelsas laudes æquare canendo?
Quæ pietas, et quanta viri? Quis fervor in illo
Relligionis erat? Quam purus cultus in illo
Cælestis patris? Quanta in Christum fidei vis
Extitit illius sacrata morte redempti?
Munera quæ rursum? Quos et libavit honores
Justitiæque speique Deo? Quæ victima laudis
Cæsa fuit? grati cordisque orisque diurna
Hostia, quam sæpe est hominum divumque parenti
Oblata in Christo. Christinam haud immemor unquam
Ille fuit, propter divinam sanguine fuso,
Mortem mortales quæ primum conciliavit,
Peccati, scelerisque ruina, et pendere pressos.

   Quid memorem HENRICUM *claro de stemmati Regem,*
HENRICUM *Octavum terræ marisque potentem?*
O! quibus hic studiis, quo illum est amplexus amore
Quem sibi subjectumque bonum, servumque fidelem
Scribat, et officia hæc haud parvo munere pensans,
Ostendit, se herumque bonum, regemque benignum.
Consiliumque lepos quantum superadditus auget,
Et juvat optatas ad res bene conficiendas,
Ille alios tantum superat, qui flectere mentem
HENRICI *potuit, miscens nunc utile dulci,*
Seria nunc levibus texens, nunc grandia parvis.
Quam facilem cursum hic aliis ad vota sequenda
Fecerat, atque aditum multis facilem patefecit?
Quam bona multa aliis, et quam mala nulla cuiquam
Intulit? Et laudem summam virtutis habebat
Hujus, qui nullos nec apertos læserat hostes.

[Hic desunt multa.]

Hic ubi dicta dedit, celeri tum concita cursu
Festinat, cytheramque novam vocemque Thalia

Præparat, ingenio divesque, et carmine felix.
Atque Jovis magni ad solium, Divosque potentes
Advolat, et vibrat tremulos ad carmina nervos.
Totum compleri tum Divis undique cælum.
Cernere erat, late sparsos ita congregat alta
Voxque sonusque Deæ, suavisque ad carmina cantus.
Tum cælum reboat totum, magnusque per alta
It clamor plaususque Deum plaususque heroum,
Nervorum fidiumque soni concentibus implent
Omnia, suffitu redolent et mascula thura,
Electra et molles aspirant pinguia odores.
Omnia DENEIUM resonant cytharæque Deique
Istos sic meritis claros accepit honores.

10. *De Nativitate Principis,* i. e. " Of the Nativity of
" the Prince." This the author of the *Heroologia* will
have to be a panegyric upon his nativity. I rather conjecture (for neither of us, I believe, saw this tract) it was
some private calculation of Prince Edward's nativity, as
Cheke studied that art, and built too much upon it.

11. *An licet nubere post Divortium,* i. e. " Whether a
" woman might marry after a divorce." A case much
handled in those times. And this seems to have been a
case put to him in behalf of a great lady, whose husband,
being a nobleman, had obtained a divorce from her.

12. *Introductio Grammaticæ.*

13. *De Ludimagistrorum Officio.* Both these seem to
have been writ primarily by him for the use of the Prince,
to whom he was schoolmaster.

14. *De Superstitione. Ad Regem Henricum.* A very
learned treatise. This was a discourse drawn up upon the
argument of *superstition,* for the use of that King, in order
to the reformation of religion, which in his reign was
much pestered with superstitions. This was set by way
of dedication before his translation of Plutarch's book of
that argument, and writ in a very elegant Latin style.

The book is extant in the library of University college,
Oxon, curiously writ, and bound up in cloth of silver:

which makes it very probable it might be the very book that he presented to the King: as hath been signified to me by Mr. William Elstob, a Fellow of that college; now the reverend and learned Rector of St. Swithin's, London. This is now published in English at the end of this work by his care.

15. *De Cineribus et Palmis. Ad Vintoniensem.* Gardiner Bishop of Winchester was earnest with the Lord Protector for the retaining the old usages in the Church, and particularly sprinkling ashes on Ash Wednesday, and

Acts and
Monum.
carrying palms on Palm Sunday. There is a letter of his writ to the Lord Protector on that subject. Perhaps the said Lord put Cheke upon giving an answer to that letter. To these books and tracts mentioned by Bale, I add these not mentioned by him:

16. *De Ecclesia; an potest errare:* i. e. " Of the " Church; whether it can err." Wrote in Latin, yet extant among the Foxian MSS. It is an argument learnedly managed by him against the Papists. Wherein he proceeded upon these questions: Whether there be a Church; what the Church is; and whether it can err.

17. His Epistles. Whereof several are extant; as his Epistle to Peter Martyr at Oxford, concerning the death of Martin Bucer. Another letter consolatory to Dr. Haddon in his sickness, very pious and devout, besides divers others before mentioned.

18. His two *recantations* might have been mentioned; but that in truth they were no further his, than as he uttered them with his mouth, but did not compose them.

19. Another branch of his labours be his *translations.* Some whereof were done out of Greek into Latin: and several undoubtedly for the use of his royal scholar, *viz.* I. Divers pieces of St. Chrysostom: as, *De Fato,* homiliæ tres; *De Providentia,* hom. tres; *Contra Observatores Novilunii,* hom. 1; *De Dormientibus in Christo,* hom. 1; together with other pieces of that ancient Father. II. Josephus's Antiquities, five books. III. Leo *de Apparatu Bellico,* lib. 1. This Leo was the Emperor Leo V. who

writ a book in Greek, *Of the Slights and Policies of War.* SECT.
From Ascham we have this account of the book, and Cheke's   IV.
translation of it: "That it was a rare book seldome heard Toxoph. f.
" of; that Cheke dedicated his translation of it to King   24 b.
" Henry VIII. while he was at Cambridge; and that of his
" gentleness would have Ascham very oft in his chamber,
" and for the familiarity he had with him, more than many
" other, would suffer him to read of it when he would.
" The which thing to do," Ascham saith, " he was very
" desirous and glad, because of the excellend handling of
" al things that ever he took in hand." *Ascham, Eng.*
Works, p. 104. IV. *Asceticum Maximi Monachi,* lib. 1.
V. *Plutarchus de Superstitione,* lib. 1. VI. Several pieces
of Demosthenes; as his *Philippics,* lib. 3. His *Olynthiacs,*
lib. 3. *Adversus Leptinem,* lib. 1. Demosthenes and
Æschines, their *adverse Orations,* lib. 1. VII. Sophocles,
translated *ad literam,* lib. 1. VIII. Euripides also, lib. 1.
IX. Aristotle *de Anima,* lib. 1. All these out of Greek
into Latin.

Other of his translations were out of English into Latin;
as the Archbishop of Canterbury's book of the Lord's Supper: this book was printed abroad. The Communion
Book: this was done for the use of Bucer, that he might
understand it, and give his judgment of it; it is extant
in his *Opuscula Anglicana.* And lastly, out of Greek into
English, he translated the Gospel of St. Matthew, before
spoken of.

Add to the rest of his writings and learned labours, that
he collected the arguments and reasons of both sides,
upon the business of the Eucharist in Parliament: where
that point was learnedly and largely debated, when the
Communion Book was appointed. He also made some
corrections of Herodotus, Thucydides, Plato, Demosthenes,
Xenophon, and other Greek authors. This is all we know
of the fruits of his learned head, though no question this
catalogue is very imperfect, and that he did write much
more than we at this distance know. But this is sufficient
to inform us what a scholar he was.

CHAP.
VII.

Cheke also translated the New Testament into English, with annotations; which was printed both in octavo and decimo sexto, but this last without the notes; which copy Christopher Barker, Queen Elizabeth's printer, gave to the Company of Stationers anno 1583, with some others, for the relief of the poor of the said Company; as appears by

Penes me.

a MS. relating to the Company in these words: " The " profit and benefit of the two most vendible volumes of " the New Testament in English, commonly called Mr. " Cheke's translation, that is, in the volume called octavo, " with annotations as they be now, and in the volume " called decimo sexto of the same translation, without " notes in the Brevier English letter onely.

" Provided that Mr. Barker himself print the said Tes- " taments at the lowest value, by the direction of the " Master and Wardens of the Company of Stationers for " the time being. Provided always, that Mr. Barker do " retein some smal number of these for divers services " in her Majesties Courts, or elsewhere."

CHAP. VIII.

Some observations upon Sir John Cheke's religion and
principles. His fortune and his fall. The Conclusion.

SECT. I.

Cheke's religion.

BUT that which advanced the value of Cheke's learning How Cheke
was, that it was seasoned with religion and the fear of came to re-
God. This sanctified his learning, and put him upon
study, to render his parts and abilities useful for the promoting and doing of good. To stay therefore a little upon
that great consideration of him, *viz.* his *religion.* Upon
good and substantial grounds, he was a hearty professor
of the reformed religion, which he took not up upon a pre-
carious account, or any secular reason or interest; but
upon mature examination and trial of the principles of
that religion that generally swayed, and was professed in
his time. He, being of an inquisitive philosophical mind,
first of all began to doubt of the great distinguishing Popish doctrine, That the body and blood of Christ is sub-
stantially and carnally present in the Sacrament; because
he saw it so far beyond all possibility of being reconciled
to reason and sense. Afterwards also, he heard other
learned men call this doctrine into question, by inquiring,
whether those words, that the Papists built their doctrine
upon, *This is my body*, were not a figurative way of
speech, as many other expressions were in Scripture, or
were to be understood in the very letter.

And for the better enlightening himself, and satisfying His course
his mind in this controversy, he took the right course, *viz.* to inform
to examine the Scriptures, which were the word of God;
and likewise the ancient Doctors of the Church, that had
their writings still extant. Many places, both in them and
in the Scripture, he found to impugn that opinion, and to

favour the figurative sense. He considered also, that whereas the literal sense made all men, and particularly the Jews, to abhor the doctrine, and consequently the religion too; the other sense would take off that abhorrency out of their minds. Then he became confirmed in this opinion of the spiritual sense, partly by reading the late books of the learned Germans, and observing what numbers in those parts fell off from Popery, and partly by taking notice of the providence of God in this realm, that is, in King Edward's days, wherein this doctrine was generally embraced; and all masses and other superstitions rejected, and thrown out of the Church. He observed also, how the Scriptures were more studied by learned men, and well examined, much beyond what was done in former times, when that doctrine was less doubted of: and he concluded, that it was brought in when men began to fall from the study of the Scriptures, and gave themselves to their own inventions, which was in the days after the Apostles and primitive age; and that as men grew more and more slack and loose in their lives, and sensibly fell short of the primitive Christians, so they sunk further into errors and mistakes in religion. And observing, how in the latest times the Clergy was visibly and fearfully apostatized from the holy lives of the ancient Fathers; and gave themselves to other studies, almost wholly neglecting the study of the Scriptures, (whereby they became by God's just judgment blind,) and that as the study of the Scriptures came into Germany and other parts, so more light in matters of religion came in with it; upon these firm and sure grounds, he concluded that the faith he stood in was the true faith of the Catholic Church. And all this was but the sum of what he confessed at his recantation; but was forced to revoke it, and to acknowledge it to have been the very ground of his running into error and heresy.

SECT. II.

His religious practices.

AND his life bore a proportion unto his principles. He His life. made it his business to do good, and to help persons in necessity, and to promote works of charity. For these ends he used his interest with the King, whensoever there was occasion, or application made to him. He was one of the three, Cecil and Cook being the two other, (to which we may add Sir John Gates, the Vice-Chamberlain, for a fourth,) noted for their furthering all good causes at Court, that respected either religion or learning. Hence it was, that Bishop Ridley called him " one of Christ's principal " proctors."

When the reverend Miles Coverdale, anno 1551, was Forwards appointed Bishop of Exeter, an excellent and able preacher Bishop Co- verdale's of the Gospel, and thence judged very fit to govern the business. Church, and to preach in those western parts, much over-run with Popery and ignorance, and to settle matters of religion there after a dangerous rebellion : yet notwith-standing his business stuck at Court, whereby his going down was hindered. Cranmer, Archbishop of Canterbury, was troubled at these delays, and sent a letter to Secre-tary Cecil, joining Cheke with him, to get this business hastened; that so he, the Archbishop, might have order for his consecration, (which some, it seems, obstructed,) and so he might go down unto his bishopric, which, the Archbishop said, needed him. And it was soon after des-patched.

But to poor strangers, chiefly divines or scholars, that Charitable had fled their country for the preserving of their religion, to poor strangers. and had left friends, and habitations, and livelihood, for the sake of their consciences; to these he had a special compassion, and was their sure friend. There is a letter I A Greek have seen in Greek of Cheke's writing to his brother Cecil, Bishop ap- plies to him. in behalf of a poor foreign Bishop, whose name indeed I cannot retrieve, but he was one that came over into England, and seemed to have business with the Protector, and applied himself first to Sir John Cheke: whose cause he espoused, and wrote earnestly in his letter to the said Cecil, who was now Master of Requests to the Lord Protector, to get him speech of the said Protector, and to assist him in his matters; adding, that what he should do for him, should be as well taken as though it were his own business. This was, I suppose, some poor persecuted Greek Bishop; and that to be the reason why Cheke wrote his letter in Greek, that this Bishop, who was the bearer of it, might understand the import of it; which, being short, I shall here insert.

Δέομαί σοι ἀδελφὲ φίλτατε βοηθεῖν τούτῳ τῷ καλῳκαγαθῷ ἀνδρὶ ἐπισκόπῳ ξένῳ, ἀπόρῳ, ἠγνοημένῳ. θέλει προθύμως ἰδεῖν καὶ λαλεῖν μετὰ τοῦ προτέκτωρος. σὺ δὲ εἰ ἀντιλαμβάνεις τῶν πραγμάτων αὐτοῦ, οὕτως χαρίεν ποιήσεις μοι, ὡς ἂν εἴη τὰ πράγματα μοῦ· ἔρρωσο τῇ δεκάτῃ τοῦ ὀκτοβροῦ. Ἀσπάζομαι τὴν ἀδελφὴν μοῦ.

τῷ ἀδελφῷ αὐτοῦ κῷ Γουλιελμῷ Σισέλλῳ   ὁ σὸς ἀδελφὸς
τῷ δούλῳ κοῦ Προτέκτωρος ἐν σχήνῃ.   Ἰωάννης Κῆκος.

Which is thus in English;

" I pray you, dearest brother, to help this good honest
" man, a Bishop, a stranger, needy, unknown. He would
" willingly see and speak with the Protector. If you are
" assisting to his affairs, you shall do me such a favour, as
" though the business were mine own. Farewel the 8th
" of October. My commendations to my sister,

To my brother Mr. Will.   " Your brother,
Sicell, servant to the L.   " JOHN CHEKE."
Protector, in Shene.

Another point of his charity appeared, in that he was so communicative of his learning and knowledge: an excellent disposition observed in some persons of the greatest learning. This generous spirit of his was taken notice of by one who had received great advantage by it; namely, Dr. Wylson before-mentioned: who occasionally speaking to Cecil concerning Cheke, after he was dead and gone,

had these words: " As the remembrance of him is dear SECT.
II.
" unto me, for his manifold gifts and wonderful virtues; so
" did I think of his most gentle nature, and so good dis- Epist. Dedi-
cat. to De-
" posed mind, to help all those with his knowledge and mosthen.
" understanding, that any ways made means unto him, Orat.
" and sought his favour. And, so I say for myself among
" others, I found him such a friend to me, for communi-
" cating the skill and gifts of his mind, as I cannot but
" during my life speak reverently of so worthy a man, and
" honour in my heart the heavenly remembrance of him."

It must be remembered for another branch of his piety, His zeal for
true reli-
gion.
his earnest care to promote the true knowledge of religion, and the profession of it: for as upon good and sure
grounds he was convinced, and abundantly satisfied of the
Reformation of the Church of England, as it was settled
and established under King Edward, so he laboured all
that he could, that it might get more and more ground.
And he was a notable instrument at the Court, to forward
it in the minds of the young nobility, as well as in the
young King: which was one of the causes of the anger of
Queen Mary's courtiers against him, of all others. And I
cannot but think, how all succeeding generations in this
kingdom are beholden to him, under God, for the settle-
ment of that mighty blessing of the Protestant religion
among us, by the means of instilling such good principles
of sound Christianity in the head and heart of that peer-
less Prince, his royal scholar.

And how fast and firm the impressions of religion were,
that he made in that good King, there is this remarkable
instance. When upon ends of policy, as the gratifying
the Emperor Charles's request, the Privy Council inclined
to yield, that the Lady Mary should have the Mass said
in her chapel, however it was abolished by statute, Archbishop Cranmer and Bishop Ridley were sent to the King, Archbishop
Cranmer's
saying to
him.
to signify, that it was the opinion and desire of his Majesty's Council, that it should be allowed her for a time,
and that he would condescend to it. And for his satisfac- Fox's Acts,
p. 1179.
tion in point of conscience in this matter, they propounded

certain reasons to him. But the King, on the other hand,
alleged Scripture for the contrary; and that so fully to
the purpose, that the Bishops allowed the same to be true.
They descended then to other arguments to persuade him,
as the fear of breaking off good friendship with the Emperor, and what evils might succeed to the realm by wars
at that time. To which the good King again replied, that
he was ready to spend his life, and all that he had, rather
than knowingly go against the truth. But the reverend
men still endeavouring to satisfy the King in this point,
as, that it was but for the present necessity, and but a
little time, the pious Prince burst forth into tears; and
they could not forbear to weep with him; and so took
their leave. Mr. Cheke was not far off, being always near
his person: the Archbishop taking him by the hand, as he
passed, said, " Ah! Master Cheke, you may be glad all
" the days of your life, that you have such a scholar."
Adding, that " he had more divinity in his little finger,
" than we have in our whole bodies." More divinity, both
in the theory and the practice too. And this was owing
in a great measure to Cheke's instructions.

SECT. III.

Cheke's fortunes.

His fortunes
various.
HAVING seen Cheke in his abilities, and in the disposition of his mind, we shall in the next place observe him
in his *fortunes*. Which were various, as usually the condition of men in Princes' Courts are, be their virtues and
merits what they will. For as his learning preferred him
to honour, so he several times felt the effects of a cour-
tier's life : and often therefore wished heartily for a retirement; though that would not be granted him. But by
the conscientious and prudent discharge of his duty towards the Prince, he was entirely beloved by him. And
as he instructed that most noble Prince, and brought him
to great perfection in learning, knowledge, and religion,
beyond his years; so a constant sense of gratitude and

love possessed his mind towards his schoolmaster. He SECT.
III.
had the favour to stand by the King's side at his chapel,
when he was present to hear sermons: which was the His favour
with the
King.
cause that he was once brought in an evidence at the ex-
amination of Bishop Gardiner, concerning a sermon which
he was appointed by the Privy Council to make: wherein
he should declare for the satisfaction of others, concerning
the King's power and authority in his *minor* age, to wit,
that it was equal, and of the same effect, as when he
should be grown up to man's estate; which the Bishop,
after he had preached his sermon, was accused not to
have done. Whereof many witnesses were sworn to tes-
tify: and among the rest Mr. Cheke, who said, " that he
" was personally present at the said Bishop's sermon,
" standing beside the King's Majesty's person; where he
" might and did perfectly hear the Bishop."

In short, the King was a grateful scholar, and Cheke Testimonies
thereof.
was a wise instructor, that had acquired the right method
of instilling knowledge into the mind of the royal youth,
while he did it with that ease and gentleness, as raised a
love, not a hatred, (a thing that often happens to school-
masters,) an esteem, not a disaffection towards his teacher.
For how many testimonies of his good will did he heap
upon him: bestowing on him ample possessions of lands
and revenues: taking him into his Privy Chamber, confer-
ring on him the honour of knighthood; and at last making
him a Privy Counsellor, and actually constituting him one
of his principal Secretaries of State, and that when there
were two Secretaries already, which was hardly ever before or since done.

For these are the words of the minutes in the Council Cheke a
principal
Secretary.
Book; " Anno 1553, Jun. 2, Sir John Cheke was sworn
" and admitted one of the principal Secretaries of State, King Ed-
ward's
" Petre and Cicil being continued." And June 11, all three Council
Book.
Secretaries sat in Council.

And among the rest of these greater gifts of the King, I The King
gives Cheke
his clock.
must not forget the mention of one smaller, a token yet of
the love he had for him; and that was of his own clock,

by which it is probable his Majesty with his schoolmaster had studied many an hour. This clock, which he gave him, I can trace for two or three removes. From Cheke it came, whether by gift or otherwise, into the hands of Dr. Edwin Sandys; who, being Bishop of Worcester in the beginning of Queen Elizabeth, about the year 1563, made a new year's gift of this old clock to Cecil the Secretary. " Which," he said, " he was sure he would the " rather accept, because it was his old master's of happy " memory, King Edward, and after, his loving and kind " brother's." Thus Cheke stood fair and flourishing in the days of King Edward.

SECT. IV.

His fall.

His saddest misfortune.
BUT upon his dear master's death, farewell all his happy days. And he is willing, out of a hearty love of true religion, to part with all his honour and all his worldly substance, and become an exile with a great many more noble and learned men. But his greatest misfortune, that far outweighed all the rest, and left some stain upon his memory, was, that he was prevailed with by fear and terror, and other temptations, to renounce his religion with his lips, and in such an open and formal manner to disclaim that good profession, which he had shewn so much zeal to before. And what shall we say for him? It was somewhat strange that he should deny and abjure that religion, that he had upon such mature study and consideration been grounded in. But neither had his philosophy nor grace (which is much more) furnished him with such a degree of courage, as voluntarily to meet death, how good soever his mind was. Cheke's falling may be considered to be of the nature of the Disciples' fall, when they forsook their master Christ in his sufferings. Which a very learned man mollified by saying,

Grot. Annot. ad Matt. xxvi. 41.
" that that φρόνημα τῆς σαρκὸς, i. e. that *lust of the flesh,* " that rebelled against their mind at that time, was not of

" those grosser dregs of the affections towards riches and
" sensual pleasures, and such like things; but desires very
" natural; as the care of life, and the avoiding of sorrow
" and pain.——And they were in the rank of those per-
" sons, who, as Aristotle[a] saith, are overcome by violent,
" excessive, and overpowering griefs, however they strive
" against them. Which he saith is especially συγγνωμονι-
" κὸν, i. e. that may admit of pardon."

Finally, therefore, in such cases as these, we should not censure too hardly, but rather say as Archbishop Matthew Parker writ upon this poor man's recantation, *Homines sumus*, i. e. " We are men;" or as one John de Hoo, an Abbot of old of Vale Royal, being a meek and compassionate man, used to say of those that were guilty of such frailties,

Peccantes dampnare cave, nam labimur omnes,
Aut sumus, aut fuimus, vel possumus esse quod hic est.

Monastic.
Anglic.
vol. ii.

Condemn not thy poor brother,
That doth before thee lay;
Since there is none but falls:
I have, thou dost, all may.

---

[a] Ἰσχυρῶν καὶ ὑπερβαλλουσῶν λυπῶν ἡττᾶσθαι, καὶ ἀντιτίνοντας.

A

TREATISE

OF

SUPERSTITION.

TO

THE REV. MR. STRYPE.

SIR,

I HAVE sent you the English of that excellent fragment
of Sir John Cheke concerning Superstition, which in Latin
has that elegance and masculine force of style and judgment, that is worthy of its author. The habit it now visits you in, is what the donor in his present circumstances
could fit it with, not such as it deserves. But you inti-
mated a willingness to take it for better for worse, and
must not be worse than your word, though some late avo-
cations would not permit him to be better than his. As
to the original discourse, it appears to have been a Dedication of the author to his Sovereign Lord King Henry
the Eighth, before that little tract of Plutarch concerning
Superstition, which he had most elegantly translated out
of the Greek. But the Dedication would have itself contained a more complete treatise on that subject, had the
favourers of the Popish cause been able to answer the
force of those arguments, with which it so strongly shook
their metropolis, and which no doubt would have been
insuperable, had they been allowed to have remained hitherto upon record. But such is the nature of that set of
men, that what is wanting to them in reason, is made
up by that diligence which they use, to uphold so weak a
cause, as could never have been able to subsist so long,
without an unwearied caution, that omits nothing that
can any way yield to its support.

It is much to be suspected, that for this cause the

reader will have occasion to lament the loss of some sheets in the following treatise, which the Romanists, not caring they should look them in the face, have despatched with their usual sleight of hand. For you know they are famed for *legerdemain,* and are noted for a clean conveyance. This might be done upon the first revolt to Popery in Queen Mary's days; but more probably in that of later date: when their celebrated champion Ob. got this MS. into his power. And it is no wonder, if he who had so good a knack at concealing, as to hide his religion for so many years, should afterwards manifest an equal dexterity in suppressing arguments against it.

The design of the Dedication in the original is congratulatory to his then Majesty, King Henry the Eighth, upon his reformation of religion, and the victories, glories, and blessings that ensued thereon, agreeable to what he had observed to have happened in the like case to the several pious kings in holy Scripture. And were it not somewhat out of countenance in this change of habit, it might with much better grace address itself to her sacred Majesty that now is, who is a most undoubted friend to the reformed religion. Yet one who seeks not reformation by distracting the revenue of the Church; but that delights in doing true and real honour to God, by providing for the true welfare of his Ministers. It is this that fills our hearts with so much joy, and our tongues with praise to Almighty God, for successes obtained by our most religious Queen, greater than those of her predecessors: whose steady example in religion, and judicious deportment in all the parts and offices of it, will, we hope, have that blessed influence, as to shame all manner of superstition from future converse amongst us, equally discouraging that kind of it, which pretends to be afraid of doing too much, and that which fears to do too little. I mean the superstitious pageantry of Rome, and the sordid superstitious meanness of the several sects. Which could not, through the grace of God, fall short of having that happy effect, which is so much her Majesty's earnest desire, and should be the endeavour of us all, our *being united at home*, nor of putting an end to those divisions, from which alone the Queen's enemies and those of our religion can have any hopes. Such, as if her Majesty's royal pattern and advice can sway any thing with us, we shall think ourselves concerned not to countenance in the least. And surely no man of reason will reject her pious admonition and example, who has either any value for his own and the public good, any loyalty to his Queen, or any honour for the name of God, who is most highly dishonoured by every kind of superstition. Now that all would think of thus behaving themselves, and be admonished by such discourses, was no doubt a very good reason for your desiring in this manner to publish this treatise, and of his complying with that desire, who is

Your assured friend,

and obliged humble servant,

W. E.

To the most illustrious and most potent Henry the Eighth of England, France, and Ireland, King, Defender of the Faith, and supreme Head upon earth of the Churches of England and Ireland. John Cheke wisheth much health.

IT is the effect of great ingenuity and judgment, (and perhaps proceeds not merely from human nature, but from divine grace,) to be able accurately to separate truth from falsehood, and to distinguish between things decent and dishonest: for so great a resemblance is there between the most distant things, and such a seeming agreement between those things that are of natures really differing one from another, that unless the best and most excellent disposition shall be enlightened by learning and supernatural grace, and be cultivated as it were by continual exercise, it will be impossible for things so much entangled and confused to be parted and discerned by it. Craftiness imitates prudence; severity is often taken for justice; boldness has a semblance of valour; stupidity is not easily distinguished from temperance; pride draws to itself the commendation of magnificence; and not only the pretence of holiness, but what is even almost a mere old wives superstition, puts itself off for religion, and for the true worship of God. *Great wisdom to distinguish things.*

And as it usually comes to pass, that swollen bodies, and such as are coloured by art, do exceed the solid bulk and natural colour of bodies; and as those things that have been tinctured with bull's gall are not far from having a kind of golden lustre; even so, such things as are in their own nature vicious, and have nothing excellent in them, have nevertheless the figure and appearance of things the most illustrious and magnificent. Concerning which there is a diligent caution to be had: and we should labour with our utmost study, that the one be not taken for the *Are not to be cheated with appearances.*

other; and that those things being quite passed by, that
have the express characters of honesty, and the image of
truth, we do not totally give ourselves over to catch at the
shadows and resemblances of things. Therefore, in the
ordering of religion, we ought to be very cautious and
circumspect, that we do not through carelessness run
headlong into any rash judgments and opinions; and that
we yield but so far to the bent of our own genius, as not
to turn out of the right way that God has prescribed,
without framing new modes of worship for ourselves; or
endeavouring to appease God with such things as he has
either not commanded to be done, or left not to be enjoined. For if even those things which are of divine pre-
script are not capable of pleasing God, unless they shall be
done as he would have them; what human reason invents,
what superstition dictates, what the heat of a man's temper hurries him on to pursue, must needs be much farther
from pleasing God, when these things neither have any
means of rendering themselves grateful to him, nor, if they
had, could they merely of themselves be worthy of the
divine care.

Religion,   But there is nothing that is of so great moment, as to
what it is. the whole concern of this or a future life, as religion:
*which instructs us in the right discipline and method of
life, and of the worship of God; and does alone comprehend the hopes of a future immortal state.*   And what is
there preferable to this?   What thing can come in com-
petition with it?   What is there that either in point of advantage, or divinity, or safety, can approach or come up to
the least part of it?   For that which as soon as we seek
after it, is not only found with as much ease as other
things; but does, over and above besides itself, draw along
with it other good things, that are the greatest, and most
abundantly such: shall we not think this chiefly to be laid
hold of, and pursue it with our utmost care?   For to what
other end should we labour with all our might, than that
having obtained those things that are greatest and most
happy, we ourselves should have a full enjoyment of true
and perfect felicity, as constantly and long as may be?

inasmuch as mankind is both naturally inclined to wish
after it, and the grace of God does likewise call upon us
to embrace it. But the religion which is now proposed by Christ's
Christ, and that is manifested to all degrees of men; which religion.
is neither hidden from the good, nor concealed from such
as are studious, nor is harsh and difficult to those that follow after it; it is not only most easily sought out, but is
even revealed to us. Which being once possessed, what
can be wanting, that may seem to any man worthy of
being desired, when wanting? what can be present to him,
that he shall think greatly deserving to be wished for?
For even our Saviour Christ has told us, that religion being
first laid hold of, other things will not with much labour
be brought in, but will naturally follow of their own ac-
cord. *Seek ye first,* says he, *the kingdom of God, and all* Matth.
these things shall be added unto you. For if he who has vi. 33.
given us Christ, will with him likewise give us all things,
since in Christ are all the treasures of wisdom and of
knowledge; how will he not, who through him hath made
secure the way to peace and reconcilement with God,
teach us also the way, whereby things less considerable,
and of lighter value, may either flow in unto us without
labour, or be present without trouble, or be taken from us
without sorrow? But if Solomon, upon his request of
wisdom and judgment, to enable him to distinguish between right and wrong, had so great an addition of riches,
power, and glory bestowed upon him, as none of his
ancestors had ever seen, and as did never again shine
forth upon any of his posterity; how great things God
Almighty will give those, who, in the true and pious worship of him, have given up themselves wholly to seek after
him; who have prepared themselves to hear his divine
voice, and with their whole will and study to live after it!
Certainly it cannot be, but that whatsoever they require
upon any occasion, they must have just so much, or what
they at present have, be it never so little, yet they require
no more; either of which, if they have once arrived to,
they are most happy: inasmuch as they are of a quiet and
contented mind; and it is a thing indifferent to them,

whether or no they have an addition of many things towards the satisfying their desire, or their desire lessened
to a moderate stint.

Reforma-
tion of reli-
gion pro-
sperous to
Kings.
This duty towards God, as often as pious and religious
Kings have observed, they have been enriched by God
with manifold and great blessings.   The memory of which
has been derived down to us with the Scripture; and the
example of them still flourishes, to excite and stir men up,
which without the Scripture would be of no force: for
1 Kings xv.
2 Chron.
xiv.
Asa, when he purged and reformed religion, that had been
oppressed and corrupted by heathen rites, and the wickedness of others; and called back his people to seek after
the Lord, and to make a new covenant with their God;
did he not defend his cities in peace, and fortify his strong
holds?   And did not all things flow in unto him prosper-
ously to his wish?   Did he not overthrow his enemies in
war, and with a small handful destroy whole armies?   And
being enriched with victory and spoils, did he not return
safe, and bring back with him the ample reward of his
having cultivated religion?   But Jehoshaphat, when he cut
down the groves, and inquired after the Lord, and went
2 Chron.
xvii.
up to him with his heart; when he sent his Princes, and
with them the Levites and Priests, to teach and instruct
the people of the Lord throughout all the coasts and cities
of Judah; and himself reformed all the people, from Beer-
sheba to Mount Ephraim; though as yet the high places
were not broken down, and although the people were not
perfectly brought back to the God of their fathers: yet,
nevertheless, how great peace and affluence of all things,
what splendor of renown, what tranquillity to the commonwealth, what provision, and abundance of military
stores, and of valiant soldiers, how great victory in battle,
and what ample spoils, and how great triumphs did he
bring back!   What need I mention to you Ezechias or
Josias, who did not only renew religion that was almost
erased and extinguished, but almost established it afresh?
How great riches, and what peace did they enjoy!   How
great a store of money, cattle, and spices, did they possess!   How did God as it were snatch them out of the

jaws of death, and transfer unto another season the time
he had appointed for his anger? How were the living
associated unto them who were the best, and the dead
gathered unto their fathers? The whole cause of which
universal prosperity is thither to be referred, whither the
Scripture leads the way. Whereas the Scripture makes
mention of them, that by following the true worship of
him whom we ought to serve, we may not only have from
him all the goods of the mind, but all other external blessings and advantages.

And since the divine providence is not tied to any one
age of mankind, or single nation, but is universally diffused
throughout all the periods of all nations and times; when
we see the same sequel of real events in those, whose
studies, and pains, and favour, have been all of them laid
out in the reformation of religion; shall we doubt in be-
lieving it to be the same cause which the Scripture assigns
to have been in the best of kings? And ought we not,
among others, to think ourselves moved by their example?

And for those who put together the authority and truth Address to
of all times, and fix their eyes upon *your most potent* King
Henry.
Majesty, they are easily made to understand, that there is
no one, either in the greatness of things already achieved,
or in the splendour of a kingdom, or in the great abundance of all those things, that are the usual objects of men's
desires, nor yet in the happy and wished for event of
things; neither in the foresight and prevention of great
evils, nor in the fruits and acquirement of the most ample
advantages; there is no one has so well succeeded in any His pros-
one of these, as you have flourished in them all: whom perity for
reforming
God has reserved to your people and your kingdom, for religion.
the expiation and cultivating as it were of religion, for
taking away and utterly destroying the errors of superstition, for the rooting out the very fibres of impiety, and
giving the utmost latitude to the propagation of Christ's
glory. So that your Majesty seems not more to have
amended religion, than your Majesty has through religion

been recommended to Almighty God. And in the future discourses of men, the mention which shall be made of religion will extol the memory of what you have done, and the often commemorating the fame of your ample praises and commendation, will bring in the discourse about religion. Whereby it comes to pass, that since the advantage of religion is of so large an extent, and since in many places of Scripture it has both the promises of this present life, and of that which is to come; they take a good and prudent course, who, labouring not unfruitfully in the lesser things, and in the single parts of religion, have bestowed all their pains, study, industry, and age, in the thorough reformation of religion, which is as it were the mother of all virtues.

Caution against mistake in religion.

But since things of a more excellent and noble nature are not so much desired by wise men, that they may have the real possession of them, as they are sought after by the imprudent, that they may induce an opinion of their having them into others; and many are not voluntarily, but through mistake, drawn after a corrupt resemblance of things, and are not easily diverted from an opinion that has taken deep root; a greater care and industry is to be laid out in giving a right tincture to our minds, than in sowing our fields. And principal caution is to be used, lest in matters of greatest moment and advantage we either slip through error, or are drawn aside by passion, or hurried on by imprudence : but of all things there is nothing surrounded with greater difficulties, or is beset with things of more different natures than *religion*. Which being the

Religion, what.

pure worship of God, for the retaining his favour, and the averting his wrath; revealed and prescribed to us by God himself, and not the device or invention of human counsel; the greater earnestness that is used by good and bad men, to be and to appear religious; so more and greater will be the contrivances and machinations of men, (if through the difficulty of the thing, or through ignorance, they cannot attain it,) to make boast even of the shadow of it by science, falsely so called; or pretend to it through hypocrisy,

or set it off by affectation, or make shew of it by innovation, or by following it give it strength. Now of this reli- Two parts
gion, since there are two parts, the one of which is placed of religion.
in the searching after *knowledge,* and in the tracing out
of these things which are grateful and well-pleasing unto
God; but the other is employed in *action,* which puts forward into life and performance, what she understands to
have the divine approbation. Each of these parts is on all
sides surrounded with so many evil and vicious motions,
that being intercepted as it were in the midst of its enemies, it comes in danger of quite overturning and distracting all religion.

But that all may be set in better order before our eyes, Religions,
and that our whole meaning may more clearly be distin- two parts.
guished, not in reality and science only, but in express
terms and words, we shall so make use of such words as
are not indeed very frequent in Scripture, yet well enough
suited to the genius of our own times, as to call that part
which consists in a thorough inquiry into the divine will,
and the method of pure worship, by the name of *sanctity ;* Sanctity, or
and that which is altogether active, and which applies speculative
theology.
itself to the fulfilling of that, which by sanctity it understands will please God, we may name *piety.* But that * Piety,
which in this place I call *sanctity,* is that knowledge which practical
divinity.
is a kind of foundation-principle of human life, and of all
our actions; and which being once well laid, if the whole
ordering of our lives be built upon it, and all things flow
out of it as from a fountain, we shall have nothing vicious
or corrupt, nothing vain or hypocritical : but if that igno- Ignorance.
rance, which is opposed to sanctity, pours out such darkness upon the mind of man, and draws such a cloud over
it, that it cannot discern that light of truth, which sanctity
uses to look into ; let men's devices and contrivances be
as they please, and let them hug themselves in them as
much as they will, yet can they not be able to free themselves from error, rashness, and deceit : for besides that it
is a most base thing to be ignorant, when man is purposely
framed for the knowledge of God, and the comprehending

him in his mind; so nothing can be imagined more unbecoming and dishonourable, than that he should voluntarily make choice of being ignorant, who is commanded to be prepared, and *ready to give a reason of that faith which is in* him. For if the benefit of Christ is so highly to be esteemed, that the very knowledge of him is eternal life, how earnestly is that ignorance to be avoided, that does most of all obstruct us in our passage unto God? And if Paul, in all his epistles, gives thanks that they are filled with knowledge, that they abound in all science, and in all wisdom; with how much labour ought we to deprecate and drive away from us such gross ignorance and thick darkness? But that is not the only ignorance, which, knowing nothing, does not think itself to know any thing. Which, although it is a fault, because it is ignorance, is nevertheless a tolerable one, and more easily to be excused. But that is a far more grievous and infectious kind of ignorance, which either knows things corruptly, and is full of error, or pretends to know what it does not. This corruption of science, is when some opiniative person does not much inquire what it is the Scripture does confirm, as how he may by novelty of invention, or subtle distinctions, either weaken what is already established, or break through and crumble the whole in pieces; and rests upon his own notions, and not the Scriptures; and thereby causes many specious and plausible errors, which, grown old with time, are scarce extinguished by their age, or taken away by his authority, who says, *Ye err, not knowing the Scriptures.* He opens not the school of Christ, but sets forth a doctrine of his own, different from all others, and repugnant to the truth, which is named *heresy.* For the truth, which cannot be other than what it is, being deserted and abandoned, he takes up with every new thing he has a mind to; nor does he follow the Scriptures, as of necessity he ought, but pursues those fancies and opinions that ought least of all to come under his choice. *The pretence of knowledge* is that which, having no knowledge or perception, does imagine itself to comprehend all things, to see

Marginal notes:

1 Pet. iii. 15.

Depraved knowledge.

Heresy.

Pretended knowledge.

into the force of all arguments, and the reason that infers
their conclusions. A delightful error to the authors, but
most dangerous to the Church, hurtful in the very delight,
and splendid in the wickedness itself; and deceiving itself,
it thinks to instruct others; making shew of wisdom, it de-
tects its own want of knowledge. And when it appears to
itself to have the clearest insight into things, yet even then
knows nothing as it ought; and being involved in the
thickest darkness of ignorance, believes itself placed in the
clearest day-light. It may in this place be styled that The bragging of the
bragging of the Gnostics, which we may term arrogance, Gnostics.
and the *tumour of science*. We may therefore make a dis- Three kinds
of igno-
tinction of these three kinds: That ignorance is like to rance.
those, whose eyes do not admit the light, who love dark- 1.
ness, and cannot endure the day; as we see it usually falls
out with owls, and persons that are sick. There is another 2.
sort, who, whatever they see, they think it to be larger
than it really is, as in a mist it commonly happens; or
judge those things to be of one colour, that are of several.
As those who behold any object through a coloured glass,
have all things represented to them of the same colour
with the glass through which they appear: and as those
who are sick of the jaundice, having their eyes overflowed
with choler, think all things appear with a saffron hue. A 3.
third kind there is, which mistake the thickest darkness
for brightest day-light: and these men think nothing is or
can be better than their own conceptions and tenets.
Such are they, who spend all their age in Plato's Cave.
So that it comes to pass, that mortal men do less perceive
the light of knowledge and sanctity, while every entrance
or passage, which to sanctity ought to be laid open, is
either intercepted or stopped up. Which things are so
much the harder to be avoided, by how much the mind of
man, in this floating and unstable motion of things, is less
qualified to look upon the true light: being so affected, as
the greatest philosophers and defenders of human nature
assert, as the owl's eyes are with the rays of the sun.
Wherefore it is less to be admired, if through the weak-

ness of nature, and the force and greatness of different
things, the true knowledge of religion, being either intermitted for some time, or corrupted by men's judgments,
or abandoned through their sloth, or let alone by reason
of the difficulty of the thing itself, is at so low an ebb with
almost all ages and degrees of men; and that men seek so
little after it with their studies, or having sought after it,
recover it, or preserve it after recovery. And, concerning
the first part of religion, this may be explication enough.

Piety, or practical divinity. The remaining part is placed in the *efficiency* of those
things which sanctity does contain. For nothing can be
fitly performed and administered, without a true notion
and foreknowledge of the thing we are in pursuit of, to
govern the whole action with counsel, and to appoint and
manage it with reason. And those things are unprofitably,
and scarce are knowingly comprehended, out of which no
consequent action buddeth forth, and in which there is not
a steadiness of reason and judgment, to curb the turbulent
and vicious insurrections of the mind.

Piety op-posed. But this *piety* is variously opposed, and is besieged with
as many kinds, on every side, of things to infest it, and
that provoke it with continual skirmishes, as we have observed *sanctity* to be for the most part attacked with. For
there are those things which manifestly oppose it, and that
wage open and perpetual war with *piety*. There are others,
who have the semblance of piety, and carry all the worth
and dignity of it in their looks, their words, and gestures,
but have nothing of solid and sincere piety in them. There
are not wanting those, who, through a mistake of the true
worship, do that which ought least of all to have been
done, and fall into a depraved and corrupt method of devotion, and account it for that which is most right and true.
For those who run out with loose inclinations, and are
hurried whithersoever their passion carries them; they are
neither restrained by reason from running headlong, nor
are reclaimed by grace from an impure and flagitious life;
who turn the grace of God into lasciviousness, and live as
if God were altogether without care of them; and who

neither consider with themselves, nor care whether there
be a God or no, or whether he has any administration or
foresight of human affairs, or that he will recompense good
men with good things, and bad men with what is evil. The
Scriptures mark them out under several titles; but it is
most agreeable to our present purpose to call them
Atheists : who know, indeed, and understand what ought Atheists,
to be done, what is good, what pleases God, and what is ^{who.}
perfect; who lay out much pains and study in the knowledge of the divine law, but perform nothing that is real;
who carry a fair outside in looks and gestures, as though
they were full of piety, while they are at the same time
internally empty of all good works; and if they are given
to alms, or fasting, or devotion, they determine not the
doing of these things upon any such grounds, but propose
to themselves another end of all their actions than God
has appointed. The Scripture calls them *hypocrites.* Hypocrites.

But those who neither openly oppose piety, nor pretend
to it, but are mistaken in it; who strive to please God in
things that he would not have, and study to worship him,
and fear him in matters wherein he is not to be feared;
who have, as it were, a kind of zeal, but without knowledge, and without sanctity; who think, that in killing
men, they in an extraordinary manner do God service;
who are afraid upon the least omission of any of those
things wherewith they fancy God to be pleased, and believe that there is no means, nor no religion, that can take
away and expiate such omission: so that they are fluctuating in perpetual fear and error. These are said to be
Δεισιδαίμονες, *vainly timorous without a cause ;* the Latins
name them *superstitious.* These kinds are very different Supersti-
from one another, and do much prejudice the soundness of ^{tious.}
religion, and are great impediments throughout the whole
course of a pure and Christian life; so that even sanctity
and piety, being associated and linked together, cannot,
with all men, make religion to be completely entire and
perfect. For wicked men seem to me to be not unlike those
who break their constitution by drunkenness and intem-

perance; they had rather be frequently sick, and be tormented with the greatest pains, than forego any part of their lust, or of those gratifications that are present.

Hypocrites. *Hypocrites* are like to them, who, being tortured with the French disease, or some such incurable and loathsome distemper, do, in the midst of this most grievous vexation, and miserable state of body, pretend that they are sound; and do by all possible means dissemble their pains, and conceal their distempers, and bear nothing with greater trouble and uneasiness, than to be called what they really are.

Superstitious. The *superstitious* are not far from being in their state and condition, who being sick to extremity, yet think themselves in good health; and who, being within the very jaws of death, through the weakness of nature have no pricking or sense of pain, feel no racking of the joints; but as nature, being vanquished and overcome by the force of the disease, yields to the greatness of the disorder, without further resistance, and blazes out a little light of health even before death, and is neither afraid of death, nor enjoys health: so these, who are in the most miserable and deplorable state, and in perpetual conflict with God, see not the danger they are in; presuming upon little matters, and not terrified with great ones; imagining themselves religious, when they are far otherwise; and whom they fear, they apprehend not how to fear in such a manner as they ought.

From all which, in this so blind and troublesome a life, whoever is free and guiltless, is not to be judged happy through any direction of nature, but blessed by the abundance of grace. For so great difficulties, such precipices of opinions, such perturbations of mind, what man can avoid? who is able to escape them? Since there is no government of life or prudence in election, going before our earliest age, but rather following us when we grow old, nor give us their company till we are in the end and passage *Not ourselves, but God.* out of life; affording us no manner of guidance and direction at our first entrance and coming into it, did not the goodness of the divine mercy choose out such as it would

save, and furnish them in order to that salvation with all
manner of grace and good things. Wherefore, as religion is
to be pursued and retained by us, with all the faculties and
affections of our minds; so the common and popular, but
uncomely and deformed sects and parties of irreligion, are
all of them to be exploded and cast out: nor is the least
room to be afforded them, I do not say in a whole kingdom, but in the single judgments and opinions of men.

And now, when every one of these parts is corrupt and
vicious, what matters it to make inquiry which of them
does most prejudice human nature, or most obstruct divine
grace, or be most corrupt and wicked of itself. But were
I now to enter into the merits of the cause, and were
necessitated to declare what I thought fit to be deter-
mined, not about all the singulars I have now mentioned,
but that alone, in particular, which above all others ought
chiefly to be avoided and declined, my judgment would be
this, that there is no one thing is nearer in resemblance,
and yet nothing really more remote and distant from reli- Supersti-
gion, than superstition; which most easily insinuates itself tion widely
distant from
into the minds of good but ignorant men, and is most religion.
deeply rooted there, and with greatest difficulty pulled
from thence. Concerning the several parts of it, several
things have been hinted here and there by many, none of
them have said all they might. Plutarch and the philosophers have attempted to treat concerning the nature of it
in general: our Christian writers have passed it over. But
it is a shame that they, in an irreligious religion, should be
more diligent to search out what reason teaches, than we,
who enjoy a most certain worship, and the truest service
of God, to search after what the sacred Scripture prescribes.

But since there may be some dispute as to the name,
while men are agreed about the thing itself; and the matter under debate is better understood, when the variety of
doubtful meanings is taken away; I shall first speak of the
name, and then take the thing under examination; that
when we are less perplexed about the signification of the

word, the thing may offer itself more fully and plainly to
be treated of.

Δεισιδαιμονία, i. e. *Superstition.*

Of the word
supersti-
tion. The word itself shews to us what notions the Grecians
had of this vice; making little difference between it and the
fear of God. Now the fear or dread of God they reckoned
in the number of those things that were worthy of praise,
and judged it to be a duty that is most becoming us towards God. Hence came these sayings of the Greeks,
Fear God, and honour your parents. Therefore is the
word *superstition* treated with equal respect; and from this
duty did the most renowned amongst the Greeks receive
their commendations: as Agesilaus is represented in Xenophon[a] " to be always possessed with the fear of God;
" esteeming these not yet happy, who live well; but be-
" lieving them to be then really blessed, who had made an
" honourable exit out of the world." So St. Paul in the
Acts praises the Athenians as men of religion, when he
calls them *Deisidæmones, such as feared God,* or *were superstitious.* And those controversies in religion, which
happened between the Jews and St. Paul, are by St. Luke
styled *certain[b] questions about superstition, or fear of
God.* These are taken in the favourable sense: but for
the most part it is taken in a different sense from such a
godly fear, and has a worse meaning; and then the word
contains in it a notion of *unprofitable fear* of God.

For as a frugal person is scarcely distinguished from one
that is covetous, because the covetous man sordidly and
corruptly imitates him: and there is a kind of wild and
rugged hardiness imitates that which is the true patience
of mind; so superstition comes very near in resemblance
to that which is the true fear of God, when it is distant
from it very widely, and would appear not to be far off:
when it cannot come in any near conjunction with it, nor

---

[a] Ἀεὶ δὲ δεισιδαίμων ἦν, νομίζων τοὺς μὲν καλῶς ζῶντας οὔπω εὐδαίμονας, τοὺς δὲ
εὐκλεῶς τετελευτηκότας ἤδη μακαρίους.

[b] Ζητήματα περὶ δεισιδαιμονίας.

conspire with it in a laudable moderation, and in a virtuous mean.

But in so many senses as the notion of fear may be Fear two-
understood, so many ways is superstition also to be taken: fold, and so
supersti-
inasmuch as everywhere, such as the shadow shews the tion.
image of the body agreeable to its opposition to the sun, so this carries an umbrage of fear, instead of that force and disposition, which is denoted by it. But although fear is variously taken in Scripture, yet there are two significations of it of greatest latitude, which will be enough for us in this place. The one of these is that which signifies our religion in general, together with our righteousness towards God. The other declares those thoughts and motions of the mind, which regard the justice of God in the punishment of evil and wicked men. For since there are two things in God, which are chiefly to be looked upon by Christians; his *justice*, whereby he restrains such as are evil; and his *mercy*, that prepares and protects the good; our confidence regards the mercy of God, takes and embraces it; fear respects the justice and severity of God in punishing and avenging evil, which it conceives not without some commotion of the mind; for so the Apostle had described both. *Be not high minded, but fear: for if* Rom. xi.
God spared not the natural branches, take heed he also 20, 21, 22.
spare not thee. Behold therefore the goodness and severity of God: on them which fell, severity; but towards thee, goodness, if thou continue in his goodness. Serve the Lord Ps. ii. 11,
with fear, and rejoice with trembling. Lay hold of in- 12.
struction, lest he being angry, ye perish from the right way, when his wrath is kindled but a little. Blessed are all they that put their trust in him. The eyes of the Lord Ps. xxxiv.
are upon the righteous, and his ears are open unto their 15.
prayer. The face of the Lord is against them that do evil, to root out the remembrance of them from the earth. But since there are those who turn the grace of God into lasciviousness, and their liberty into licentiousness, and an occasion to the flesh; so there are those who traduce the justice of God, as being severe, and who esteem his mercy

to be too much lenity, and remissness, and indulgence : and thus, while they trust too much to themselves, and are hurried on by their own inclinations, and hope, while they commit sin, that God will remit their offences ; they have not confidence in God, but a bold presumption. Against whom it is wisely and wholesomely written, *Say not, I have transgressed, what trouble shall come unto me? the Lord indeed is slow to wrath, yet will he not let thee go unpunished. Because thine offence is forgiven thee, be not careless in thy prosperity, so as to add sin to sin. Nor say, that his compassion is manifold, he will forgive the multitude of my sins. For mercy and wrath proceedeth from him, and his anger resteth upon sinners.* Those who do not reckon this confidence and security amongst the greatest of sins, understand not what the true trust and confidence in God is : so those who, rejecting the true fear of God, look upon him as a fierce and cruel punisher and avenger of wickedness, and whose minds are not vigilant to escape his just wrath ; but are tortured with an opinion of God's austerity and cruelty ; what else will they answer to our Lord, or what other account will they deliver up to him, than that of the foolish servant in the Gos-

Matt. xxv. 24. pel? *Lord, I knew thee that thou art an hard man, reaping where thou hast not sown, and gathering where thou hast not strawed.*

Superstition an immoderate dread of God. Such as have this not only useless but pernicious fear, and who turn aside out of the right course of true fear, are called *superstitious ;* and this fear, which is vehement beyond the just measure, is termed *superstition.* Which superstition is hinted at by the Apostle whom our Saviour loved. *There is,* says he, *no fear in love :* for those whom we heartily love, how can we be possessed with any vain terrors, or entertain any needless fears of them?

And when the end of the law is love, that which wanders at the greatest distance from the end, how can it possibly be confined within the bounds of love? There is nothing more wide and distant, than that him, whom on the account of his great and many benefits, we ought to love and reverence, we should have the most horrid dread and terror of, in our whole hearts and wills, by reason of an opinion of his being severe and cruel. And this is one kind of *superstition* and *fear*.

The Scripture sometimes, under the name of fear, comprehends religion in general, and the devout worship of God. So that nothing is signified under the name of religion, that is not included also in the name of fear. Hence it is that we have so large and so remarkable a description of it in Ecclesiasticus. Hence it is that we have so ample commendations of it in so many places of Scripture. And hence is that of the Prophet: *Come, ye children, hearken unto me: I will teach you the fear of the Lord. What man is he that desireth life, and would see good days? Let him refrain his tongue from evil, and his lips that they speak no guile.* And St. James says the same thing in other words: *Pure religion and undefiled before God and the Father is this, To visit the fatherless and widows in their affliction, and to keep himself unspotted from the world.* And therefore the two Evangelists did fitly translate these words of the law, *Thou shalt fear the Lord thy God,* in this manner, *Thou shalt worship the Lord thy God:* that hereby they might demonstrate *fear* and *worship* to be the same.

But the Prophet, celebrating the praises of the law of God, while he would distinguish it not only with ornaments of matter, but with variety of expressions, saith, *The law of the Lord is perfect, converting the soul: the testimony of the Lord is sure, making wise the simple. The statutes of the Lord are right, rejoicing the heart: the commandment of the Lord is pure, enlightening the eyes. The fear of the Lord is clean, enduring for ever: the judgments of the Lord are true and righteous altogether.* But though the Psalms exhibit to us a repeated way of writing, they do not always furnish us with new matter, but they retain the same weighty things, under a variety of devout expressions. Whence it comes to pass, that by joint words and phrases, different things are not signified,

Fear is religion.

Ps. xxxiv. 11.

James i. 27.

Ps. xix. 7, 8, 9.

but the same matter aggravated and enlarged. And thus is religion oftentimes joined with fear; not as two things of a separate nature, but that two words of like importance might answer in discourse to one another: for it is in the law, *And now, Israel, what doth the Lord thy God require of thee, but to fear the Lord thy God, and to walk in all his ways, and to love him, and to serve the Lord thy God with all thy heart, and with all thy soul?* And again, *Thou shalt fear the Lord thy God, and him shalt thou serve, and to him shalt thou cleave, and swear by his name.* And in the speech of Joshua, *Now therefore fear the Lord, and serve him in sincerity and in truth.* And Samuel, *If ye will fear the Lord, and serve him, and obey his voice, and not rebel against the commandment of the Lord.* And King Jehoshaphat, *Let the fear of the Lord be with you, be circumspect, and do your duty.* And St. Peter in the Acts, *He that feareth God, and worketh righteousness.* Hence it is that St. Luke styles those who are religious and devout, not only εὐλαβεῖς, as being men of caution and circumspection, and who did not undertake any thing without great provision and foresight; but he calls them likewise σεβόμενοι, *worshippers;* such who, deliberately resolving and foreseeing what ought to be done, perform it with all dutifulness and diligence. For Simeon was called εὐλαβῆς, *a devout man;* and they are termed ἄνδρες εὐλαβεῖς, *who are the devout men of every nation under heaven;* and in several places of the Acts they are sometimes called σεβόμενοι, *worshippers,* sometimes εὐλαβεῖς, *devout men.* But why should Ecclesiasticus call the fear of the Lord, the holiness of knowledge or wisdom itself, and discipline? or in other places should name the performance of the law with the highest wisdom, and with the knowledge of the precepts of the Lord? unless he intended hereby both parts of religion, *sanctity* and *piety;* and so believed universal religion to be contained under the name of *fear.* But of a thing that is not over difficult we have been too tedious: for the result of all that has been said is this, that the name of *fear* does comprehend

Deut. x. 12, 13.

v. 20.

Joshua xxiv. 14.
1 Sam. xii. 14.

Acts x. 35.

Luke ii. 25.
Acts ii. 5.

under it all religion, and is sometimes taken for religion itself.

This being laid down, this follows, which we are now chiefly concerned about, that superstition, which is the rival of *fear*, is universal error in religion. So that the notion of fear does not extend itself with a greater latitude to all manner of good, than superstition shoots itself into all the branches and fibres of error. For as fear stands with respect to universal religion; so superstition regards not the errors of each part separately considered, but the complex error both of *sanctity* and *piety*. Therefore, such who define superstition to be, when any one fears God in things not to be feared, or places the worship of God in such things as he will not be worshipped in; these men, in my opinion, rightly and prudently discover wherein the whole power and nature of superstition does consist. And they do not amiss, who define an endeavour after piety, without sanctity, to be superstition. For since all matters are discerned in these three things, in knowledge, in action, and in endeavour; neither is knowledge, nor yet action, right in superstition; notwithstanding there remains endeavour, which, if it be approvable without the rest, is all the praise that superstition deserves. And there is in it perhaps somewhat to soften and allay in some measure the greatness of the evil that is in the other two. So St. Paul testifies of his brethren and kinsmen, *That they had a zeal of God, but not according to knowledge:* that in the midst of their so great wickedness, and such blindness of their understandings, he might not take away the evil, but qualify it, and shew that there was some spark of good among all that evil. In which St. Paul endeavoured not to favour ignorance, which does corrupt zeal; but to correct zeal, that it might come to knowledge.

But superstition cannot be without ignorance; for did it really know what it thinks it does, and put in practice what it knows, with all the powers of the mind, it would then be no longer superstition, but religion. Therefore, while the Scripture does not name superstition, but de-

An approved definition of superstition.

Rom. x. 2.

Superstition supposeth ignorance.

scribe it, it always makes mention of ignorance, as in this
John xvi.
2, 3.
example : *The time cometh, that whosoever killeth you will
think that he doth God service. And these things will they
do unto you, because they have not known the Father, nor*
Rom. x. 3.
me. And again, *For they being ignorant of God's righteousness, and going about to establish their own righteousness, have not submitted themselves unto the righteousness
of God.* But where knowledge is wanting, who can hope
to have any action entire and perfect? For a man will
either act rashly and at adventures, if he does any thing
ignorantly; or else unsteadily, in case he be at a loss what
he ought chiefly to adhere to; or with some doubting, if
so be he understand not the true quality of the thing he
has undertaken. But those persons are void and destitute
of all knowledge of divine worship, that have once yielded
up themselves to superstition : for they do those things,
the nature of which did they but thoroughly know and
perceive, not so much from the judgment of right reason,
as from the aid of the grace of God, they would, as much
as it were possible, have them in the greatest abhorrence.

For what a thing is it, to render good men and Ministers, as the Evangelist words it, ἀποσυναγώγους, *excommu-
nicate,* or *thrown out of the synagogue?* How great a
matter is it to condemn them to death, and deliver them
up to be torn asunder with all manner of tortures? What
a thing is it to provide for the establishing their own
righteousness? What a fearful thing is it, as much as in
them lies, to betray Christ their Lord and Saviour, and to
fix on him the extremest disgrace, and to crucify him?
But the superstitious, while they think they desire to
please God, kill, destroy, and betray those, whom with
duty, kindness, and favour, they ought rather to embrace.
And while they stand fixed in their own righteousness, as
Rom. x. 4.
in a strong hold, they never arrive at *that law of righteousness, the end of which is Christ :* and him, whom had
they known to be the Lord of life and glory, they had not
crucified as a traitor and malefactor, they put to the most
cruel and shameful death.

From these things we understand, that there can neither be true *knowledge* nor right *action* in superstition; and that it is tossed to and fro with ignorance and error, entertaining a depraved opinion of that which is right. For how can it otherwise come to pass, if men will worship God with things not to be worshipped? If, leaving the commandment and the word of the Lord, (wherein is contained, as it were, the fountain of knowledge and wisdom,) they follow after their own inventions, and their own wills? If they determine otherwise about things than God Almighty has appointed and prescribed; and direct them not to that end and use for which they were designed by him? Thus it comes to pass, that the whole matter in which superstition is concerned, is either this, that such things are applied to the worship and service of God as ought to be thrown out altogether and rejected; or else that mean and little things are had in greater price and esteem than is fit; or are bent and distorted to some other way than ought, and to which they were intended. But if those things are alone to be made use of, and applied to the service of God, which he has commanded; if nothing is to be added, nothing taken away; if we are not to incline to either side, but are to keep on right in the way of his commandments; all those things which have not the word of God and the Scriptures, either commanding *men*, or approving the *things*, must necessarily be rejected and taken away, if so be the service of God be sought by us, and we apply ourselves to God's pure and sincere worship, and propose to ourselves such a religion as is holy and undefiled.

Nor are we here to attribute too much to our own inventions, or tread too close upon the footsteps of our ancestors, or be led on by the example of the most powerful nations. Our own *inventions* are such, that when we follow them, we hearken not to the voice of the Lord; we approve what is our own, and reject what is from others: but are not therefore the wiser, because we applaud our-

How to avoid superstition.

1.
Human inventions.

P

selves; but therefore may justly be punished by God, because we reject what comes from him.

For as in the past ages of men he suffered all nations to walk in their own ways, so will he suffer all our counsels to be ineffectual, our endeavours fruitless, our service to be vain: and he will deservedly bring that of the Psalmist against us; *My people would not hear my voice, and Israel would not obey me. So I gave them up unto their own hearts' lust: and let them follow their own inventions.* This branch of superstition St. Paul fitly names ἐθελοθρησκεία, *will-worship:* which is wholly contained in those voluntary inventions and judgments of ours, framed after our own lusts. This vice is so reprehended in Scripture, that to will any indifferent thing is hardly allowed there. Hence is that grave and severe reprehension of St. Paul, *Tell me, ye that would be under the law.* Hence that sacrifice of Saul, which he offered prudently, as he thought himself, but yet inconsiderately, and without any command of God; nay, without and contrary to his will. This turned away the favour and clemency of God, and armed his anger and his fury against him. Let us learn, therefore, what we are to hold to, *that obedience is better than sacrifice, and to hearken is more excellent than the fat of rams.* Let us learn that *rebellion is as the sin of witchcraft, and not to acquiesce in the word of the Lord is as great a crime as idolatry.* Let us learn, that *the Lord will have mercy and not sacrifice, and that the knowledge of God is better than whole burnt-offerings.* But, lastly, which is the greatest of all, we think this will-worship to be the perversest idolatry, because they who feign new kinds of worship, think God to be other than he really is; and so they do in effect frame to themselves a new deity in their own minds.

2. There is another kind of the superstitious persons, who seek not novelties, but are content with what is ancient; who trouble not their inventions to contrive, but follow what has been in use; and what has been left them by

Marginalia:

Ps. lxxxi. 11, 12.

Will-worship.

Gal. iv. 21.

1 Sam. xv. 22, 23.

2. Ancestors.

their ancestors, they judge to be firm and sure; they admit not of other things, but adhere to that alone. But it is a grievous thing to establish that which your forefathers have used, to hold that certain and fixed, and to reject and set at nought what Christ, elder than all your ancestors, commanded. Christs saith, *Before Abraham was, I am.* John viii. But how wicked and abominable were it to relate those 58. things which the Prophet had said, *As for the word that* Jer. xliv. *thou hast spoken to us in the name of the Lord, we will* 16, 17, 18. *not hearken unto thee. But we will certainly do whatsoever thing goeth forth out of our own mouth, to burn incense to the* frame *of heaven, and to pour out drink-offer-* Queen. *ings unto it, as we have done, we, and our fathers, our kings, and our princes, in the cities of Judah, and in the streets of Jerusalem: for then had we plenty of victuals, and were well, and saw no evil. But since we left off to burn incense to the* frame *of heaven, and to pour out drink-offerings unto it, we have wanted all things, and have been consumed by the sword and by the famine.* These things said the men of Judah, while they sojourned in Egypt. Ah, miserable men! How mistaken were they, not knowing the Scriptures! How did they harden their hearts, disbelieving Jeremiah! How did they through blindness turn away the true cause of their miseries! For Moses had foretold it to them: *Not for thy righteousness,* Deut. ix. 5. *or for the uprightness of thine heart, dost thou go to possess the land: for thou art a stiff-necked people, when thou provokedst the Lord, when thou didst worship idols, when thou refusedst to put thy trust in the Lord. Remember, and for-* 7, 8. *get not, how thou provokedst the Lord thy God to wrath in the wilderness: from the day that thou didst depart out of the land of Egypt, and till ye came unto this place, ye have been rebellious against the Lord. Also in Horeb ye provoked the Lord to wrath, so that the Lord was angry with you to have destroyed you.* And the Psalmist cries out, *They kept not the covenant of God, and refused to walk in his law; and forgot his works, and his wonders that he* Ps. lxxviii. *had shewed them. Marvellous things did he in the sight of* 10.

their fathers. Nevertheless they sinned yet more against him by provoking the Most High in the wilderness. And they tempted God in their heart by asking meat for their lust. Yea, they speak against God in these words, Can God furnish a table in the wilderness?

Our fore-fathers not to be fol-lowed in their faults.

Let us not therefore approve the vices of our forefathers, as if they were virtues, but of whatever quality their vices are, let us acknowledge them: and let us place our confidence in God, and not forget the things that he has done; let us do his commandments, lest we become, as the Psalmist speaks, *like unto our fathers, a people, who turned back and rebelled, a generation that set not their heart aright, and whose spirit was not stedfast with God.* But why hearkened they not to Jeremiah, whom the Lord set apart, whom he had ordained a Prophet to the nations, in whose mouth God had placed his word? Why did they not rather turn the cause of their misfortunes, as Jeremy commanded, upon their own actions? Why did they not ascribe it to their own perverseness, to their own wickedness; that they obeyed not the voice of the Lord; that they walked not in his laws, and that they offered incense unto strange gods; but that this very opinion of their ancestors, which stuck so close, and was difficult to be removed, had taken such deep root, that it was not to be plucked away, or drawn out? They thought that their fathers were to be necessarily followed, their ancestors imitated, and all their words and actions towards God to be approved and confirmed.

How we are to follow our fathers.

But if our fathers are to be followed, there is one who is our heavenly Father, who is not only King of kings, and Lord of lords, but Father of fathers also, who ought chiefly to be followed. If our fathers are to be followed, why do we rather reckon their numbers, than weigh their worth? Why do we rather take after the most in number, than wisest in understanding, and most holy in life? It is not following the fathers, to imitate their faults; but to be willing to express their virtues and knowledge, propounded to our imitation, in our own life and endeavour. The commendation of the kings of Israel, is not that they walked in the sins of Jeroboam, and the other kings; but in that they directed all their actions according to the example of David. The greatest reproofs of the kings of Israel and Judah were, that they did not those things which were well-pleasing to the Lord, as David their father had done; but walked in the ways of the kings of Israel. The best way to acknowledge God, and to know true religion, is to think that it may fall out, and almost in all ages doth, which they in the Book of Psalms confess to God, *We have sinned with our fathers.* This is that part of superstition, which St Peter calls ᵃ*vain conversa-* 1 Pet. i. 18. *tion received by tradition from the fathers,* which judges of the strength of any thing, from its having been in use and reputation with their ancestors: not understanding, that as in the ages of men, so in the succession of ages it happens, those are not always the wisest that are oldest in years, but that possess that cause of wisdom, which the Psalmist produceth, *I have understood more than the aged, because I sought thy commandments.* And when the psalm declares that God was angry with the generation of their fathers forty years; yet the same spirit did as truly prophesy, that *the people which should be born should praise the Lord.*

Hence it comes to pass, that not because some things After-times went before, therefore any thing is better; but because it have advantage of correcting the follows that which has been prescribed by the most wise recting the and good God, therefore it is good. And following ages former. being taught by the ignorance of the former, correct many things, and make many alterations, not for the worse, but for the better. This the wisest Prophet saw and took notice of, and left it to be observed by us. *Day unto day* Ps. xix. 2. *uttereth speech, and night unto night sheweth knowledge.* But if any one would reckon up all the ages, yea centuries from Seth to Noah, and from thence to the times of the Patriarchs, then to Moses and Joshua, from them to the memory of David, afterwards to Ezechias and Josias, and

ᵃ Μάταιαν ἀναστροφὴν πατροπαράδοτον.

so on to Esdras and Nehemiah; from them to Christ, after Christ, and the certain succession of the Apostles to this very age; he will perceive mighty declensions of times, and the greatest ignorance and impiety prevailing in them. And at these certain spaces of time limited by God, they have been repulsed, and again called back to some light of divine religion; and that again by the authority of men, and by neglect often extinguished.

For as there are in the body certain joints and ligaments, by which it is tied together, and in these the greatest firmness and stability of strength is esteemed to consist; so in a long tract of years, and in the ages of the world, there have always been, and ever will be certain periods, wherein will be the greatest force and weight of truth; the divine Providence, either repelling the ignorance, or quickening the sloth, or lessening the wickedness and naughtiness of men. *And thus* much of the *vain conversation received from the fathers.*

3.
Example of
nations, not
to be de-
pended on.

And why should the example of any nation withdraw you from God, when all of them are his, and created to serve the living God? *For all nations shall serve him.* If those nations which excel others in exquisite learning and in good religion, are not to be drawn into example; and a pattern of life and manners is not to be taken from them; then no human discipline, no institution ought to prevail to establish worship, or bring any authority to constitute religion. For if those things which in men's opinions are of greatest excellence, and to the wits of men seem most admirable, have no place, no right here, things of less weight, and more inconsiderable, are much less to be introduced and applied to any part of piety and divine worship. But God rejected the imitation of the best and most flourishing nations, proposed his own word to be followed, and taught us, that all other religions are empty,

Lev. xviii.
3, 4, 5.

false, and vain. For he saith by Moses, *After the doings of the land of Egypt, wherein ye dwelt, shall ye not do, and after the doings of the land of Canaan, whither I am about to bring you, shall ye not do, neither shall ye walk*

in their ordinances, ye shall do my judgments, and keep
mine ordinances to walk therein; I am the Lord your
God, ye shall therefore keep my statutes, and my judg-
ments, which if a man do, he shall live in them. Not only The learn-
profane histories set forth most magnificent and famous ing of the
things concerning Egypt; but even Scripture supposed all Egyptians.
the fountains of all human wisdom flowed thence, which
watered almost all the world with its precepts and opinions.
For the Scripture, when it would commend the learning
and education of Moses, says, that he was trained up and
instructed in all the *learning of the Egyptians.* And
when the wisdom of Solomon was shewn to have far sur-
passed the wit and prudence of all others; his understanding is not only set forth to have been greater than
the wisdom of all the men in the East, but is declared to
have exceeded the cunning of those in Egypt. So that
the being accomplished in the arts and learning of Greece,
was not a thing of greater esteem and reputation among
the Romans, and with the other nations of Europe, and of
Asia the Less, than was the glory of those who were
masters of the wisdom and learning of Egypt, throughout
India, and over the Greater Asia and Africa.

Away therefore with them, and let us put far from us Admonition
the ordinances of all nations of what kind, and how great to follow no
soever they be; lest they draw us off from the word of the prescrip-
Lord, and from the true religion prescribed and appointed tions.
us. For as there is no respect of single persons, so neither is there of particular nations with God. For in him
that made us, there is *neither Greek nor Jew, circumcision* Col. iii. 11.
nor uncircumcision, Barbarian, Scythian, bond nor free;
but Christ is all and in all.

But if neither Jew be any thing, nor Greek, if circum- Christ alone
cision be nothing, nor uncircumcision, but Christ be all to be fol-
and in all; why do we set before us their example for our lowed.
authority and imitation, who are not only without Christ,
but against him? And why do we not rather follow him,
who, being *all in all*, hath suffered death for all, that whether we live or die, we might all be his. But what need

we say more: they whose whole life is transacted in a blind ignorance, who neither hold to what they should follow, nor see what they should hold to; what can these persons have to draw men over to imitate them in religion? But unless all had been in ignorance, why was it commanded the Apostles, that *they should go and teach all nations?* Forasmuch as we do not teach the knowing, but admonish them; we do not punish the ignorant, but instruct them.

To this part of superstition, the Scripture has not assigned an universal name, yet from the Scripture there may one be given it. For as among the Greeks they are said Κρητίζειν, Σικιλίζειν, Ἰσθμιάζειν, Λυδίζειν, to *Cretize,* to *Sicilize,* &c. who imitate the customs and vanities of those countries, the Cretans, the Sicilians, the Isthmians, the Lydians; and they are said in Latin *pergræcari,* to be *thorough-paced Greeks,* who follow the levity and good fellowship of that people in their lives; so those who run after the superstition of the Jews, are said by St. Paul Ἰουδάζειν, to *Judaize.* And those who propose to themselves the laws and ceremonies of other nations, are said Ἐθνικῶς ζῆν, καὶ οὐκ Ἰουδαικῶς, *to live after the manner of the Gentiles, and not as the Jews.* And since the greatest controversies at the beginning in the Church, while yet a growing, were concerning the law of Moses, concerning the ceremonies, concerning the rites of the Jews; as in other matters, so in this particular, I shall have a right to be excused, if that which is most famous in its kind I make to serve for all, and name the imitating the manner of that nation in point of worship, *Judaizing,* or *playing the Jew.*

How to call this part of superstition.

Therefore, so far as was convenient to be said summarily, concerning the things to be rejected, (that neither our own *devices,* nor the practice of our *ancestors,* nor the example of any *nations,* ought to call us off, or slacken us from the word of God,) I think it has been sufficiently declared in this place. It remains that the things going before be throughly handled, which are things in nature.—

I suppose he was going to apply the premises to the Roman Church: but here being a chasm in the original, and divers pages wanting, so far I presume as he touched Popery; the other sheets were in all probability conveyed away by Mr. O. W. and that party, during their reign in University college; being ashamed of those arguments they could not answer, and resolved that they should never again be produced against them, for their reproach and conviction.

The fragment that is left is as follows:

Your Majesty, who every day brings to light the defaced and oppressed parts of religion for the use of men, that things most wholesome and sound being by you discovered, may drive away these miseries of ignorance and error, and that true religion may by degrees shoot up till it arrive to full perfection and maturity. Thus shall ignorance give place to the knowledge of the Lord; the flesh offer less resistance unto holiness; the judgment of men shall prevail in civil causes; the word of the Lord shall bear the sway in religion; the custom of our forefathers shall assume nothing to itself, unless the force of truth do establish it, and the examples of nations shall not pervert the rule of life. So shall such things as are great be esteemed for great, and light and trivial things be reckoned as they are. The imitation of our fathers shall not tend towards error; but the conservation of its own state will tend to soundness. There shall be no confusion of things, but things of different natures shall be distinguished. So every thing shall go directly towards its end, and not be diverted some other way by the depravations of men's judgments. Thus regard will be had, not only what is done, but wherefore it is done: and things being joined with their causes shall not be rashly and at haphazard administered. And it shall be known for what end God hath appointed every thing, not whither our wills would hurry all things. That we may give praise and thanks unto God, and enumerate all his benefits; that we

The benefit of knowing the truth.

Q

may perform that worship, which he prefers before all sacrifices, and offerings, and slaughterings of beasts; that we may remember the righteousness of God alone, and perpetually praise and call upon his holy name, who only doth wondrous works.

Conclusion, with thanks and prayers for the King and Prince.' And let us yield him our greatest and most earnest acknowledgments, that he hath given his *judgments*, as we see, to your Majesty, and that he hath imparted *righteousness*, as we hope, to our Prince, that ye both may administer right with justice to the people, and may help in judgment the afflicted. For from these things we promise ourselves, what in greatest part we see effected, that there may be neither ignorance, nor hypocrisy, nor corruption of any part in religion; that there may neither be any perverseness in life, nor error in worship, nor counterfeiting in our actions; but that all parts being rightly and entirely constituted, we may not be esteemed maimed before God, with some piece of religion cut off, but being upright in heart, we may be found perfect and complete.

The Lord Jesus preserve your Majesty in most flourishing estate.

Hartford, December 30.